Procedures and Methodologies

EC-Council | Press

Volume 2 of 5 mapping to

E|CSA™

EC-Council | **Certified Security Analyst**

Certification

COURSE TECHNOLOGY
CENGAGE Learning™

Australia • Brazil • Japan • Korea • Mexico • Singapore • Spain • United Kingdom • United States

COURSE TECHNOLOGY
CENGAGE Learning™

Procedures and Methodologies
EC-Council | Press

Course Technology/Cengage Learning
  Staff:

Vice President, Career and Professional
  Editorial: Dave Garza

Director of Learning Solutions:
  Matthew Kane

Executive Editor: Stephen Helba

Managing Editor: Marah Bellegarde

Editorial Assistant: Meghan Orvis

Vice President, Career and Professional
  Marketing: Jennifer Ann Baker

Marketing Director: Deborah Yarnell

Marketing Manager: Erin Coffin

Marketing Coordinator: Shanna Gibbs

Production Director: Carolyn Miller

Production Manager: Andrew Crouth

Content Project Manager:
  Brooke Greenhouse

Senior Art Director: Jack Pendleton

EC-Council:

President | EC-Council: Sanjay Bavisi

Sr. Director US | EC-Council:
  Steven Graham

For product information and technology assistance, contact us at
Cengage Learning Customer & Sales Support, 1-800-354-9706

For permission to use material from this text or product,
submit all requests online at **www.cengage.com/permissions**.
Further permissions questions can be e-mailed to
permissionrequest@cengage.com

Library of Congress Control Number: 2010925634

ISBN-13: 978-1-4354-8367-5

ISBN-10: 1-4354-8367-7

Cengage Learning
5 Maxwell Drive
Clifton Park, NY 12065-2919
USA

Cengage Learning is a leading provider of customized learning solutions with office locations around the globe, including Singapore, the United Kingdom, Australia, Mexico, Brazil, and Japan. Locate your local office at: **international.cengage.com/region**

Cengage Learning products are represented in Canada by
Nelson Education, Ltd.

For more learning solutions, please visit our corporate website at **www.cengage.com**

NOTICE TO THE READER

Printed in the United States of America
1 2 3 4 5 6 7 12 11 10

Brief Table of Contents

Table of Contents

Hacking and electronic crimes sophistication has grown at an exponential rate in recent years. In fact, recent reports have indicated that cyber crime already surpasses the illegal drug trade! Unethical hackers better known as *black hats* are preying on information systems of government, corporate, public, and private networks and are constantly testing the security mechanisms of these organizations to the limit with the sole aim of exploiting it and profiting from the exercise. High profile crimes have proven that the traditional approach to computer security is simply not sufficient, even with the strongest perimeter, properly configured defense mechanisms like firewalls, intrusion detection, and prevention systems, strong end-to-end encryption standards, and anti-virus software. Hackers have proven their dedication and ability to systematically penetrate networks all over the world. In some cases *black hats* may be able to execute attacks so flawlessly that they can compromise a system, steal everything of value, and completely erase their tracks in less than 20 minutes!

The EC-Council Press is dedicated to stopping hackers in their tracks.

About EC-Council

The International Council of Electronic Commerce Consultants, better known as EC-Council was founded in late 2001 to address the need for well-educated and certified information security and e-business practitioners. EC-Council is a global, member-based organization comprised of industry and subject matter experts all working together to set the standards and raise the bar in information security certification and education.

EC-Council first developed the *Certified Ethical Hacker,* CIEH program. The goal of this program is to teach the methodologies, tools, and techniques used by hackers. Leveraging the collective knowledge from hundreds of subject matter experts, the CIEH program has rapidly gained popularity around the globe and is now delivered in over 70 countries by over 450 authorized training centers. Over 80,000 information security practitioners have been trained.

CIEH is the benchmark for many government entities and major corporations around the world. Shortly after CIEH was launched, EC-Council developed the *Certified Security Analyst,* EICSA. The goal of the EICSA program is to teach groundbreaking analysis methods that must be applied while conducting advanced penetration testing. EICSA leads to the *Licensed Penetration Tester,* LIPT status. The *Computer Hacking Forensic Investigator,* CIHFI was formed with the same design methodologies above and has become a global standard in certification for computer forensics. EC-Council through its impervious network of professionals, and huge industry following has developed various other programs in information security and e-business. EC-Council Certifications are viewed as the essential certifications needed where standard configuration and security policy courses fall short. Providing a true, hands-on, tactical approach to security, individuals armed with the knowledge disseminated by EC-Council programs are securing networks around the world and beating the hackers at their own game.

About the EC-Council I Press

The EC-Council I Press was formed in late 2008 as a result of a cutting edge partnership between global information security certification leader, EC-Council and leading global academic publisher, Cengage Learning. This partnership marks a revolution in academic textbooks and courses of study in Information Security, Computer Forensics, Disaster Recovery, and End-User Security. By identifying the essential topics and content of EC-Council professional certification programs, and repurposing this world class content to fit academic programs, the EC-Council I Press was formed. The academic community is now able to incorporate this powerful cutting edge content into new and existing Information Security programs. By closing the gap between academic study and professional certification, students and instructors are able to leverage the power of rigorous academic focus and high demand industry certification. The EC-Council I Press is set to revolutionize global information security programs and ultimately create a new breed of practitioners capable of combating the growing epidemic of cybercrime and the rising threat of cyber-war.

Penetration Testing Series

The EC-Council | Press *Penetration Testing* series preparing learners for E|CSA/LPT certification, is intended for those studying to become Network Server Administrators, Firewall Administrators, Security Testers, System Administrators and Risk Assessment professionals. This series covers a broad base of topics in advanced penetration testing and security analysis. The content of this program is designed to expose the learner to groundbreaking methodologies in conducting thorough security analysis, as well as advanced penetration testing techniques. Armed with the knowledge from the Penetration Testing series, learners will be able to perform the intensive assessments required to effectively identify and mitigate risks to the security of the organization's infrastructure. The series when used in its entirety helps prepare readers to take and succeed on the E|CSA, Certified Security Analyst certification exam.

Books in Series:
- *Penetration Testing: Security Analysis*/1435483669
- *Penetration Testing: Procedures and Methodologies*/1435483677
- *Penetration Testing: Network and Perimeter Testing*/1435483685
- *Penetration Testing: Communication Media Testing*/1435483693
- *Penetration Testing: Network Threat Testing*/1435483707

Procedures and Methodologies

Procedures and Methodologies coverage includes techniques and tools to perform a thorough penetration test. Discussion includes legal requirements, rules of engagement, how to plan and schedule a test, how to perform vulnerability analysis, external and internal penetration testing, and techniques to conduct an advanced penetration test.

Chapter Contents

Chapter 1, *Penetration Testing Methodologies,* explains the fundamentals of penetration testing including what make a good penetration test, common techniques, and the process for conducting a test. Chapter 2, *Customers and Legal Agreements*, focuses on various legal issues involved in penetration testing. Chapter 3, *Duties of a Licensed Penetration Tester*, discusses the professional duties of a Licensed Penetration Tester including legal standards. It also covers the importance of a clear understanding of the rules of engagement (ROE) between organization and penetration tests including how to define the scope of the ROE. Chapter 4, *Penetration Testing Planning and Scheduling*, explains how to prepare and execute a test plan. Chapter 5, Pre-Penetration Testing Checklist, describes this essential tool including a clear explanation of each item on the checklist.

Chapter 6, *Information Gathering and Social Engineering Penetration Testing*, explains the steps required to ensure that complete information is gathered, defines social engineering and explains how to conduct a search for information via the Internet. Chapter 7, *Vulnerability Analysis*, explains the process on how to conduct a vulnerability assessment including how to recognize, measure and prioritize vulnerabilities in a system. Chapter 8, *External Penetration Testing*, explains the evaluation of the strengths and weaknesses of an organizations internal and external architecture through the Internet. Chapter 9, *Internal Network Penetration Testing*, discusses how to test the security weaknesses and strengths of an organization computers and devices from within the company. Chapter 10, *Penetration Testing Deliverables*, describes the components of a penetration testing report and describes how a tester creates the final report. Chapter 11, *Post-Testing Actions*, focuses on the actions that an organization should take following the completion of a penetration test. Chapter 12, *Advanced Exploits and Tools*, explains the concept of simulating an attack by experienced hackers including techniques to conduct the testing.

Chapter Features

Many features are included in each chapter and all are designed to enhance the learner's learning experience. Features include:

- *Objectives* begin each chapter and focus the learner on the most important concepts in the chapter.
- *Key Terms* are designed to familiarize the learner with terms that will be used within the chapter.

- *Chapter Summary*, at the end of each chapter, serves as a review of the key concepts covered in the chapter.
- *Hands-On Projects* encourage the learner to apply the knowledge they have gained after finishing the chapter. Chapters covering the Licensed Penetration Testing (LPT) materials do not have Hands-On Projects. The LPT content does not lend itself to these types of activities. Files for the *Hands-On Projects* can be found on the Student Resource Center. Note: you will need your access code provided in your book to enter the site. Visit *www.cengage.com/community/eccouncil* for a link to the Student Resource Center.

Student Resource Center

The *Student Resource Center* contains all the files you need to complete the *Hands-On Projects* found at the end of the chapters. Chapters covering the Licensed Penetration Testing (LPT) materials do not have Hands-On Projects. The LPT content does not lend itself to these types of activities. Instructions for logging onto the Student Resource Site are included with the access code. Visit *www.cengage.com/community/eccouncil* for a link to the Student Resource Center.

Additional Instructor Resources

Free to all instructors who adopt the *Procedures and Methodologies* book for their courses is a complete package of instructor resources. These resources are available from the Course Technology web site, *www.cengage.com/coursetechnology*, by going to the product page for this book in the online catalog, click on the Companion Site on the Faculty side; click on any of the Instructor Resources in the left navigation and login to access the files. Once you accept the license agreement, the selected files will be displayed.

Resources include:

- *Instructor Manual*: This manual includes course objectives and additional information to help your instruction.
- *ExamView Testbank*: This Windows-based testing software helps instructors design and administer tests and pre-tests. In addition to generating tests that can be printed and administered, this full-featured program has an online testing component that allows students to take tests at the computer and have their exams automatically graded.
- *PowerPoint Presentations*: This book comes with a set of Microsoft PowerPoint slides for each chapter. These slides are meant to be used as a teaching aid for classroom presentations, to be made available to students for chapter review, or to be printed for classroom distribution. Instructors are also at liberty to add their own slides.
- *Labs*: Additional Hands-on Activities to provide additional practice for your students.
- *Assessment Activities*: Additional assessment opportunities including discussion questions, writing assignments, internet research activities, and homework assignments along with a final cumulative project.
- *Final Exam*: Provides a comprehensive assessment of *Procedures and Methodologies* content.

Cengage Learning Information Security Community Site

This site was created for learners and instructors to find out about the latest in information security news and technology.

Visit *community.cengage.com/infosec* to:

- Learn what's new in information security through live news feeds, videos and podcasts.
- Connect with your peers and security experts through blogs and forums.
- Browse our online catalog.

How to Become E|CSA Certified

EC-Council Certified Security Analyst (E|CSA) complements the Certified Ethical Hacker (C|EH) certification by exploring the analytical phase of ethical hacking. While C|EH exposes the learner to hacking tools and technologies, E|CSA takes it a step further by exploring how to analyze the outcome from these tools and technologies.

E|CSA is a relevant milestone towards achieving EC-Council's Licensed Penetration Tester (LPT), which also ingrains the learner in the business aspect of penetration testing. The LPT standardizes the knowledge base for penetration testing professionals by incorporating the best practices followed by experienced experts in the field. The LPT designation is achieved via an application/approval process. LPT is obtained by holding both the CEH and ECSA, then completing the application process for LPT found here at *http://www.eccouncil.org/lpt.htm*.

E|CSA Certification exams are available through Authorized Prometric Testing Centers. To finalize your certification after your training, you must:

1. Apply for and purchase an exam voucher from the EC-Council Community Site at Cengage: *www.cengage.com/community/eccouncil*.

2. Once you have your Exam Voucher, visit www.prometric.com and schedule your exam.

3. Take and pass the E|CSA certification examination with a score of 70% or better.

About Our Other EC-Council | Press Products

Ethical Hacking and Countermeasures Series

The EC-Council | Press *Ethical Hacking and Countermeasures* series is intended for those studying to become security officers, auditors, security professionals, site administrators, and anyone who is concerned about or responsible for the integrity of the network infrastructure. The series includes a broad base of topics in offensive network security, ethical hacking, as well as network defense and countermeasures. The content of this series is designed to immerse the learner into an interactive environment where they will be shown how to scan, test, hack and secure information systems. A wide variety of tools, viruses, and malware is presented in these books, providing a complete understanding of the tactics and tools used by hackers. By gaining a thorough understanding of how hackers operate, ethical hackers are able to set up strong countermeasures and defensive systems to protect their organization's critical infrastructure and information. The series when used in its entirety helps prepare readers to take and succeed on the C|EH certification exam from EC-Council.

Books in Series:
*   *Ethical Hacking and Countermeasures: Attack Phases*/143548360X
*   *Ethical Hacking and Countermeasures: Threats and Defense Mechanisms*/1435483618
*   *Ethical Hacking and Countermeasures: Web Applications and Data Servers*/1435483626
*   *Ethical Hacking and Countermeasures: Linux, Macintosh and Mobile Systems*/1435483642
*   *Ethical Hacking and Countermeasures: Secure Network Infrastructures*/1435483650

Computer Forensics Series

The EC-Council | Press *Computer Forensics* Series, preparing learners for C|HFI certification, is intended for those studying to become police investigators and other law enforcement personnel, defense and military personnel, e-business security professionals, systems administrators, legal professionals, banking, insurance and other professionals, government agencies, and IT managers. The content of this program is designed to expose the learner to the process of detecting attacks and collecting evidence in a forensically sound manner with the intent to report crime and prevent future attacks. Advanced techniques in computer investigation and analysis with interest in generating potential legal evidence are included. In full, this series prepares the learner to identify evidence in computer related crime and abuse cases as well as track the intrusive hacker's path through client system.

Books in Series:
- *Computer Forensics: Investigation Procedures and Response*/1435483499
- *Computer Forensics: Investigating Hard Disks, File and Operating Systems*/1435483502
- *Computer Forensics: Investigating Data and Image Files*/1435483510
- *Computer Forensics: Investigating Network Intrusions and Cybercrime*/1435483529
- *Computer Forensics: Investigating Wireless Networks and Devices*/1435483537

Network Defense Series

The EC-Council | Press *Network Defense* Series, preparing learners for INSA certification, is intended for those studying to become system administrators, network administrators and anyone who is interested in network security technologies. This series is designed to educate learners, from a vendor neutral standpoint, how to defend the networks they manage. This series covers the fundamental skills in evaluating internal and external threats to network security, design, and how to enforce network level security policies, and ultimately protect an organization's information. Covering a broad range of topics from secure network fundamentals, protocols & analysis, standards and policy, hardening infrastructure, to configuring IPS, IDS and firewalls, bastion host and honeypots, among many other topics, learners completing this series will have a full understanding of defensive measures taken to secure their organizations information. The series when used in its entirety helps prepare readers to take and succeed on the NISA, Network Security Administrator certification exam from EC-Council.

Books in Series
- *Network Defense: Fundamentals and Protocols*/1435483553
- *Network Defense: Security Policy and Threats*/1435483561
- *Network Defense: Perimeter Defense Mechanisms*/143548357X
- *Network Defense: Securing and Troubleshooting Network Operating Systems*/1435483588
- *Network Defense: Security and Vulnerability Assessment*/1435483596

Cyber Safety/1435483715

Cyber Safety is designed for anyone who is interested in learning computer networking and security basics. This product provides information cyber crime; security procedures; how to recognize security threats and attacks, incident response, and how to secure internet access. This book gives individuals the basic security literacy skills to begin high-end IT programs. The book also prepares readers to take and succeed on the Security|5 certification exam from EC-Council.

Wireless Safety/1435483766

Wireless Safety introduces the learner to the basics of wireless technologies and its practical adaptation. *Wireless|5* is tailored to cater to any individual's desire to learn more about wireless technology. It requires no pre-requisite knowledge and aims to educate the learner in simple applications of these technologies. Topics include wireless signal propagation, IEEE and ETSI Wireless Standards, WLANs and Operation, Wireless Protocols and Communication Languages, Wireless Devices, and Wireless Security Network The book also prepares readers to take and succeed on the Wireless|5 certification exam from EC-Council.

Network Safety/1435483774

Network Safety provides the basic core knowledge on how infrastructure enables a working environment. Intended for those in an office environment and for the home user who wants to optimize resource utilization, share infrastructure and make the best of technology and the convenience it offers. Topics include foundations of networks, networking components, wireless networks, basic hardware components, the networking environment and connectivity as well as troubleshooting. The book also prepares readers to take and succeed on the Network|5 certification exam from EC-Council.

Disaster Recovery Series

The *Disaster Recovery Series* is designed to fortify virtualization technology knowledge of system administrators, systems engineers, enterprise system architects, and any IT professional who is concerned about the integrity of the their network infrastructure. Virtualization technology gives the advantage of additional flexibility as well as cost savings while deploying a disaster recovery solution. The series when used in its entirety helps prepare readers to take and succeed on the E|CDR and E|CVT, Disaster Recovery and Virtualization Technology certification exam from EC-Council. The EC-Council Certified Disaster Recovery and Virtualization Technology professional will have a better understanding of how to setup Disaster Recovery Plans using traditional and virtual technologies to ensure business continuity in the event of a disaster.

Books in Series:
- *Disaster Recovery*/1435488709
- *Virtualization Security*/1435488695

Acknowledgements

Michael H. Goldner is the Chair of the School of Information Technology for ITT Technical Institute in Norfolk Virginia, and also teaches bachelor level courses in computer network and information security systems. Michael has served on and chaired ITT Educational Services Inc. National Curriculum Committee on Information Security. He received his Juris Doctorate from Stetson University College of Law, his undergraduate degree from Miami University and has been working over fifteen years in the area of Information Technology. He is an active member of the American Bar Association, and has served on that organization's Cyber Law committee. He is a member of IEEE, ACM and ISSA, and is the holder of a number of industrially recognized certifications including, CISSP, CEH, CHFI, CEI, MCT, MCSE/Security, Security +, Network + and A+. Michael recently completed the design and creation of a computer forensic program for ITT Technical Institute, and has worked closely with both EC-Council and Delmar/Cengage Learning in the creation of this EC-Council Press series.

## Chapter 1

Penetration Testing Methodologies

Objectives

After completing this chapter, you should be able to:

- Frame a guideline that a penetration tester can adopt while performing a penetration test
- Differentiate between penetration testing and vulnerability scanning
- Illustrate the differences between white-, black-, and gray-box testing
- Describe social-engineering techniques
- Calculate the effective costs and benefits of a penetration test
- Conduct passive reconnaissance
- Explain the functions of the three phases of a penetration test
- Illustrate the profile of a good penetration tester
- Outline basic penetration testing methodologies

Key Terms

Black-box testing a type of penetration testing in which the tester has no information or assistance from the client

Gray-box testing a type of penetration testing in which the tester simulates an attack made by someone inside the client's company

Passive research a penetration testing technique that provides information on the configuration of the organization's system by using public-domain sources

Penetration testing a form of security testing that assesses the security model of a network as a whole

Return on investment (ROI) the ratio of the net gain from a planned project to its total costs

Social engineering   a technique used by attackers to exploit the human vulnerabilities within a network

Vulnerability scanning (or testing)   a process that examines the security of individual computers, network devices, or applications

White-box testing   a type of penetration testing in which the tester has full access to the client's information

Introduction to Penetration Testing Methodologies

Penetration testing goes a step beyond vulnerability testing in the field of security assessments. Unlike *vulnerability scanning*—a process that examines the security of individual computers, network devices, or applications—penetration testing assesses the security model of the network as a whole. Penetration testing can reveal to network administrators, IT managers, and executives the potential consequences of a real attacker breaking into the network. Penetration testing also sheds light on the security weaknesses missed by a typical vulnerability scan.

A penetration test will point out vulnerabilities and document how those weaknesses can be exploited. It also shows how an attacker can exploit several minor vulnerabilities to compromise a computer or network. Penetration testing exposes the gaps in the security model of an organization and helps organizations strike a balance between technical prowess and business functionality from the perspective of potential security breaches. This information is also useful during disaster recovery and business continuity planning.

Most vulnerability assessments are carried out solely based on software and do not assess other types of potential security problems. People and processes can be the source of security vulnerabilities as much as technology or software vulnerabilities can. Using social-engineering techniques, penetration tests can reveal whether employees routinely allow people without identification to enter company facilities and gain unauthorized access to a computer system. Practices such as the patch management cycle can be evaluated during a penetration test. A penetration test can also reveal process problems, such as delaying security updates until three days after they are released, which would give attackers a three-day window to exploit known vulnerabilities.

A penetration tester can be differentiated from an attacker only by intent and lack of malice. Therefore, employees or external experts must be cautioned against conducting penetration tests without proper authorization. Incomplete and unprofessional penetration testing can result in a loss of services and disruption of business continuity.

The management of the client organization should provide clear written permission to perform penetration testing. This approval should include a clear description of what will be tested and when the testing will take place. Because of the nature of penetration testing, failure to obtain this approval might result in committing a computer crime, despite best intentions.

Penetration Testing

Hacking, as it is typically defined, portrays a streak of genius or brilliance in the ability to conjure previously unknown ways of doing things. In this context, to advocate a methodology that can be followed to simulate a real-world hack through ethical hacking or penetration testing might come across as a contradiction. The reason behind advocating a methodology in penetration testing arises from the fact that most attackers follow a common underlying approach when it comes to penetrating a system.

In the context of penetration testing, the tester is limited by resources: namely time, skilled resources, and access to equipment as outlined in the penetration testing agreement. The paradox of penetration testing is that the inability to breach a target does not necessarily indicate the absence of a vulnerability. In other words, to maximize the returns from a penetration test, testers must be able to apply their skills to the resources available in such a manner that the attack area of the target is reduced as much as possible.

A penetration test simulates methods used by intruders to gain unauthorized access to an organization's networked systems and then compromise them. It involves using proprietary and open-source tools to conduct the test. Apart from automated techniques, penetration testing involves manual techniques for conducting targeted testing on specific systems to ensure that there are no security flaws that may have gone undetected earlier.

Penetration testing is performed in an organization to accomplish the following goals:

- To test and validate the efficiency of security protections and controls

- To enable vulnerability perspectives for the organization, internally and externally

- To provide usable information to audit teams gathering data for regulatory compliance

- To minimize the costs of security audits by providing comprehensive and detailed realistic evidence of an enterprise's abilities
- To help in prioritizing the application of proper patches for reported or known vulnerabilities
- To find out the existing risks of an organization's networks and systems
- To evaluate the efficiency of network security devices such as firewalls, routers, and Web servers
- To provide a comprehensive approach for preparing steps that can be taken to prevent future exploitation
- To discover if existing software, hardware, or network infrastructure needs a change or upgrade

What Should Be Tested?

An organization should conduct a risk assessment before the penetration test, which will identify the main threats to the network, including the following:

- Communications failure, e-commerce failure, and loss of confidential information
- Public systems: Web sites, e-mail gateways, and remote-access platforms
- Mail, DNS, firewalls, passwords, FTP, IIS, and Web servers
- Important production systems
- Systems belonging to important as well as regular customers

Testing should be performed on all hardware and software components of the network security system.

What Makes a Good Penetration Test?

The following activities will ensure a good penetration test:

- Establishing the parameters for the penetration test, such as objectives, limitations, and justifications of the procedures
- Hiring highly skilled and experienced professionals
- Appointing a legal penetration tester who follows the rules in the nondisclosure agreement
- Choosing a suitable set of tests that balances costs and benefits
- Following a methodology with proper planning and documentation
- Documenting the results carefully and making them comprehensible for the client. The penetration tester must be available to answer any queries whenever there is a need.
- Clearly stating findings and recommendations in the final report

Common Penetration Testing Techniques

- *Passive research*: Passive research is normally carried out during the start of an external penetration test and provides information on the configuration of the organization's system by using public-domain sources such as the following:
  - DNS (Domain Name Service)
  - USENET (newsgroups)
  - ARIN (American Registry for Internet Numbers)
- *Network mapping and OS fingerprinting*: Network mapping and OS fingerprinting provide an overview of the configuration of the entire network being tested. These techniques are designed to specify different types of services present on the target system.
- *Spoofing*: Spoofing is the act of using one machine to pretend to be another. Spoofing techniques are used in both internal and external penetration testing to access computers that are configured to reply only to specific computers.
- *Network sniffing*: Sniffing techniques are used to capture data as it travels across a network. Sniffed data packets may help a tester analyze traffic connections and data flow across a network. Network sniffing is usually performed as a part of internal penetration testing, as it is very easy to capture data packets from within a network.

- *Trojan attack*: Trojans are malicious code or programs that are usually sent to a network as e-mail attachments or transferred via chat rooms. A penetration test attempts to send specially crafted Trojans to a network.

- *Brute-force attack*: A brute-force attack is the most commonly known password-cracking method; the attacker basically tries to use all possible character combinations to crack the password effectively. It can overload a system and possibly stop it from responding to legal requests.

- *Vulnerability scanning*: Vulnerability scanning is a comprehensive examination of the targeted areas of an organization's network infrastructure. It is performed with automated tools that test a large number of weaknesses present in the system against known database vulnerabilities and security holes. It provides hands-on tools to network administrators that can be used to identify vulnerabilities before an attacker exploits them.

- *Scenario analysis*: This final phase of testing makes risk assessment of vulnerabilities much more accurate.

Penetration Testing Process

The process for performing a penetration test in an organization must be determined before testing the networking devices and system vulnerabilities. The penetration testing process includes the following procedures:

- Defining the scope
- Performing the penetration test
- Reporting and delivering results

Defining the Scope

Before performing a penetration test, it is necessary to define the range of the testing. For different types of penetration testing, different types of network devices exist. The testing criteria can target the entire network and systems, or it can simply target devices such as Web servers, routers, firewalls, DNS servers, mail severs, and FTP servers.

The following elements must be determined to properly define the range of a test:

- Extent of the test
- Target of the test
- Geographical location of the test
- Personnel to conduct the test

Performing the Penetration Test

Each company ensures that the processes they are implementing for a penetration test are appropriate. This involves gathering all the information significant to security vulnerabilities. It is the responsibility of the tester to make sure the applications, networks, and systems are not vulnerable to a security risk that could allow unauthorized access.

Reporting and Delivering Results

Once the penetration testing is completed, security testers examine all information derived from the testing procedure. The delivery report contains the following information:

- List of prioritized vulnerabilities and risks
- Information pertaining to the strong and weak points of the existing security system
- Risks categorized as high, medium, or low
- Information about each device's vulnerabilities

Testers make recommendations for repairing found vulnerabilities and provide technical information on how to fix vulnerabilities found in the system. They can also provide some useful resources to the organization, such as Internet links that may be helpful for finding additional information or patches to repair found vulnerabilities.

Announced Testing/Unannounced Testing

Announced Testing

Announced testing is an attempt to compromise systems on the client's network with the full cooperation and knowledge of the IT staff. This type of testing examines the existing security infrastructure for possible vulnerabilities. Announced penetration testing helps a penetration tester in the following ways:

- A penetration tester could easily acquire a complete overview of the infrastructure of the organization.
- A penetration tester may be given the kind of physical access provided to different employees in the organization.
- A penetration tester may get a clearer picture of measures applied to information and system security of the organization.

Security staff usually joins the penetration testing teams to conduct these audits. This type of penetration testing is quite effective for the physical security of the penetration testing.

Unannounced Testing

Unannounced testing is an attempt to compromise systems on the client's networks without the knowledge of IT security personnel. Unannounced penetration testing is quite effective for testing the security of an organization against social-engineering attempts. In unannounced penetration testing, only the top management is aware of these tests. Unannounced penetration testing helps the organization to check for organizational security threats that may arise due to human errors and ignorance. Unannounced penetration testing examines the agility of the security infrastructure and the responsiveness of the IT staff and how much they are aware of the sensitivities of the organization's information security.

Types of Penetration Testing

The three types of penetration testing are as follows:

1. *Black-box testing* (zero-knowledge testing): In order to simulate real-world attacks and minimize false positives, penetration testers can choose to undertake black-box testing (or zero knowledge testing, with no information or assistance from the client) and map the network while enumerating services, shared file systems, and operating systems discreetly. Additionally, the penetration tester can undertake wardialing to detect listening modems and wardriving to discover vulnerable access points, provided these activities are within the scope of the project.

2. *White-box testing* (complete-knowledge testing): If the organization needs to assess its security against a specific kind of attack or a specific target, complete information about the organization's network may be given to the penetration testers. The information provided can include network-topology documents, asset inventory, and valuation information. Typically, an organization would opt for this when it wants a complete audit of its security. It is critical to note that despite all this, information security is an ongoing process and penetration testing gives a snapshot of the security posture of an organization at any given point in time. White-box testing can be done with and without the knowledge of the IT staff. Only the top management is kept in the loop when a test is conducted without the involvement of the organization's IT staff.

3. *Gray-box testing*: Gray-box penetration testing is the most common approach to test the vulnerabilities that an attacker can find and exploit. This testing process functions in a similar way to black-box testing. Both the attack team and normal users are provided with the same privileges. The purpose of these tests is to simulate an attack by a malicious insider.

Black-Box Penetration Testing

In black-box testing, the testers have no prior knowledge of the infrastructure that is to be tested. The tester uses fingerprinting methods to acquire information about the inputs and the expected outputs but is not aware of the internal workings of a system.

This test is carried out only after extensive research related to the organization is done. It is carried out from the user's point of view. Designing test cases is difficult without clear and concise specifications, but it is done once the specifications are complete.

This test simulates the process of a real hacker. Black-box testing is quite time-consuming and expensive. It is also known as functional testing.

White-Box Penetration Testing

White-box testing is also known as complete-knowledge testing. The tester is provided with various pieces of information about the organization before the white-box testing is started. This test simulates the process of the company's employees.

The following information is often provided during white-box testing:

- *Company infrastructure*: This includes information related to the different departments of the organization. Information related to hardware, software, and controls are also revealed to the penetration tester.

- *Network type*: The network-type information could be regarding the organization's LAN and the topology used to connect the systems. It could also be information regarding access to remote networks or the Internet.

- *Current security implementations*: Current security implementations are the various security measures adopted by the organization to safeguard vital information against any kind of damage or theft.

- *IP address/firewall/IDS details*: This information includes details of the IP addresses the organization uses, the firewalls used to protect data from unauthorized users, and other important technical details about the network. The firewall and IDS policies are made available to the penetration tester.

- *Company policies*: The various policies that the organization has adopted to carry out business could be made available, depending on the nature of the test. Security policies, legal policies, and labor policies can all be useful to the penetration tester.

Gray-Box Penetration Testing

Gray-box penetration testing involves a security assessment and internal testing; the process of testing examines the scope of access by insiders within the organization's network. Both the attack team and normal users are provided with the same privileges, and the purpose is to simulate an attack by a malicious insider. Here, the tester usually is given limited information.

Strategies of Penetration Testing

Penetration testers use the following strategies when conducting a test:

- *External penetration testing*: External penetration testing is mainly done on servers, core software, and other infrastructure components. It is a conventional method of penetration testing.

- *Internal security assessment*: The internal security assessment offers a clear view of the site's security. Internal security assessments have a methodology similar to external penetration testing.

- *Application security assessment*: Application security assessment has a methodology similar to external penetration testing.

- *Network security assessment*: The network security assessment identifies risks and vulnerabilities that may harm network and security policies. It also provides information that is needed to make network security decisions.

- *Wireless/remote-access security assessment*: Wireless/remote-access security assessment deals with the security risks associated with wireless devices. Some of the wireless devices that are under security threat are 802.11 wireless networking and Internet access through broadband. Precautions must be taken so that the architecture, design, and deployment of such solutions are secure.

- *Telephony security assessment*: Telephony security assessment deals with the security issues of voice technologies. Penetration testers may attempt to exploit the PBXs to route calls at the target's expense or check mailbox deployment and security, voice over IP (VoIP) integration, unauthorized modem use, and associated risks.

- *Social-engineering assessment*: **Social engineering** is a technique used by attackers to exploit the human vulnerabilities within a network. Social engineering is a procedure where the weaknesses and the amicability of people are exploited. Testers may use techniques such as eavesdropping, dumpster diving, cracking employee passwords through guessing, and trying to memorize access codes by observing people.

External Penetration Testing

External penetration testing does not require any prior knowledge of the site, the topology of the network, or the platform. Extensive analysis of security devices such as Web servers, routers, and firewalls is required. In this type of testing, the vulnerabilities and deployments in the target hosts must be evaluated. The strengths and weaknesses of the company's internal and external architecture are tested through the Internet. Finding such flaws in the organization enables an organization to defend itself against exploitation of vulnerabilities by an intruder. This technique is also called a black-box security scan.

External penetration testing involves a comprehensive analysis of publicly available information about the target, such as the following:

- Web servers
- Mail servers
- Firewalls
- Routers

Internal Security Assessment

Internal penetration testing involves testing the security weaknesses and strengths of the computers and devices within a company. It involves checking the site's location and connecting to the internal network. It is mainly done to check the existence of known vulnerabilities that could be exploited by authorized internal users.

A penetration tester, disguised as an authorized user, attacks the system to check for vulnerabilities. The tester scans internal servers to identify hosts, open ports, services, and the network configuration. The tester also sniffs network traffic for sensitive data like user passwords. Internal penetration testing is more like white-box testing. The same tools and methods are used for internal penetration testing as external penetration testing. This test highlights the following vulnerabilities:

- Protocol and network infrastructure vulnerabilities
- Server operating system and application vulnerabilities, internal controls, and procedures
- Unsuitable user privileges
- Internal intrawalls separating subnetworks

Application Security Assessment

It is not possible to prevent a weak application from exposing an organization's assets, even in a well-deployed and secure infrastructure. Network points depict each logical and physical segment. The goal of this type of assessment is to ensure that an application does not reveal or grant access to the core servers and software within a network.

Software testing is an essential part of the software development process and helps to identify the superiority, accuracy, and totality of the software developed. In other words, software testing ensures error-free and reliable software. Application testing involves software-application testing and Web-application testing.

The vulnerabilities of a Web application can be identified with the help of Web-application testing, which involves executing an application remotely without knowing the inner workings of the application. The best way to perform a test is by exploiting various vulnerabilities of an application through a series of systematic and repetitive tests.

Application Security Assessment Components Some important components of application testing are the following:

- *Source-code review*: A source-code review helps to ensure that the application does not contain any important information that an attacker might use to exploit an application. For instance, clearly available application code may include test comments, names, or cleartext passwords that can reveal essential data or information about the application to the intruder.

- *Authorization testing*: Authorization testing tests the systems responsible for the commencement and maintenance of user sessions. It involves testing of the input authentication of login fields, cookie security, and lockout testing to ensure that valid sessions cannot be hijacked. Authorization testing is performed to identify the permission status of logged-in systems and helps to identify unauthorized access.

- *Functionality testing*: Functionality testing tests the systems that are responsible for an application's functionality. It involves testing of the input validation of characters and specific URLs.

- *Web penetration testing*: Web penetration testing involves checking a Web application written in languages such as J2EE, ASP.NET, and PHP. In this testing, the team is given a set of accounts on an application at different levels of privilege so that the team members can find OWASP-type vulnerabilities. Web penetration testing helps identify Web-application vulnerabilities such as SQL injection problems, XSS, XSRF, weak authentication, and source-code exposure.

Network Security Assessment

Network penetration testing is critical for an organization's computer network. It is designed to assess an organization's network and system security risks and vulnerabilities in a way that an attacker might assess a network. Network penetration testing uses processes and tools to scan the network for vulnerabilities and helps organizations develop security policies.

This test attempts to compromise systems from the network in the same way that an attacker would and then prepares a detailed report of the findings. It uncovers network security faults that can lead to data or equipment being manipulated or destroyed by Trojans, DoS attacks, and other intrusions.

The testers involved in network penetration testing are experienced in network programming and security, and thus have a deep understanding of vulnerabilities, the way to exploit those vulnerabilities, and the ways to fix them. This test ensures that the security implementation actually provides the protection that the enterprise requires when any attack takes place on a network, generally by exploiting a system vulnerability in an organization.

Wireless/Remote-Access Assessment

Wireless/remote-access assessment is used for assessing the security levels of an organization that uses a mobile workforce. To ensure effective management of the associated risks, it is essential to secure the architecture, design, and deployment of solutions.

IEEE expanded the original 802.11 standard to form an 802.11b specification with a bandwidth of up to 11 Mbps. It uses a frequency of about 2.4 GHz. 802.11a has a bandwidth of about 54 Mbps and a frequency of about 5 GHz, is least commonly used due to its high cost, and is commonly found on business networks. The 802.11g specification supports the best features of both 802.11a and 802.11b. It has a bandwidth of 54 Mbps and a frequency of 2.4 GHz. Most 802.11g access points are compatible with 802.11b.

Bluetooth technology supports wireless networking and is compatible with a wide range of operating systems and devices. Various devices like PDAs, laptops, cell phones, printers, and so on are Bluetooth enabled. Bluetooth is a simple and easy way to communicate among various computer devices. The radio communication channel is a fast-fading mobile radio channel.

Telephony Security Assessment

Telephony security assessment helps in assessing security issues related to corporate voice technologies. These security threats can include the following issues:

- Numerous modem vulnerabilities such as the authorized and unauthorized use of modems. For example, wardialing allows malicious users to uncover modems and to gain access to them.

- Voice over IP (VoIP) integration

- Mailbox deployment and security

- Abuse of PBXs by outsiders to route calls at the target's expense

Social Engineering

Social engineering is the use of influence and persuasion to mislead people for the purpose of gathering information. It is often referred to as people hacking. Social engineers use psychological tricks on a target to gain sensitive information such as contact addresses, passwords, usernames, and credit card details.

The human tendency to help and trust can be exploited in many ways to collect information. It depends on the environment or circumstances whether social engineering is computer-based or conducted through direct contact. The information could be from the trash or it could be from a sweeper. Some social-engineering tricks are false telephone calls, e-mail hoaxes, and phishing. Social engineers can pose as temporary employees or cleaning crews and walk around looking at the notes stuck to monitors. Other techniques include giving a bogus survey in a mailbox with an offering of a cash reward or a prize, or asking some seemingly innocent questions that could reveal personal information. The most popular means of social engineering is human-based. People have been conditioned not to be exceedingly suspicious. They correlate certain behavior and appearance to known persons. A good social engineer will perform background research on a company to get an idea of its basic nature and even obtain some employees' names. Such information helps attackers bypass controls to gain physical access to the organization's information systems and steal important information.

Penetration Testing Consultants

The quality of the penetration test is directly proportional to the kind of expertise that the penetration testing agency has. Any penetration testing task is successful only if qualified penetration testers with enough skill perform the test. A penetration test of a corporate network examines numerous different hosts with a number of different operating systems, network architectures, and policies and procedures. It is of the utmost importance to explain the requirements clearly to the penetration testing firm.

Before getting into the contract, it is the job of the penetration testing firm to learn about the various requirements of the target organization. It should be understood by the testing team that a penetration test to be performed for a corporate firm would necessitate probing into various networks and multiple platforms.

A penetration tester should be well versed in the target organization's policies and procedures so that the tester will not upset any of the rules and procedures that may affect the client.

There is no benchmark to label an individual as a skilled penetration tester. It is the duty of any good penetration tester to examine the various setups of networks, the architectures, and the various connections in which they are involved. All these tasks require continued exposure to such environments and extensive learning.

It is not enough for penetration testers to know various methods and procedures of hacking or for them to be well versed in the usage of various hacking tools. It is important on their part to gain knowledge about various business procedures and essential risks that may follow when businesses are probed through penetration testing. The scope of testing ranges from internal system testing to external review of various enterprise assets and consultants. By doing so, the penetration tester should gain enough knowledge of what is required and what the various methods are to perform the test as well as the issues involved in those tasks.

Required Skill Sets

A professional penetration tester should possess the following skill sets:

- Should be well versed in the following hardware concepts:
  - Networking concepts such as TCP/IP and cabling techniques
  - Routers, firewalls, and IDS
- Should be proficient in the following software concepts:
  - Ethical hacking techniques: exploits, hacking tools, etc.
  - Databases: Oracle, MSSQL
  - Open-source technologies: MySQL, Apache
  - Operating systems: Windows, Linux, Mac
- Should have knowledge of the following applications:
  - Wireless protocols and devices: Bluetooth, WAPs
  - Web servers, mail servers, SNMP stations, and access devices
- Should possess knowledge of the following services:
  - Telecommunication skills: Broadband, ISDN, ATM, and VoIP
  - Troubleshooting skills

Hiring a Penetration Tester

Companies usually ask the following questions before hiring a penetration tester:

- Is the supplier a specialist, or is the security practice a secondary concern?
- Does the supplier offer a comprehensive suite of services, tailored to the client's specific requirements?
- Does the supplier's methodology follow and exceed those of OSSTMM, CHECK, and OWASP?

- Does the supplier have a policy of employing former hackers?
- Are the supplier's staff experienced security professionals, holding recognized certifications such as CISSP, CISA, and CHECK?
- Can the staff distinguish and articulate between infrastructure and application testing?
- How many technical consultants does the supplier have who work on security and assessments, and how many of those are dedicated solely to security?
- Does the supplier present the deliverables, such as the final report, in an informed manner, with concise and practical information for technical and nontechnical parties?
- Is the supplier a recognized contributor within the security industry?
- Are references available to attest to the quality of past work performed?

Responsibilities of a Penetration Tester Some of the critical responsibilities of a penetration tester are as follows:

- Performing penetration testing and risk assessment of the target system
- Presenting reports to superiors regarding the efficiency of penetration tests and risk assessments, and making proposals for risk mitigation
- Interfacing with user groups to understand their security needs
- Exploiting the system vulnerabilities and justifying the vulnerabilities found
- Clearly defining the goals of the penetration test, ensuring superior quality, and effectively communicating the results
- Understanding the security of the organization's servers, network systems, and firewalls relevant to specific business risks

Profile of a Good Penetration Tester Good penetration testers will have the following elements in their resume:

- Conducted research and development in the security area
- Published research papers
- Made presentations at various local and international seminars
- Possess various certifications
- Possess membership/affiliation/accreditation of many respected organizations, such as:
  - EC-Council
  - IEEE
  - $(ISC)^2$
- Written and published security-related books
- Earlier achievements
- Projects handled
- Professional skill set

Companies make decisions based on the information available to them about the deployment of the penetration tester. The penetration tester must include and highlight the above-mentioned criteria to obtain a contract.

Generally, companies receive many applications if they post a particular position on job sites. In such a highly competitive scenario, the organization would naturally consider the most qualified person. So the critical features any organization would look for in a candidate would be:

- *Qualification*: Organizations look for a related graduate or postgraduate degree from a reputed institute, with a considerably good skill set and a consistent academic record.
- *Work experience*: A good candidate must have already worked for some other organization in a related field for a considerable duration. The projects handled earlier, which are related to the particular domain, also play a vital role in short-listing the candidate. For example: Nick worked for XSecurity as a network engineer for five years and is seeking career growth.

- *Cutting-edge technical skills*: The candidate should be technically proficient and should have acquired some of the leading certifications such as CCNA, CEH, CHFI, CCNP, MCSE, and CISA.
- *Communication skills*: The default requisite for any candidate would be good communication skills, both written and verbal; good interpersonal skills; confidence; and other related traits.
- *Attitude*: The attitude of the candidate toward work, the organization, and life in general speaks volumes about the individual.
- *Teamwork skills*: The candidate should be a team player who knows how to deal with both seniors and subordinates, and can bridge the gap between them. He or she should also possess good managerial skills.

Other than the above-mentioned assets, good references from former employers, superiors, and customers are beneficial.

Companies' Concerns The following can be the concerns of any company:

- Companies usually work in collaboration with reputed and well-established firms like Foundstone, ISS, TruSecure, and EC-Council.
- Companies will verify the tools that are being used, the environments in which the tools run, and the number of tools running.
- Companies ask for references from candidates who seek employment from them or who want to enter into business dealings with them.
- Business proposals submitted to companies must be in written form for evidence purposes. E-mail proposals are usually avoided from the security aspect point of view.
- Companies are particular about having security-related services.
- Companies demand security-related certifications like CISSP, CEH, and TICSA, to confirm the authenticity of business partners and clients.
- Companies are always particular about not recruiting candidates who are hackers, as they fear that their company's sites and assets will be exposed.
- Companies can ask for a security clearance in countries such as the United States.
- Companies usually focus on whether data will be stored after testing and the duration for which it has to be stored to avoid any misuse.

Methodology

It has been observed that even hackers go about their attacks in a strategic manner. A methodology ensures that the process is a standard manner with documented and repeatable results for a given security posture. This helps testers plan their testing/attack strategy according to the input gained in the preceding phases of the testing process.

A penetration test involves the systematic analysis of all the security measures in place. A full project should include some or all of the following areas:

- *Network security*: Penetration testers should check for the following things to secure a network:
  - Network surveying
  - Port scanning
  - System identification
  - Services identification
  - Vulnerability research and verification
  - Application testing and code review
  - Router testing
  - Firewall testing
  - Intrusion-detection-system testing
  - Trusted-systems testing

- Password cracking
- Denial-of-service testing
- Containment-measures testing
- *Information security*: Penetration testing to check the security of sensitive information of the organization includes the following activities:
  - Document grinding
  - Competitive intelligence scouting
  - Privacy review
- *Social engineering*: Security of the organization against social-engineering attacks may be ensured by:
  - Request testing
  - Guided suggestion testing
  - Trust testing
- *Wireless security*: A penetration tester should perform the following tasks to check the security of wireless devices and networks:
  - Wireless-networks testing
  - Cordless-communications testing
  - Privacy review
  - Infrared-systems testing
- *Communications security*: The following penetration testing methods are used for communications security:
  - PBX testing
  - Voice-mail testing
  - Fax review
  - Modem testing
- *Physical security*: Security of the organization against physical attacks may be ensured by implementing the following procedures:
  - Access-controls testing
  - Perimeter review
  - Monitoring review
  - Alarm-response testing
  - Location review
  - Environment review

Penetration Testing Methodologies List

The cornerstone of a successful penetration test is the methodology involved in devising it. The underlying methodology should help the tester by providing a systematic approach to the testing pattern. The consistency, accuracy, and efficiency of the test must be met and should be up to the mark of the testing methodology. This does not mean that the entire framework should be restrictive, however.

The following are two important types of penetration testing methodologies:

1. Proprietary methodologies
2. Open-source and public methodologies

Proprietary Methodologies There are many organizations that work on penetration testing and who offer services and certifications. These network-security organizations have their own methodologies that are kept confidential. Examples of some proprietary methodologies are:

- IBM
- ISS

- Foundstone
- EC-Council LPT

Open-Source and Public Methodologies There is a wide range of methodologies that are publicly available. Anyone can use these methodologies. Figure 1-1 illustrates a typical methodology. The following methodologies can be accessed online:

- *OSSTMM*: OSSTMM is the Open-Source Security Testing Methodology Manual, compiled by Pete Herzog. OSSTMM is a standard set of penetration tests to achieve security metrics. It is considered to be a de facto standard of the highest level of testing, and it ensures high consistency and remarkable accuracy.

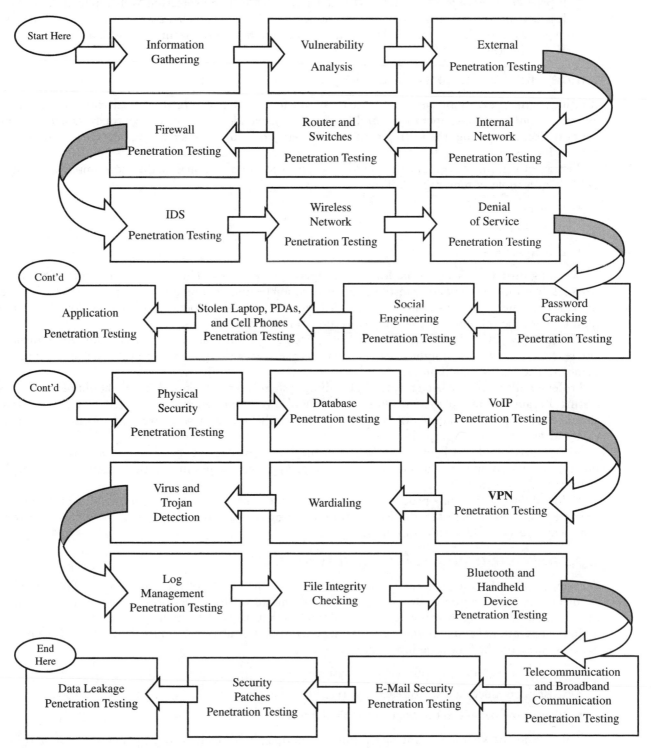

Figure 1-1 Methodologies make penetration testing more reliable.

- *CISSP*: CISSP is a certification program governed by the International Information Systems Security Certifications Consortium [(ISC)^2]. It aims at maintaining high management-level information and network security.

- *CISA*: The Certified Information Systems Auditor program is sponsored by ISACA and is accepted worldwide.

- *CHECK*: This methodology tries to spot all the vulnerabilities of a system that may cause the loss of sensitive information stored on that system.

- *OWASP*: OWASP is the Open Web Application Security Project, which is an open-source methodology. It provides a set of tools and a knowledge base, which help in protecting Web applications and services. It is beneficial for system architects, developers, vendors, consumers, and security professionals who might work on designing, developing, deploying, and testing the security of Web applications and Web services.

Guidelines for Security Checking

Routine testing prevents any incidents from occurring in the first place. Testing of network security in areas such as system configurations, operations, and administration should be conducted routinely. During the process of network security testing, the testing team should verify that all the systems are configured properly with the proper devices.

Testing of significant equipment should be performed initially. Some of the more important and common publicly accessible systems are as follows:

- Firewalls

- Web servers

- E-mail servers

Warning instructions should be followed properly while testing. There are certain types of testing, such as network scanning, vulnerability testing, and penetration testing, that require strict caution to be followed. Testing can reproduce the signs of an attack, so it is essential that the process of testing be done in a coordinated manner with the full knowledge and permission of appropriate officials.

The security policy should serve as a proper guideline for the organization's needs and requirements. Testing can reveal unknown vulnerabilities, so incorporating security-testing events into the procedures of risk management can decrease vulnerabilities.

Professionals who have been trained in handling system and network operations should perform the security testing. Because the task of system administration is also very complex and not limited to systems, organizations should have a sufficient number of administrators with the necessary skill level to perform system administration and security testing properly.

All systems should be kept up-to-date with the proper patches. It may become essential to patch numerous systems based on the results of security testing. Applying patches in a suitable manner can sharply reduce vulnerability exposure.

Vulnerability testing may produce false-positive scores or may not spot some types of problems exceeding the detection capabilities of the tools. Penetration testing is a valuable complement to vulnerability testing that is aimed to reveal hidden vulnerabilities.

Operational Strategies for Security Testing

The object of performing a security test is to maximize the benefit of the organization. From an operational point of view, penetration testing helps in determining information security strategies by identifying vulnerabilities and measuring their impact and likelihood so that they can be managed proactively.

In the operational and maintenance phases, penetration testing types and frequencies involve a prioritization process based on the following information:

- Security category of the information system
- Cost of conducting tests for each test type
- Identifying benefit to the organization's systems

The decision of what to test during the implementation phase involves all the systems present in the organization. The senior IT manager should be involved in the prioritization process.

Security Category of the Information System

FIPS 199 is Federal Information Processing Standards Publication 199. It provides standards to establish the security essentials for an organization's information systems that help in upgrading the ranking of the systems for the testing process. The risks to an organization can be evaluated by using security categories along with information about vulnerabilities and threats.

FIPS Publication 199 defines three levels of potential impact on organizations or individuals if there is a breach of security (e.g., a loss of confidentiality, integrity, or availability):

- Low

- Moderate

- High

The potential impact is low if the impact of loss of confidentiality, integrity, and availability on organizational assets, operations, or individuals may be limited. This limited effect could have the following impacts:

- Degradation in mission capability and capacity of the organization to perform major functions within the stipulated time period is somewhat affected

- Degradation in efficiency of the functions of the organization

- Little damage to the assets of the organization

- Little loss of income

- Damage to individuals

The potential impact is moderate if the impact of potential loss of confidentiality, integrity, and availability could be adverse on organizational assets, operations, or individuals. This adverse effect could have the following impacts:

- Degradation of mission capability and capacity of the organization to perform major functions within the stipulated time period is extensively affected

- Little damage to assets of the organization

- Significant loss of income

- Harmful to individuals and may lead to loss of life or serious injuries

The potential impact is high if the impact of potential loss of confidentiality, integrity, and availability could be severe or catastrophic on organizational assets, operations, or individuals. A high level of impact could produce the following effects:

- Severe degradation or loss of mission capability and failure of the organization to perform even one or two of its primary functions

- Major damage to the assets of the organization

- Major loss of resources and income

- Severe harm to individuals and possible loss of life or serious injuries

Identifying Benefits of Each Test Type

To make sure that the cost of penetration testing does not go beyond its value to the organization, the advantage of performing testing must be qualified or quantified.

The overall benefit of penetration testing is to identify vulnerabilities before an attacker exploits them. The following factors should be considered to assess the benefits of testing:

- The knowledge gained about systems and networks while performing the test process will improve the organization's control of its assets.

- By testing and correcting revealed deficiencies, an organization significantly decreases the possibility of any intrusion or business interruption and thereby reduces the amount of vulnerabilities that can be exploited.

Prioritizing the Systems for Testing

The results of the security category, the cost of conducting a test, and the benefits are evaluated and ranked to prioritize the systems. These results serve as a detailed analysis of the weaknesses present in the organization that require immediate attention. The analysis must provide a list of systems based on the following factors:

- Cost of testing
- Security category
- Benefits

The list will include required resources for conducting each type of test for each system. Initially, the organization needs to determine the minimum required resources for minimum testing (for those systems with the highest level of impact). Then, it should identify and compare the resources of security testing with the required resources. If both of these resources are not sufficient to carry out the test process for high-impact systems, then the organization should gather additional resources to complete the security testing. The calculated cost for security testing will be the quantitative evidence for using more resources. After identifying the funding for most critical systems, objects with less priority are tested in descending order. The result of the final step is based on the highest impact systems that are tested with related frequency and testing techniques.

ROI for Penetration Testing

ROI is a traditional financial measure based on historic data. It is a retrospective metric that yields insights into how to improve business results in the future. In reality, most organizations use one or more financial metrics that they refer to individually or collectively as ROI. These metrics include:

- *Payback period*: The amount of time required for the benefits to pay back the cost of the project
- *Net present value (NPV)*: The value of future benefits reported in terms of today's money
- *Internal rate of return (IRR)*: The benefits reported as an interest rate

Return on investment (ROI) is the ratio of the net gain from a planned project to its total costs. The purpose of a penetration test in an organization is to discover and expose vulnerabilities in an organization's security system, considering the company's information assets and how those assets are related to the business value of the organization.

For the calculation of the TCO (total cost of ownership), a comparison of security investment and the potential damage prevented is performed. This compares the cost of the loss to the company's assets with the cost of preventing that loss.

Through a penetration test, the knowledge of possible risk, vulnerabilities, or threats to information assets (IA) and the information required to mitigate those risks is acquired.

Determining the Cost of Each Test Type

The cost of a penetration test depends on the following factors:

- Size of the organization's system to be tested, such as a local area network (LAN), wide area network (WAN), single database, or major application
- Complexity of the system for testing
- Skills of the penetration testers engaged
- Level of human interaction required for each test
- Selecting sample hosts for penetration testing
- Duration of time spent in performing penetration testing
- Scope of the engagement and travel expenses

Phases of Penetration Testing

- *Pre-attack phase*: This phase is focused on gathering as much information as possible about the target to be attacked. It can be invasive, such as gathering information through scanning, or it can be noninvasive, such as reviewing public records.

- *Attack phase*: The information gathered in the pre-attack phase forms the basis of the attack strategy. During the attack phase, the attack strategy is developed and carried out.

- *Post-attack phase*: The post-attack phase is a crucial part of the testing process, as the tester needs to restore the network to its original state. This involves cleaning up testing processes and removing vulnerabilities created (not those that existed originally), exploits crafted, and so on, until all systems tested are returned to their original state prior to testing.

Pre-attack Phase

The pre-attack phase consists of the hacker's attempts to investigate or explore the potential target. Ultimately, it boils down to information gathering and may involve competitive intelligence gathering, social engineering, breaching physical security, etc. This is often done stealthily, and attackers typically spend more time in the pre-attack phase than in the actual attack phase.

Beginning with passive reconnaissance, the tester will gather as much information as possible about the target company. Most leaked information is related to the network topology and the types of services running on the network. The tester can use this information to provisionally map out the network for planning a more coordinated attack strategy later.

Regarding publicly available information, access to this information is independent of the organization's resources and thus can be effectively accessed by anyone. This information can even be contained on systems unrelated to the organization.

Best Practices It is vital to maintain a log of all the activities carried out and the results obtained. Testers must ensure that their work is time-stamped and communicated to the appropriate person within the organization if it is so agreed upon in the rules of engagement.

While planning an attack strategy, testers should also make sure to correlate their strategic choices to the input or output obtained from the pre-attack phase. The system logs are a good guide to start either developing or acquiring the tools based on need.

Results That Can Be Expected Information obtained during this phase may include:

- *Physical and logical location of the organization*: Footprinting tools and techniques can be utilized during this phase. Examples include using the WHOIS database, using search engines such as Google, finding the network block using RIRs, and searching the company Web site. This phase incorporates analysis of the data returned during normal interaction with the organization. This includes the banners and other system messages displayed when a user connects to a Web or mail server.

- *Analog connections including phone lines, fax lines, dialup lines, and other out-of-band connectivity*: These can be recorded for later use with wardialers such as PhoneSweep and ToneLoc. The most important function of this is to bypass the conventional security provided by firewalls, DMZs, and the like by taking advantage of an unprotected modem.

- *Personal information*: The tester can scout other media, such as print media, to obtain personal information (people's names and phone numbers). The tester can use social-engineering techniques to extract information. This can include breaching physical security (tailgating), dumpster diving, impersonation, and so on.

- *Information about other organizations that are connected to the target being profiled*: As security is only as good as the weakest link, it is possible to breach security by taking advantage of a weak link. Examples include third-party merchant sites or partners using default installations of Web-application components known to have vulnerabilities.

- *Any other information that has the potential to result in a possible exploitation*: This can include job postings, message group postings, press releases, and even casual conversations.

Passive Reconnaissance Passive reconnaissance involves the following activities:

- Mapping the directory structures of Web servers and FTP servers.

- Gathering competitive intelligence over newsgroups for references to and submissions from within the organization, bulletin boards, and industry feedback sites. Related information can be obtained from job postings, number of personnel, published resumes, and responsibilities. This can also include estimating the cost of support infrastructure.

- Determining the worth of infrastructure interfacing with the Web. Asset classification, as it is described under ISO 17799, may also be carried out here. This is to ensure that the penetration test is able to quantify acceptable risk to the business.

- Retrieving network registration information from WHOIS databases, critical asset information from financial Web sites, and information about business services related to the registered party.

- Determining the product range and service offerings of the target company that are available online or can be requested online. A tester can estimate the threat level posed to these by checking for available documentation, associated third-party product vulnerabilities, cracks, and versions.

- Document sifting: This refers to gathering information solely from published material. This includes skimming through a Web page's source code; identifying key personnel; investigating them further through background checks based on published resumes and affiliations; and publicly available information such as personal Web pages, personal e-mail addresses, job databases, and properties pages of soft copies of any documents.

- Social engineering can be done by identifying a conduit (a person who can be targeted easily based on the information gained about personnel) and profiling that person. This may be in terms of position, habits, preferences, weak traits, etc. The objective here should be to extract sensitive information and catalog it in the log.

Active Reconnaissance The information gathering process encroaches on the target territory. In this case, the perpetrator may send probes to the target in the form of port scans, network sweeps, enumeration of shares and user accounts, etc. The hacker may adopt techniques such as social engineering and use tools that automate these tasks, such as scanners and sniffers. The footprint left by the attacker is larger, and novices can be easily identified.

- *Network mapping*: Map the network by getting the information from the server domain registry numbers unearthed during the passive reconnaissance phase. The IP block forms the backbone of the network. Investigate the network linkages both upstream and downstream. These include the primary and secondary name servers for hosts and subdomains. Steps include:
  - Interpreting broadcast responses from the network.
  - If ICMP is not blocked, use ICMP to sweep the network.
  - Use reverse name lookups to verify addresses.

- *Perimeter mapping*: Map the perimeter by tracerouting the gateway to define the outer network layer and routers, and tracing system trails in the Web logs and intrusion logs. The tester may also follow system trails from Web postings and bulletin boards. Steps include:
  - Analyzing the traceroute response and mapping the perimeter using firewalking techniques.
  - Using online sources such as Netcraft to find out more about the information systems (IS) infrastructure and historical performance data. This will give server uptime for the latest patch releases. Verify them.

- *System and service identification through port scans*: This will essentially result in the identification of live systems and their IP addresses, port states (open, closed, or filtered), protocols used (routing or tunneled), active services and service types, service application types and patch levels, OS fingerprinting, version identification, internal IP addressing, etc. Steps include:
  - Deploying a connect scan for all hosts on the network. Use this through port 1024 to enumerate ports.
  - Deploying a stealth SYN scan for ports 20, 21, 22, 23, 25, 80, and 443. Extend this scan to live systems to detect port states.
  - Deploying an ACK scan for ports 3100–3150, 10001–10050, and 33500–33550 using TCP port 80 as the source to get past the firewall. Additional ports may be scanned randomly for ports above 35000 on the network.
  - Deploying a fragment scan in reverse order with FIN, NULL, and XMAS flags set for ports 21, 22, 25, 80, and 443. This can also be used for enumerating the subset of ports on the default packet fragment testing ports.

- Deploying FTP bounce and idle scans for ports 22, 81, 111, 132, 137, and 161 in order to infiltrate the DMZ.

- Deploying UDP scans to check for port filtering on a small subset. If it is not filtered, this can also be used to enumerate ports. Additionally, send Trojan scans to those ports and note responses.

- Cataloging all the protocols being used. Note any tunneled or encapsulated protocols.

- Cataloging all services identified for ports discovered—whether filtered or not. Note service remapping and system redirects.

- Cataloging all applications identified using scanners such as Nmap. Additional information such as patch level and version fingerprinting may also be retrieved. Note TCP sequence predictability for the scans.

- *Web profiling*: This phase will attempt to profile and map the Internet profile of the organization. Information gleaned will be used for later attack techniques such as SQL injection, Web server and application hacking, session hijacking, denial-of–service, etc. Steps include:

  - Cataloging all Web-based forms, types of user input, and form-submission destinations.

  - Cataloging Web privacy data including cookie types (persistent or session), nature and location of information stored, cookie expiration rules, and encryption used.

  - Cataloging Web error messages, bugs in services, third-party links, and applications. Locate the destination.

Attack Phase

The attack phase involves the actual compromise of the target. The attacker may exploit a vulnerability discovered during the pre-attack phase or use security loopholes such as a weak security policy to gain access to the system. The important point here is that while the attacker needs only one port of entry, organizations are left to defend several. Once inside, the attacker may escalate privileges and install a backdoor to sustain access to the system and exploit it.

Perimeter Testing Social engineering will be an ongoing activity through the testing phase, as sensitive information can be gleaned at any stage of testing. The tests that can be carried out in this context include, but are not limited to, making impersonating or mock phone calls to capture sensitive information, verifying information gathered through activities like dumpster diving, and so on. Other means include e-mail testing, trusted-person acquisition, and attempts to retrieve legitimate authentication details such as passwords and access privileges. Information gathered here can be used later in Web-application testing as well.

Firewall Testing The information gained during the pre-attack phase using techniques like firewalking is further exploited here. Attempts to evade the IDS and bypass the firewall are made. This includes crafting and sending packets to check firewall rules—for example, sending SYN packets to test stealth detection. This will determine the nature of various packet responses through the firewall. A SYN packet can be used to enumerate the target network. Similarly, other port scans with different flags set can be used to attempt enumeration of the network. This will also give an indication of source port control on the target.

   Usually, perimeter testing measures the firewall's ability to handle fragmentation, big packet fragments, overlapping fragments, a flood of packets, etc. Testing methods for perimeter security include, but are not limited to, the following techniques:

- Evaluating error reporting and error management with ICMP probes

- Checking access control lists with crafted packets

- Measuring the threshold for denial of service by attempting persistent TCP connections, evaluating transitory TCP connections, and attempting streaming UDP connections

- Evaluating protocol filtering rules by attempting connection using various protocols such as SSH, FTP, and telnet

- Evaluating the IDS capability by passing malicious content (such as malformed URLs) and scanning the target variously for response to abnormal traffic

- Examining the perimeter security system's response to Web server scans using multiple methods such as POST, DELETE, and COPY

Web-Application Testing I The Web-application testing phase can be carried out as the tester proceeds to acquire the target.

- *Input validation*: Tests include OS command injection, script injection, SQL injection, LDAP injection, and cross-site scripting. Other tests include checking for dependency on external data and source verification.

- *Output sanitization*: Tests include parsing special characters and verifying error checking in the application.

- *Checking for buffer overflows*: Tests include attacks against stack overflows, heap overflows, and format-string overflows.

- *Access control*: Access control checks for access to administrative interfaces, sends data to manipulate form fields, attempts URL query strings, changes values on the client-side script, and attacks cookies. Other tests include checking for authorization breaches, lapses in event-handling sequences, proxy handling, and compliance with the least-privilege access rule.

- *Denial of service*: A test for a DoS vulnerability is induced through malformed user input, user lockout and application lockout due to traffic overload, transaction requests, or excessive requests on the application.

Web-Application Testing II

- *Component checking*: Check for security controls on Web server/application components that might expose the Web application to vulnerabilities such as basic authentication.

- *Data and error checking*: Check for data-related security lapses such as storage of sensitive data in the cache or input of sensitive data using HTML. Check for verbose error messages that give away more details of the application and error types than necessary.

- *SQL-injection techniques*: SQL injection may be attempted against a Web application to gain access to the target system.

- *Confidentiality check*: For applications using secure protocols and encryption, check for lapses in key-exchange mechanisms, inadequate key length, and weak algorithms. Validate authentication scheme by attempting user enumeration through login or recovery process. Check digital certificate and signature verification process.

- *Session management*: Check time validity of session tokens, length of tokens, and expiration of session tokens while transiting from SSL to non-SSL resources; presence of any session tokens in the browser history or cache; and randomness of the session ID (check for use of user data in generating the ID).

- *Configuration verification*: Attempt manipulation of resources using HTTP methods such as DELETE and PUT, check for version content availability and any visible restricted source code in public domains, attempt directory and file listing, and test for known vulnerabilities and accessibility of administrative interfaces in server and server components.

Wireless Testing If the organization has a wireless network, the following activities may be undertaken. This is not an exhaustive list, and the tester is encouraged to update the list with new testing methods. Activities include the following methods:

- Check if the access point's default Service Set Identifier (SSID) is easily available. Test to see if any access point broadcasts the SSID, and see if it is possible to access the LAN through this. Tests can include brute forcing the SSID character string using tools like Kismet.

- Check for vulnerabilities in accessing the WLAN through the wireless router, access point, or gateway. This can include verifying if the default Wired Equivalent Privacy (WEP) encryption key can be captured and decrypted.

- Audit for broadcast beacon of any access point and check all protocols available through the access points. Check if layer-2 switched networks are being used instead of hubs for access point connectivity.

- Subject authentication to playback of previous authentications in order to check for privilege escalation and unauthorized access.

- Verify whether access is granted only to client machines with registered MAC addresses.

Acquiring the Target Usually, target acquisition refers to all the activities that are undertaken to unearth as much information as possible about a particular machine or system so that it can be used later in the actual process of exploitation. Acquiring a target refers to the set of activities in which the tester subjects the target machine to more-intrusive challenges such as vulnerability scans and security assessments. This is done to gain more information about the target that can be used in the exploit phase.

Examples of such activities include subjecting the machine to the following procedures:

- *Active probing assaults*: This can use results of network scans to gather further information that can lead to a compromise.
- *Running vulnerability scans*: Vulnerability scans are completed in this phase.
- *Trusted systems and trusted process assessment*: This involves attempting to access the machine's resources using legitimate information obtained through social engineering or other means.

Escalating Privileges Once the target has been acquired, the tester attempts to exploit the system and gain greater access to protected resources.

Activities include the following techniques:

- The tester may take advantage of poor security policies, e-mails, or unsafe Web code to gather information that can lead to escalation of privileges.
- Use of techniques such as brute force to achieve privileged status. Tools for this purpose include GetAdmin and password crackers.
- Use of Trojans and protocol analyzers.
- Use of information gleaned through techniques such as social engineering to gain unauthorized access to privileged resources.

Execute, Implant, and Retract In this phase, the tester effectively compromises the acquired system by executing arbitrary code. The objective here is to explore the extent to which security fails. The tester will attempt to execute arbitrary code, hide files in the compromised system, and leave the system without raising alarms. The tester will then attempt to reenter the system stealthily. Activities include the following processes:

- Executing exploits already available or specially crafted to take advantage of the vulnerabilities identified in the target system.
- Subjecting the system to denial-of-service attacks. This can be carried out in the previous phase as well.
- Exploiting buffer overflows in order to trick the system into running arbitrary code. The tester may spawn a remote shell, and attempt to upload files and conceal them within the system.
- Executing activities that are usually subjected to containment measures such as the use of Trojans and rootkits. The tester may also use viruses that take advantage of vulnerabilities to exploit the system. Establishing a rootkit or a Trojan that can lead to access of more critical systems can also be part of the testing process.
- Erasing log files or camouflaging modifications to escape legal ramifications. Activities in the retract phase include manipulation of audit log files to remove traces of the activities. Examples include use of tools such as Auditpol. The tester may also change settings within the system to remain inconspicuous during a reentry, change of log settings, etc.
- Reentering the system by using the backdoor implanted by the tester.

Post-attack Phase and Activities

This phase is critical to any penetration test, as it is the responsibility of the tester to restore the systems to the pretest state. The objective of the test is to show where security fails, and unless there is a scaling of the penetration test agreement whereby the tester is assigned the responsibility of correcting the security posture of the systems, this phase must be completed.

Activities in this phase include the following processes:

- Removing all files uploaded to the system
- Cleaning all registry entries and removing any vulnerabilities created

- Reversing all file and settings manipulations done during the test
- Reversing all changes in privileges and user settings
- Removing all tools and exploits from the tested systems
- Restoring the network to the pretest stage by removing shares and connections
- Mapping the network state
- Documenting and capturing all logs registered during the test
- Analyzing all results and presenting them to the organization

 It is important that the penetration tester document all activities and record all observations and results so that the test can be repeated and verified for the given security posture of the organization.

For the organization to quantify the security risk in business terms, it is essential that the tester identify critical systems and critical resources, and map the threats to these.

Chapter Summary

- Adopting a methodology while performing a penetration test is advisable.
- The methodology should be open, flexible, and applicable at a broad level.
- Each test is unique, and attack strategies need to be carefully planned.
- The basic difference in the approaches of vulnerability testing and penetration testing makes it impractical to rely on checklists and templates alone in the latter context.
- Passive research is normally carried out during the start of an external penetration test and provides information on the configuration of the organization's systems by using public-domain sources.
- Penetration tests can be announced or unannounced.
- Gray-box penetration testing examines the scope of access by insiders within the organization's network.
- Penetration tests have three phases: pre-attack, attack, and post-attack.
- Social engineering is the use of influence and persuasion to mislead people for the purpose of gathering information.

## Chapter 2

Customers and Legal Agreements

Objectives

After completing this chapter, you should be able to:

- Explain the need for penetration testing, stages of penetration testing, and customer requirements
- Describe the rules of behavior and risks associated with penetration testing
- Read and understand various legal agreements involved in penetration testing

Key Terms

Complete-knowledge test   a type of penetration test in which the testing team is given complete knowledge about the target organization's network and security systems

Confidentiality agreement   a type of agreement that states that the information provided by the target organization will be treated as confidential and proprietary; this agreement also covers key aspects of negligence and liability for many potential issues

DMZ (demilitarized zone)   an area that is open to all network traffic, beyond the protection of the firewall and proxies

HIPAA (Health Insurance Portability and Accountability Act) of 1996   an act that mandates that all health and human-services organizations incorporate security standards to protect Electronic Protected Health Information (ePHI)

Negligence claim   a claim made against a testing firm asserting that the firm failed to exercise minimum required protective measures regarding or care of the target organization's electronic information systems and other electronic information assets

Nondisclosure agreement (NDA)   a document that protects an organization's confidential information during business dealings with customers, suppliers, employees, and the press

Partial-knowledge test   a type of penetration test in which the target organization provides basic information to the testing team in order to save time and expenses; the information provided to the team may include policy and network topology documents, assets, inventory, and other valuable information

Rules of behavior   an agreement that details the internal and external aspects surrounding the testing procedure

Zero-knowledge test   a type of penetration test in which the testing team has no information and will have to start from scratch

Introduction to Customers and Legal Agreements

This chapter focuses on customers and legal agreements. It deals with the various legal issues involved in penetration testing. It also covers the need for penetration testing, the stages of penetration testing, and customer requirements for penetration testing.

Why Organizations Need Penetration Testing

In today's digital data arena, in which so much of a corporation's foundations depend upon its information strategy, it is necessary for every organization to have a secure network. Organizational data needs to be protected from misconfigurations, exploits, damaging update patches, backdoors, disgruntled employees, and other possible risks.

Penetration testing helps trace vulnerabilities and weaknesses in a target network. It also enables the identification of strengths, weaknesses, threats, and defenses on the network. The scope of a typical penetration test includes the following:

- Setting up a penetration testing team of trusted and knowledgeable individuals
- Locating and preparing the *demilitarized zone (DMZ)* (an area that is open to all network traffic, beyond the protection of the firewall and proxies) for the test
- Observing what systems and data can be compromised
- Identifying possible network breaches via the intranet
- Determining whether penetration and database server access is possible

By defining the scope of the penetration test:

- Critical areas to be tested can be identified
- Legal issues can be addressed
- An unbiased test can be run against a working network, and both systems and system administration can be strengthened and improved

A penetration testing team can be either in-house or an outside party. In most cases, an outside party is hired to conduct the test. This option provides an unbiased penetration test of the network security measures employed. This will help the in-house network team trace vulnerabilities and take measures against them. It is essential to show the in-house staff their network's vulnerabilities. Legal requirements such as HIPAA make it necessary to conduct penetration testing.

Penetration testing helps organizations be compliant with HIPAA. *HIPAA* is the *Health Insurance Portability and Accountability Act of 1996*. It mandates that all health and human-services organizations incorporate security standards to protect Electronic Protected Health Information (ePHI). It requires that the information architecture be designed to protect and conceal personal details about an individual's health whenever the ePHI of a person is created, received, maintained, or transmitted.

This requires health organizations to maintain system architecture that is capable of protecting sensitive personal information from unexpected threats and hazards. The HIPAA Privacy Rule 34 does not inhibit the reasonably predicted use of ePHI. Compliance to HIPAA ensures that the employees of the organization will respect, keep, and abide by the privacy and security policies established by HIPAA.

Initial Stages in Penetration Testing

It is important to identify the customer's requirements and the objectives of the penetration test; the test should be developed based on those requirements. To prepare a penetration test, a tester should perform the following tasks:

- Provide a complete checklist of services that are provided in a penetration test to the client
- Draft a contract, a "Get Out of Jail Free Card," NDA agreements, and other initial legal agreements
- Prepare any other legal agreements that address issues raised during negotiations
- Set a date for authorized individuals from both parties to sign the agreements and contract
- If terms and conditions of the service being offered change after the contract is signed, prepare mutual-understanding agreements and have them signed by authorized, knowledgeable personnel before testing begins

Understand Customer Requirements

It is important to fully understand the customer's requirements to ensure that the penetration test addresses them completely.

- Identify what needs to be tested:
  - Servers
  - Workstations
  - Routers and firewalls
  - Networking devices
  - Cabling
  - Databases and applications
  - Physical security
- Select the specific sectors to be tested, and prepare users and administrators.
- Create a checklist of testing requirements.
- Identify the time frame and testing hours.
- Develop an emergency plan.
- Make sure all information is securely backed up before beginning anything.
- Decide on the format for reporting.
- Identify who will be involved in the reporting and document delivery.

Create a Checklist of Testing Requirements

The following is an example checklist of penetration testing requirements to be given to the customer:

- Do you have any security-related policies and standards?
- If yes, do you want them to be reviewed?
- Do you want a review of the physical security of your servers and network infrastructure to be performed?
- How many Internet domains do you have?
- How many Internet hosts do you have?
- Do you want your Internet presence to be mapped? Otherwise, can you provide us with a detailed diagram of your Internet presence, including addresses, host OS types, and software in use on the hosts? We will also need addresses in use on both sides of the hosts if they connect to both the Internet and the internal network.
- Do you want the security of your routers and hubs to be reviewed?

- If yes, how many routers and hubs exist on your network?
- Do you want a security review of the workstations on the network to be performed? If yes, what operating systems are the workstations running?
- If yes, how many workstations would you like to be tested?
- Five or fewer servers of each type (NT, UNIX, and Novell) will be accessed; do you want more to be reviewed?
- If yes, how many of each?
- Do you want denial-of-service testing to be conducted? This testing can have adverse effects on the systems tested. We can arrange to perform this testing during nonproduction hours.
- Do you want a modem scan of your analog phone lines to be performed?
- What kind of RAS server are you using and how many modems are used?
- Do you want other sites to be visited to perform assessments on systems?

Penetration Testing "Rules of Behavior"

Penetration testing involves an in-depth analysis of an organization's information technology expertise. It is a series of testing procedures that audits the entire network. The target organization's requirements and expectations are the most important criteria in preparing "rules of behavior" under which the penetration test will be performed.

The *rules of behavior* are an agreement that details the internal and external aspects surrounding the testing procedure. Before the test is performed, authorized representatives from both parties should sign this agreement. This paves the way to a common understanding regarding the limitations, liabilities, and indemnification considerations of the test.

The rules-of-behavior agreement addresses various aspects of the penetration test. They include the following:

- Approaches
- Technique of attack
- Success criteria
- Reporting and response

Approaches

Penetration tests must run on all networking environments, such as Internet, intranet, extranet, and dial-up. There are three types of approaches:

1. In the *zero-knowledge test*, the testing team does not have any information and has to start from scratch. It is an exactly realistic approach.

2. In a *partial-knowledge test*, the target organization provides basic information to the testing team in order to save time and expenses. The information provided to the team may include policy and network topology documents detailing assets and inventory, and other valuable information.

3. In a *full-knowledge test*, the testing team is given complete knowledge about the target organization's network and security systems.

Techniques of Attack

It is important to plan out the attack so that the correct type of information is gathered about the systems. That way, inadvertent information loss from target systems can be avoided. The basic techniques involved in a penetration test include the following:

- *Social engineering*: This technique involves using various methods to manipulate an employee into revealing information or performing certain actions.
- *Enumeration*: The penetration testing team actively tries to gain information such as usernames, network-share information, and application version numbers of currently running services.

- *Vulnerability mapping*: The testing team maps the profile of the environment to publicly known vulnerabilities.
- *Hacking*: The testing team attempts to gain privileged access to a target system. To do so, it attempts to exploit all known vulnerabilities. This phase includes using various testing tools and techniques for identifying vulnerabilities, exploiting them, and tracing all discovered loopholes in the target system's security.

Success Criteria

A mutually agreed-upon success rate is essential to the rules-of-behavior document. This rate states the beginning and completion of the test period and the expected benefits derived from testing. It shows the study time frame and safe termination period. Some of the goals may include the following:

- Accessing internal resources
- Reading and altering restricted files
- Reading and executing a program, or reading transaction data
- Accessing any user account and gaining administrator privileges
- Controlling network management systems

Reporting and Response

There should be a detailed report, and proper documentation procedures should be followed throughout the penetration testing period. The report should state the various procedures and techniques being used and their respective outcomes. All information, including the scheduled completion of each phase, must be in journal form. The representatives of both parties involved in the penetration test should have a common point of contact to facilitate reporting and updating their observations during and after the test.

Release and Authorization Form

Along with the rules-of-behavior test agreement, the release and authorization form must also be acknowledged and signed. This form states that the team or organization responsible for the penetration test should not be held responsible for any unintentional interruptions in service and loss or damage to any equipment. It should also state that the penetration testing team is not liable for criminal actions in the penetration test being performed. Note, however, that this form protects against criminal actions, but not liability due to unintentional wrongdoing, or tort.

Penetration Testing Risks

Penetration testing can have serious repercussions if not performed correctly. Testing is conducted against the target organization's security systems and involves penetration into various networking environments, which may pose many risks.

Normally, companies continue to conduct business when these tests are performed, so it is the company's responsibility to safeguard its information systems during this period. Their properties are at risk of attack and prone to be affected by the penetration test.

If the systems are affected by the attack, it may lead to loss of information, system breakdown, loss or misconfiguration of the company's systems, and so on. Any damage to the systems or to the information in them may cause losses to the organization. Costs can run high on electronic assets such as client databases, proprietary code, documentation, and intellectual property.

Penetration Testing by Third Parties

Organizations concentrate on keeping their systems secure. They may conduct penetration tests to check the security of these systems. An organization may hire a third party to perform the penetration tests for the following reasons:

- A third-party group may find vulnerabilities unable to be identified by internal testing.
- There may be a lack of skilled penetration testers in the organization.

- The organization may want to provide third-party assurance to customers.
- The organization can ensure that experienced testers perform the tests.
- It may be more cost effective than recruiting skilled penetration testers.

Using outside penetration testers may come with risks. It is important to take precautions to avoid these risks.

Precautions When Outsourcing Penetration Testing

The following are some of the precautions to be taken in selecting a third-party service provider:

- The third party should provide details of the team performing the penetration test, and the team members should agree to a background check and reference check.
- Representatives from each organization should meet, and a representative from the third party should be available before, during, and after the penetration test.
- The third party should maintain and provide ongoing logs and traces of actions during the penetration test. A knowledgeable representative from the company should check the logs.

The following should be considered when a third-party service provider performs a penetration test:

- Ensure that the service provider is prevented from misusing organizational confidential data during testing.
- Ensure that the service provider does not leave any vulnerabilities.
- Check that the service provider does not pass any information about the organization to the outside.
- Ensure that the service provider has the experience and credentials needed to perform the penetration test.
- Make sure that the penetration tester is capable of communicating issues and results to management in a nontechnical way after the test.

Legal Consequences

Both parties involved in a penetration test must prepare and agree upon a penetration testing contract.

- Authorization for a test must come from a senior director of each company and not from just any employee.
- Authorized representatives from both parties should sign the contract.
- Prior to signing, legal advisors or lawyers of the respective firms should examine the contract.
- Senior directors must authorize requests from an employee to add, change, or stop penetration testing.
- Legal fees for damages will have to be paid if any penetration testing activity is carried out without proper authority.

Various legal requirements and agreements will be discussed in this section.

Get Out of Jail Free Card

A "Get Out of Jail Free Card" is a legal agreement signed by an authorized representative of an organization that indemnifies the tester against any loss or damages that may result from the testing. In other words, a "Get Out of Jail Free Card" is a letter from the company to a penetration tester giving legal authority to test the network and stating legal release from inadvertent damages caused to the network during the test. For this reason, it is called a "Get Out of Jail Free Card." Any firm that plans to test its Internet applications and e-commerce initiatives should have this agreement drafted, but it is the tester's responsibility to make sure that it contains the provisions required, is signed, and is specific as to what the tester may and may not do. A sample "Get Out of Jail Free Card" is shown in Figure 2-1.

Permitted Items in a Legal Agreement

Table 2-1 is a sample list of tests that the testing agency can perform. It also lists whether or not each item is permitted by the organization ordering the test.

```
┌─────────────────────────────────────────────────────────────┐
│                                                          ⚜    │
│        ┌─────────────────────────────────────┐               │
│        │      Get Out Of Jail Free Card      │               │
│        └─────────────────────────────────────┘               │
│                                    Place:_____           │
│                                    Date:_____           │
│                                    Type: Filing Memo          │
│                                                               │
│   SUBJECT: AUTHORIZED LIABILITY WAIVER AGREEMENT              │
│                                                               │
│   Contracting the act of securing information technology      │
│   assets of MYZ Pvt. Ltd to PP-Licensed Penetration          │
│   Testers Pvt. Ltd. The testing team is required to          │
│   trace vulnerabilities in our resources, penetrate through   │
│   them, and try to access various resources available. It    │
│   is required that the team scan our desktops, laptops,       │
│   servers, network elements, and other computer systems       │
│   owned by this organization on a regular, periodic basis     │
│   to discover vulnerabilities present on these systems and    │
│   suggest measures to secure them. In the above-mentioned     │
│   process of performing the pen-test, the testing team will   │
│   not be held liable for any damage caused to our             │
│   organization's electronic assets.                           │
│   Hereby, document to be attested by following individuals:   │
│                                                               │
│                                                               │
│   Signature of                  Signature of                 │
│   Test Team In-charge: _____  Organizational In-charge: ___ │
│                                                               │
│                                                               │
│   Full Name: _____          Full Name: _____         │
│   Date: _____             Date: _____            │
│                                                               │
└─────────────────────────────────────────────────────────────┘
```

Figure 2-1   This is a sample "Get Out of Jail Free Card."

Confidentiality and NDA Agreements

Two important documents that should be completed before any penetration testing begins are a confidentiality agreement and a nondisclosure agreement.

A *confidentiality agreement* states that the information provided by the target organization will be treated as confidential and proprietary. This agreement also covers key aspects of negligence and liability for many potential issues. The target organization should be careful in wording the agreement because many testing firms would not want to be held liable even in the case of negligence. Ensure that the service-providing firm has insurance coverage for damages.

A *nondisclosure agreement (NDA)* protects an organization's confidential information during business dealings with customers, suppliers, employees, and the press. A written NDA is a powerful legal tool that states that the signer will not disclose any trade secrets, patents, or other proprietary information to anyone outside the company. Legal action can be taken against the signer for any violation of the documented agreement. The organization can sue for damages and compensation. Many documents and other information regarding penetration testing contain critical information that could damage one or both parties if improperly disclosed.

Both parties bear responsibility to protect tools, techniques, vulnerabilities, and information from disclosure beyond the terms specified by a written agreement. Nondisclosure agreements should be narrowly drawn to protect sensitive information. Specific areas to be considered include the following:

- Ownership of the information flowing on the network (internally and in the DMZ)
- Use of the evaluation reports
- Use of the testing methodology in customer documentation

Test	Permitted
Electronic mapping—external	Yes
Electronic mapping—internal	Yes
Social engineering by telephone	Yes
Social engineering by mail	No
Adopt employee identity—remote	No
Adopt employee identity—on-site	Yes
Prepare a computer to meet upgrade requirements	No
Break into employee workstations	Yes
Read corporate e-mail	No
Pretend to be a technical supplier	Yes
Dumpster diving—on-site outside	Yes
Dumpster diving—on-site inside	No
Dumpster diving—off-site	No
Target sensitive corporate resources	No
Personnel extortion, blackmail, and coercion	No
Investigate backgrounds of staff	Yes
Penetration of business partners	No
Denial of service of web server	Yes
Denial of service of mail server	Yes
Sniffing and spoofing of host network	Yes
Man-in-the-middle attack	No
Forced reinstall; restart	Yes
File manipulation	No

Table 2-1 This shows a sample list of the types of attacks the testing team can perform

The following are some points to be considered when crafting an NDA:

- Identify truly valuable information and information that is critical to the company.
- Clearly specify that the person signing the agreement should not disclose the things mentioned in it.
- Clearly identify all parties to the agreement.
- Specifically include the starting date and length of the nondisclosure period.

All the parties involved in the NDA agreement should have it reviewed by their respective legal advisors.

The Contract

A contract for penetration testing should include all needed clauses and other information and conditions to be followed by both parties involved in the penetration test. It should clearly state the rights and responsibilities of both parties. Figure 2-2 shows a sample contract.

A well-constructed contract must clearly state all points, such as:

- *Objective of the penetration test*: Reasons for performing the penetration test and the goals to be met by performing the test have to be clearly identified.

Penetration Testing Contract

The below text is a sample contract only and does not obligate XSECURITY to perform services under any specified terms or conditions. This contract is for educational purposes only. Only valid signed contracts will be considered binding.

This contract is between XSECURITY (hereinafter referred to as the "provider") and Penetration Testing Services buyer (hereinafter referred to as the "client") for the supply of Penetration Testing services by the provider for the client.

Whereas the provider provides certain computer and systems security consulting and testing services including Penetration Testing services, and

Whereas the client wishes to retain the provider to provide computer and systems security services, specifically Penetration Testing services, therefore

The client does hereby retain the provider for the purpose of providing Penetration Testing services on the client's computers and/or systems.

The objective of the Penetration Testing service is to identify and report on security vulnerabilities to allow the client to close the issues in a planned manner, thus significantly raising the level of their security protection. The client understands that Internet security is a continually growing and changing field and that testing by XSECURITY does not mean that the client's site is secure from every form of attack. There is no such thing as 100% security

Figure 2-2   This is a sample penetration testing contract.

- *Sensitive information*: This includes information related to the target organization's electronic assets, developing applications, network security parameters, or other sensitive information that is required by the penetration testing team.
- *Indemnification clause*: This clause protects the penetration tester/agency from any legal or financial liabilities in case the penetration test results in loss or damage to the assets of the organization.
- *Nondisclosure clause*: This clause is drafted by the target organization to safeguard its confidential information from being publicized.
- *Fees and project schedule*: These are the payment and pricing options of the service being offered.
- *Reporting and responsibilities*: Contract guidelines state the methodology for performing the test and reporting procedures and scheduling period for the task assigned.

Liability Issues

When entering into a service relationship, both parties should review their liability with respect to the outlined tasks. A company's legal liability can arise as a result of the following:

- Standards and penalties imposed by federal, state, or local governments
- Breach of contractual agreements

- Other noncontractual civil wrongs (torts) ranging from fraud, invasion of privacy, and conversion to deceptive trade practices and negligence
- Federal and state statutes that may impose criminal penalties as well as form the basis for private lawsuits

Many times, penetration testing leads to unexpected consequences under which the target organization's systems may start to malfunction, services may be interrupted, and information may be corrupted. In the case of any such potential mishap, the testing firm should have a liability waiver signed by the authorized personnel of the client organization that states that the testing firm cannot be held responsible for such consequences. To create a liability waiver, both parties should consult their legal advisors.

A liability waiver should address aspects such as the following:

- Damages to systems
- Denial of services
- Information corruption
- Hacked access to passwords and account information during the test
- Grounds for recourse in the case of damage
- A maximum amount given for damages incurred
- The method of dispute resolution in case any problems arise

A letter of authorization is needed when an outside firm hosts the target organization's network. The testing team may mistakenly access networks of other companies hosted by that company. In such a case, this letter would protect the testing firm legally.

A master services agreement is another agreement that serves as a warranty to both parties involved in the penetration test. This addresses issues such as changes in work scope, pricing, testing tools, time frame, and other concerns.

Applicable Laws: Computer Fraud & Abuse Act

(a) Whoever

(1) knowingly accesses a computer without authorization or exceeds authorized access, and by means of such conduct obtains information that has been determined by the United States Government pursuant to an Executive order or statute to require protection against unauthorized disclosure for reasons of national defense or foreign relations, or any restricted data, as defined in paragraphy. of section 11 of the Atomic Energy Act of 1954, with the intent or reason to believe that such information so obtained is to be used to the injury of the United States, or to the advantage of any foreign nation;

(2) intentionally accesses a computer without authorization or exceeds authorized access, and thereby obtains information contained in a financial record of a financial institution, or of a card issuer as defined in section 1602(n) of title 15, or contained in a file of a consumer reporting agency on a consumer, as such terms are defined in the Fair Credit Reporting Act (15 U.S.C. 1681 et seq.);

(3) intentionally, without authorization to access any computer of a department or agency of the United States, accesses such a computer of that department or agency that is exclusively for the use of the Government of the United States or, in the case of a computer not exclusively for such use, is used by or for the Government of the United States and such conduct affects the use of the Government's operation of such computer,

(4) knowingly and with intent to defraud, accesses a Federal interest computer without authorization, or exceeds authorized access, and by means of such conduct furthers the intended fraud and obtains anything of value, unless the object of the fraud and the thing obtained consists only of the use of the computer; shall be punished as provided in subsection (c) of this section.

(5) intentionally accesses a Federal interest computer without authorization, and by means of one or more instances of such conduct alters, damages, or destroys information in any such Federal interest computer, or prevents authorized use of any such computer or information, and thereby

(A) causes loss to one or more others of a value aggregating $1,000 or more during any one year period; or

(B) modifies or impairs, or potentially modifies or impairs, the medical examination, medical diagnosis, medical treatment, or medical care of one or more individuals; or

(6) knowingly and with intent to defraud traffics (as defined in section 1029) in any password or similar information through which a computer may be accessed without authorization, if

(A) such trafficking affects interstate or foreign commerce; or (B) such computer is used by or for the Government of the United States;

(b) whoever attempts to commit an offense under subsection (a) of this section shall be punished as provided in subsection (c) of this section. (c) The punishment for an offense under subsection (a) or (b) of this section is

(1)(A) a fine under this title or imprisonment for not more than ten years, or both, in the case of an offense under subsection (a)(1) of this section which does not occur after a conviction for another offense under such subsection, or an attempt to commit an offense punishable under this subparagraph; and

(B) a fine under this title or imprisonment for not more than twenty years, or both, in the case of an offense under subsection (a)(1) of this section which occurs after a conviction for another offense under such subsection, or an attempt to commit an offense punishable under this subparagraph; and

(2)(A) a fine under this title or imprisonment for not more than one year, or both, in the case of an offense under subsection (a)(2), (a)(3) or (a)(1) of this section which does not occur after a conviction for another offense under such subsection, or an attempt to commit an offense punishable under this subparagraph; and (B) a fine under this title or imprisonment for not more than ten years, or both, in the case of an offense under subsection (a)(2), (a)(3) or (a)(6) of this section which occurs after a conviction for another offense under such subsection, or an attempt to commit an offense punishable under this subparagraph; and

(3)(A) a fine under this title or imprisonment for not more than five years, or both, in the case of an offense under subsection (a)(4) or (a)(5) of this section which does not occur after a conviction for another offense under such subsection, or an attempt to commit an offense punishable under this subparagraph; and

(B) a fine under this title or imprisonment for not more than ten years, or both, in the case of an offense under subsection (a)(4) or (a)(5) of this section which occurs after a conviction for another offense under such subsection, or an attempt to commit an offense punishable under this subparagraph.

(d) The United States Secret Service shall, in addition to any other agency having such authority, have the authority to investigate offenses under this section. Such authority of the United States Secret Service shall be exercised in accordance with an agreement which shall be entered into by the Secretary of the Treasury and the Attorney General.

(e) As used in this section

(1) the term "computer" means an electronic, magnetic, optical, electrochemical, or other high speed data processing device performing logical, arithmetic, or storage functions, and includes any data storage facility or communications facility directly related to or operating in conjunction with such device, but such term does not include an automated typewriter or typesetter, a portable hand held calculator, or other similar device;

(2) the term "federal interest computer" means a computer

(A) exclusively for the use of a financial institution or the United States Government, or, in the case of a computer not exclusively for such use, used by or for a financial institution or the United States Government and the conduct constituting the offense affects the use of the financial institution's operation or the Government's operation of such computer; or (B) which is one of two or more computers used in committing the offense, not all of which are located in the same State;

(3) the term "State" includes the District of Columbia, the Commonwealth of Puerto Rico, and any other commonwealth, possession or territory of the United States;

(4) the term "financial institution" means

(A) an institution with deposits insured by the Federal Deposit Insurance Corporation;

(B) the Federal Reserve or a member of the Federal Reserve including any Federal Reserve Bank;

(C) a credit union with accounts insured by the National Credit Union Administration;

(D) a member of the Federal home loan bank system and any home loan bank;

(E) any institution of the Farm Credit System under the Farm Credit Act of 1971;

(F) a broker-dealer registered with the Securities and Exchange Commission pursuant to section 15 of the Securities Exchange Act of 1934;

(G) the Securities Investor Protection Corporation;

(H) a branch or agency of a foreign bank (as such terms are defined in paragraphs (1) and (3) of section l (b) of the International Banking Act of 1978); and

(I) an organization operating under section 25 or section 25(a) of the Federal Reserve Act.

(5) the term "financial record" means information derived from any record held by a financial institution pertaining to a customer's relationship with the financial institution;

(6) the term "exceeds authorized access" means to access a computer with authorization and to use such access to obtain or alter information in the computer that the accesser is not entitled so to obtain or alter; and

(7) the term "department of the United States" means the legislative or judicial branch of the Government or one of the executive departments enumerated in section 101 of title 5.

(f) This section does not prohibit any lawfully authorized investigative, protective, or intelligence activity of a law enforcement agency of the United States, a State, or a political subdivision of a State, or of an intelligence agency of the United States. (Added Pub.L. 98-473, Title II,' 2102(a), Oct. 12,1984,98 Stat. 2190, and amended Pub.L.99-474,' 2, Oct. 16,1986, 100 Stat. 1213; Pub.L. 100-690, Title VII,' 7065 Nov. 18, 1988, 102 Stat. 4404; Pub.L. 101-73, Titie IX,' 962(aX5), Aug. 9, 1989 103 Stat. 502-Pub.L. 101-647, Title XII,' 1205(e), Titie XXV,' 2597(j), Title XXXV,' 3533, Nov. 29, 1990, 104 Stat. 4831, 4910, 4925.)

Negligence Claim

In law, negligence arises when a party owes a legal duty to another, that duty is breached, and the breach causes damage to the injured party. A *negligence claim* of liability is based on a charge that the company, its officers, and directors acted negligently.

In penetration testing, the testing firm will be considered negligent if it fails to exercise minimum required protective measures regarding or care of the target organization's electronic information systems and other electronic information assets. If the testing team fails to put in the minimum effort that any reasonable and responsible service provider would have under such circumstances, the organization can claim negligence of the testing firm. In such a case, any lawsuit would be termed a negligence claim.

To launch a negligence claim, the petitioner should include four important elements:

- *Duty of care*: In this element, the petitioner should be able to prove that the testing firm did not inform the petitioner that such damage might occur in such time as any other responsible service provider might have been able to inform the petitioner.

- *Breach of duty*: In this element, the petitioner can claim that the testing team did not exercise the remedial action that any other professional would have taken to avoid the damage to some extent.

- *Casual occurrence*: The target organization should be able to prove that the damage incurred is not due to any casual coincidence or mere mishap.

- *Actual loss incurred*: In this element, the petitioner should be able to prove the actual loss incurred by the petitioner is due to the negligence of the testing firm.

The licensed penetration testing firm can defend itself from negligence claims. To do so, the firm would have to attack each of the four elements in the negligence claim:

1. It can challenge the petitioner's claim and the duty-of-care clause.

2. It can defend itself by proving that the incident or damage had been acted upon with the appropriate amount of responsibility based on best practices within the industry.

3. It can defend itself by proving that the damage incurred was casual and not due to their negligence.

4. It can question whether the plaintiff suffered any actual loss.

Best Practices

The information obtained during the penetration test could come from various departments within an organization, such as finance, research and development, personnel, legal, and security. Lost or compromised information can invite lawsuits and create liability despite proof of a reasonable standard of care in protecting information. The penetration tester should plan for all the possible consequences that could arise while conducting the tests.

The penetration tester/agency should be prepared for a worst-case scenario. The team that undertakes this work should be careful while performing the test, as a slight mistake could trigger legal action from the client.

Avoiding liability involves planning for problems. The team should plan a crisis management and communications strategy. Activities of crisis management include forecasting potential crises that may occur before the real experience and plan methods and ways to tackle such events. Planning generally includes the following:

- Identification of the real nature of the crises that may occur

- Assuring stakeholders that crisis recovery is well planned

- Making intervening arrangements to minimize damage and recover from crises

- Remaining focused on public relations to recover any damage to public image

A well-planned crisis-management strategy will help an organization respond to such situations promptly and appropriately and will result in the following:

- Enhanced safety of staff and customers
- Conformity in meeting necessary regulation requirements
- Mitigation of effects from a major incident or emergency
- Improved employee morale and confidence in the organization
- Protection and enhancement of reputation
- Reduction of risk of litigation and corporate liability

Drafting Contracts

As mentioned earlier, representatives of both parties should draft a contract to address various issues that may emerge from the penetration test and should state all the agreements that have been made. A contract is a powerful legal tool that protects both parties from misunderstandings and should clearly allocate liability in case of unforeseen or unintended consequences, such as a system crash, loss of access, compromised proprietary or sensitive information, and damage to the network or information residing on the network.

Due to the importance of the contract, both parties should do the following:

1. Verify the accuracy of the description of various agreements addressed in the contract.
2. Verify whether the draft is clearly written and documented, and contains sufficient details defining the rights and responsibilities of both parties.
3. Engage legal counsel early in the process to help prepare and review the proposed contract. The most important elements addressed in the draft would be as follows:

   - *Scope of test*: The contract should clearly describe the activities, time period required to conduct the test, rights and responsibilities of the parties to the contract, and other logistical information.
   - *Performance standards*: Both parties should define the requirements of the test and the minimum required standard of performance expected from the penetration test.
   - *Security and confidentiality*: The contract should address the testing team's responsibility for security and confidentiality of the target organization's resources and information, etc. It should address agreements such as an NDA.
     - Some of the security and confidentiality components required include:
       - Access to internal controls
       - Compliance with applicable regulatory requirements
       - Access to various records or databases for the testing team
       - Access of testing team's records by the target organization
       - A notification requirement for material changes to services, systems, controls, key project personnel, and service locations and approval agreements for the changes implemented
       - Insurance coverage maintained by the testing team
   - *Audit information*: Various auditing reports must be included, such as financial, security reviews, and standards of quality.
   - *Reporting*: Contractual terms should include the frequency and type of reports the target organization will receive and the fees required to be paid for such reports.
   - *Costs*: The contract should fully describe the fees for services that include any development, conversion, and recurring services, and any other special requests and additional costs that may be incurred.
   - *Ownership and license*: It should address the ownership, rights to, and allowable use of the target organization's data, equipment/hardware, system documentation, system and application software, and other intellectual property rights.

- *Dispute resolution*: The target organization should include required provisions for any dispute resolution processes that attempt to resolve problems in a prompt manner and even include provision for continuation of services during the dispute resolution period.

- *Indemnification*: Indemnification provisions, also known as "Get Out of Jail Free Cards," should be prepared. These state that the testing team will not be held liable for any damages or loss of information.

- *Help desk*: This is an agreement to extend support to the target of the penetration test as and when necessary, and to exchange information as required.

The contract will be subject to the laws of the local, state, and federal governments. All disputes arising out of that contract shall be subject to the exclusive jurisdiction of those respective governments. It is important to have an attorney review the contract in the contexts of local, state, and federal government statutes.

How Much to Charge?

Penetration test pricing varies. A penetration test firm should provide several choices when it comes to pricing. The target organization should be given choices among various packages with different pricing options and allowed to choose the elements they want and can afford.

Pricing will usually be based on the number of work days required to fulfill the scope of the project. It can also be based on the number of IP addresses that need to be tested. Another item to be considered when pricing the test scope is the manpower required.

The number of servers to be tested incurs more cost per unit than client computers do because servers have to be much more extensively attacked. They also include more information to be safeguarded as well as analyzed.

Penetration test pricing is dependent on the techniques used to perform the test, such as social engineering, gathering competitive intelligence, stealing laptops, and evading physical security.

Chapter Summary

- Penetration testing helps to trace the vulnerabilities and weaknesses that exist in a network. It also enables an organization to identify strengths, weaknesses, threats, and defenses on the network.

- Rules of behavior are an agreement that details the internal and external aspects surrounding the testing procedure.

- A "Get Out of Jail Free Card" agreement outlines the types of activities to be performed and indemnifies the tester against any loss or damage that may result from the testing.

- Nondisclosure agreements (NDAs) protect an organization's confidential information during business dealings with customers, suppliers, employees, and the press.

- Penetration testing teams should develop a crisis management and communications strategy. In the event of lost or compromised information, they should provide a track record showing the team exercised a reasonable standard of care in trying to protect information.

## Chapter 3

Duties of a Licensed Penetration Tester

Objectives

After completing this chapter, you should be able to:

- Explain the professional duties of an LPT
- Recount the important legal standards for an LPT
- List the compliance checklists necessary for conducting a penetration test
- Delineate the rules of engagement (ROE) between an organization and penetration testers
- Define the scope of the ROE
- Outline the steps for framing the ROE
- Recount the clauses in the ROE

Key Terms

Licensed penetration tester (LPT) an individual who has been certified by EC-Council as a professional penetration tester

LPT-audited logo a logo used to notify users that Web sites and networks are thoroughly audited by an LPT

Rules of engagement (ROE) the formal permissions given to conduct a penetration test

Introduction to Duties of a Licensed Penetration Tester

A *licensed penetration tester (LPT)* is an individual who has been certified by EC-Council as a professional penetration tester. An LPT is expected to adhere to ethical and professional standards and be fully acquainted with the duties of a penetration tester. LPTs are expected to conduct themselves professionally and be fully acquainted with the legal standards set by the local and national governments that have jurisdiction over any projects. LPTs must also be acquainted with the rules of engagement for every project that they are involved in. Ethical and professional standards attempt to ensure the reliability of LPTs and the quality of the licensed penetration tester certification program.

Duties of a Licensed Penetration Tester

LPTs must do the following:

- Constantly analyze work
- Approach work with the will to improve it
- Learn from mistakes as well as successes
- Motivate, compliment, and reward team members
- Understand the reasons for doing things a certain way
- Work toward the common goal of a project
- Use calendars and keep a well-organized schedule
- Write down tasks
- Keep checklists
- Carry pens and pads to take notes
- Carry voice recorders to record findings
- Record all activities
- Share information with team members
- Ask questions and admit mistakes
- Use all available resources to adequately address the needs of a project
- Always dress professionally

Licensed penetration testers must stay up to date on the technologies in their fields. The following activities should be followed to stay current in the field:

- Constantly update knowledge and skill set
- Look outside the workplace for information
- Read books, journals, and trade magazines
- Attend conferences, workshops, and training sessions
- Visit various security Web sites and forums
- Join various security discussion groups
- Visit libraries and bookstores

LPT-Audited Logos

LPTs are authorized to use the LPT-audited logos in Figure 3-1. *LPT-audited logos* are used to notify users that Web sites and networks are thoroughly audited by an LPT. The "LPT Audited" mark appears only when a Web site's security meets the highest security scanning standards of EC-Council's LPT methodology.

Standards and Compliance

Laws

The following list of statutes may govern information security consultants and their customers:

- Gramm-Leach-Bliley Act (GLBA)
- Health Insurance Portability and Accountability Act (HIPAA)
- Sarbanes-Oxley Act
- Federal Information Security and Management Act (FISMA)

Figure 3-1   LPT-audited logos can be used on any Web site or network that has been thoroughly reviewed by an LPT.

- Family Educational Rights and Privacy Act (FERPA)
- Electronic Communications Privacy Act (ECPA)

GLBA Compliance Checklist

The following are some of the major components of GLBA:

- Financial Privacy Rule
- Safeguards Rule
- Pretexting Protection

The following checklist should be used for GLBA compliance:

- Ensure whether the written security program includes:
  - Program policy
  - Issue-specific policies
  - System-specific policies
- Perform risk assessment to detect the threats to the customer's data or to the systems that store the data.
- Create written incident response plans to take action when any unauthorized access is detected.
- Document business continuity plans covering those systems that support customer information.
- Checklist for Safeguard Rule:
  - Does the organization have appropriate disciplinary policies?
  - Does the written document contain the policies and procedures for handling the confidential information?
  - Are the employees made aware of the information security policies and practices?
  - Does the organization maintain record retention policies for those files that consist of customer information and identity verification?
  - Is the storage area secured from unauthorized access and protected against physical hazards like fire or floods?
  - Are the organization's electronic records stored securely?
  - How does the organization transmit and receive sensitive customer information?
- Checklist for administrative safeguards:
  - Does the organization have official sanctions against their employees who fail to comply with security policies and procedures?
  - Does the organization implement policies to review audit logs, access reports, and track records of security incidents?
  - Does the organization check the references or background of potential employees?
  - How does the organization ensure that employees are updated about applicable policies and expectations?
  - Does the organization conduct scheduled and unscheduled training with their employees on security policies?
  - Does the organization have specific policies, procedures, and tools for defending against, detecting, and reporting malicious software?
  - Has the organization established procedures for restoring any loss of customer information stored electronically?
  - Has the organization implemented procedures for periodic testing and correction of contingency plans?
- Checklist for physical safeguards:
  - Has the organization implemented policies and procedures for the protection of the facility and the equipment from unauthorized access and theft?
  - Is there any facility to lock rooms and file cabinets where customer information is kept?
  - Has the organization implemented physical safeguards for all of their workstations that access customer information to authenticate access by authorized users?
  - Does the organization implement policies and procedures to address the final nature of the customer's information and the hardware or storage media on which it is stored?
  - Does the organization maintain records about the movements of hardware and electronic media, and the entities that do the moving?

- Does the organization create a retrievable, exact copy of customer information, when needed, and before moving the equipment?
- Checklist for technical safeguards:
  - Does the organization essentially manage all the security tools and keep employees informed about security risks and breaches?
  - Has the organization established a written contingency plan addressing breaches of safeguards?
  - Has the organization established procedures for obtaining essential customer information during an emergency?
  - Does the organization store electronic customer information on a protected server that is accessible through a password only and is in a physically secure area?
  - Has the organization implemented mechanisms for encrypting and decrypting customer information?
  - Does the system administrator of the organization regularly scan, obtain, and install patches that resolve software vulnerabilities?
  - Does the organization have procedures and controls for preserving both secure backups of media as well as secure archived data?

HIPAA Compliance Checklist

Administrative safeguards:

- Has the organization implemented procedures for the approval or supervision of employees who work with Electronic Protected Health Information (ePHI) or in locations where it might be accessed?
- Does the organization implement policies for granting access to ePHI, such as access to a workplace, transaction, program, or process?
- Does the organization establish procedures for creating and maintaining retrievable, correct copies of ePHI?
- Has the organization established procedures for restoring any loss of ePHI data that is accumulated electronically?

Physical safeguards:

- Has the organization implemented policies and procedures for the protection of the facility and equipment from unauthorized access and theft?
- Does the organization implement procedures to control and check access to facilities based on the role or function of an individual?
- Does the organization implement policies and procedures stating the proper functions that are to be performed?
- Has the organization implemented physical safeguards for all of their workstations that access ePHI to authenticate access by authorized users?
- Do the policies and procedures implemented by organizations address the final disposition of ePHI and the storage media on which it is recorded?

Technical safeguards:

- Is there a procedure for assigning a unique name or number for identifying and following a user's identity in the organization?
- Does the organization establish procedures for acquiring necessary ePHI during an emergency?
- Has the organization implemented any method for encrypting and decrypting ePHI?
- Does the organization perform audit control, using a hardware, software, or a procedural system, that include or use ePHI?
- Has the organization implemented any electronic mechanisms to verify that ePHI has not been modified or destroyed in an unauthorized manner?
- Is there a procedure implemented to verify that a particular person is the one who accessed ePHI?

Sarbanes-Oxley Compliance Checklist

The following checklist should be used for Sarbanes-Oxley compliance:

- Does the audit committee create communication procedures that guarantee safe, secure, and anonymous communications with employees?
- Does the audit committee create record retention procedures that safeguard employee reports of fraud?
- Are all frauds, whether material or nonmaterial, reported to the audit committee?
- Are the disclosure controls defined for financial reporting?
- Does the financial disclosure reflect all material correcting adjustments and off–balance sheet transactions?
- Is a code of ethics established for the financial function and financial officers?
- Has the organization implemented a code of ethics for its senior financial officers?
- Has the management reviewed the effectiveness of the organization's internal controls and procedures for financial reporting?

FISMA Compliance Checklist

The following checklist should be used for FISMA compliance:

- Does the organization regularly review the risks pertaining to the information system?
- Does the organization develop policies and procedures based on the results of risk assessments?
- Does the organization follow the policies that are based on risk assessments?
- Does the organization plan to acquire proper information about facilities, the network, and information systems?
- Does the organization provide security-awareness training to all employees?
- Does the organization evaluate the effectiveness of information security policies annually?
- Does the organization plan, implement, evaluate, and document the remedial actions for deficiencies in the information security policy?
- Does the organization plan the procedures of detecting, reporting, and responding to incidents?
- Does the organization plan procedures for the operational stability of information systems that maintain the operations and assets of the organization?

FERPA Compliance Checklist

The following checklist should be used for FERPA compliance:

- Each program must have release-of-confidential-information forms on the program's letterhead.
- Do not share confidential information outside an organization.
- Electronic transfer methods are not permissible for transfer of confidential information.
- Applications and enrollment forms must be free of confidential questions.
- Do not share confidential information with students. Each program must have all confidential information in locked files with monitored access only.
- Confidential information files should be maintained for a period of five years.
- Confidential files should be maintained properly.
- Does the university have a written policy about the student's academic records?
- Does the university annually notify students of their rights and the institution's policies pertaining to FERPA?
- What are the rights of inspection and review of a student's educational records?
- What are the procedures for modifying educational records?

- Do students have the right to modify or check their educational records? Does the yearly notification to the presently enrolled students regarding their rights under FERPA contain the following information?
  - The student's right to inspect and review educational records
  - The student's right to change or modify any part of the educational record
  - The student's right to manage the disclosure of sensitive identifiable information present in his or her educational record
- Does the university hold the right to deny a student's access to the following records?
  - The financial statements and tax returns of the student's parents
  - Letters and statements of recommendation for which the student has waived access
  - Those records that are not educational records, as defined by FERPA

ECPA Compliance Checklist

The following checklist should be used to ensure ECPA compliance:

- Block all P2P file sharing.
- Ensure that employees follow an authorized IM usage policy.
- Restrict the transmission of confidential information over such channels.
- Ensure that only authorized personnel can access confidential and sensitive information.
- Only authorized personnel should have the authority to transmit and receive the information.
- Maintain the confidentiality of data.
- Monitor and audit the activities of those who are using IM and other communication channels.
- Provide training to employees.

Rules of Engagement (ROE)

Rules of engagement (ROE) are the formal permissions to conduct a penetration test. They provide certain rights and restrictions to the test team for performing the test, and help testers to overcome legal, federal, and policy-related restrictions to use different penetration testing tools and techniques.

ROE may allow the testers to conduct some technical and nontechnical activities such as port scanning, social engineering, and network sniffing, and may restrict conducting certain activities, such as password cracking or SQL-injection attacks, which an organization might think are detrimental to the normal function of the organization or are too intrusive. These activities are explicitly defined in the ROE as a guide to penetration testers. Penetration testers might be allowed to conduct certain activities that otherwise may be considered illegal or against established legal, federal, and policy guidelines.

Scope of ROE

The ROE act as guidelines for penetration testers. They should clearly explain the allowed and restricted activities during a test.

The ROE include:

- Specific IP addresses/ranges to be tested
- Any restricted hosts (i.e., hosts, systems, or subnets not to be tested)
- A list of acceptable testing techniques (e.g., social engineering, DoS, etc.) and tools (password crackers, network sniffers, etc.)
- Times when testing is to be conducted (e.g., during business hours, after business hours, etc.)
- Identification of a finite period for testing
- IP addresses of the machines from which penetration testing will be conducted so that administrators can differentiate legitimate penetration testing attacks from actual malicious attacks
- Points of contact for the penetration testing team, the targeted systems, and the networks
- Measures to prevent law enforcement being called with false alarms (created by the testing)
- Handling of information collected by the penetration testing team

Steps for Framing the ROE

The following steps should be used for framing the ROE:

1. Estimate the cost, time, and effort that the organization can invest:
    - Based on the scope of the project, estimate the cost required to perform the penetration testing. The estimated cost will depend on the size of the team, type of testing carried out, resources required, and so on.
    - Estimate the time required to complete the penetration testing process. If the estimated costs and resources are high, then the time required to complete the project will be greater, and vice versa.

2. Decide the desired depth for penetration testing:
    - Rules of engagement include the depth of penetration testing and type of testing, including DoS testing, database testing, firewall testing, and so on. The depth includes the resources required to accomplish the project in the time required.

3. Have precontract discussions with different penetration testers:
    - Before performing the penetration testing, have a precontract discussion with different penetration testers and generate a quote that provides detailed information on the resources required, type of testers involved, budget required, and expected time required to finish the project.

4. Conduct brainstorming sessions with top management and technical teams:
    - Based on the quote provided by the team of penetration testers, conduct a meeting with the top management and technical teams, and have a discussion with them about the rules of engagement, including the resources required, type of testing to be carried out, budget required, and testers needed to perform the penetration testing process.

Clauses in ROE

The ROE include the list of allowed and prohibited activities in which the organization may allow some activities, such as port scanning, and prohibit others, such as password cracking, SQL injection, and DoS attacks. They may also explicitly prohibit some activities that might cause risk to the system, such as installation of executable files. ROE protect the penetration testing team by guaranteeing the organization's support.

ROE must specify the systems and networks that need to be tested. They should clearly specify the IP addresses, number of systems, and address ranges used by the systems. ROE must detail the following elements:

- Definitions of test scope, limitations, and other activities for protecting the test team
- Authorization of penetration testers for systems and network testing
- Details about the level and reach of the penetration test
- Definition of different types of allowed testing techniques

ROE should provide detailed and clear specifications for the following activities:

- Port and service identification
- Vulnerability scanning
- Security configuration review
- Password cracking

ROE should furnish the following information:

- Details on how organizational data is treated throughout and after the test
- Details on how data should be transmitted during and after the test
- Techniques for data exclusion from systems upon termination of the test
- Clear guidance on incident handling

Chapter Summary

- LPTs must motivate, compliment, and reward team members.

- LPTs must stay up to date in their field.

- LPT-audited logos are used to indicate that a Web site or network has been thoroughly audited by an LPT.

- The GLBA compliance checklist ensures that penetration testers create written incident response plans to take action when any unauthorized access is detected.

- The HIPAA compliance checklist asks whether the organization has implemented any methods to encrypt and decrypt ePHI.

- The FISMA compliance checklist makes sure that penetration testers develop security policies and procedures based on the results of risk assessments.

- The FERPA compliance checklist makes sure that penetration testers do not share confidential information outside an organization.

- Rules of engagement are the formal permissions to conduct a penetration test.

- The scope of the ROE clearly explains the limits associated with the security test.

- The ROE may prohibit activities such as installing and using executable files that pose a risk to the system.

- The rules of engagement list allowed and prohibited activities.

- The ROE help testers overcome legal, federal, and policy-related restrictions to use different penetration-testing tools and techniques.

## Chapter 4

Penetration Testing Planning and Scheduling

Objectives

After completing this chapter, you should be able to:

- Explain how a penetration test plan and schedule is made
- Complete test deliverables
- Conduct a penetration testing planning phase
- Determine the project scope
- Organize a penetration testing team
- Organize a tiger team
- Use the proper scheduling tools

Key Terms

IEEE Standards Association   an organization with members working voluntarily to develop standards for various products

Test deliverables   documents that include a specification document, design document, test-plan document, user's manual, and installation manual

Test plan   a document that details the structure of a penetration test

Test-plan identifier   specifies the scope and purpose of a test along with the resources that are needed, the activities involved, and the scheduling

Tiger team   a group of people uncovering details on the vulnerabilities present in the system, the attack methods, and the skills to defend against these vulnerabilities

Work breakdown structure   a hierarchical tree structure that arranges the entire project in a well-organized fashion

Introduction to Penetration Testing Planning and Scheduling

Penetration testing requires extensive planning and scheduling to be effective. The steps of a penetration test must be planned in a sequence that will make the results trustworthy, the client must be consulted on all aspects of the project, and a testing team that meets the needs of the specific project must be organized. A well-constructed plan will constitute a great deal of the work of an actual penetration test.

A *test plan* is a document that details the structure of a penetration test. A test plan could be structured according to an industry standard such as the Institute of Electrical and Electronics Engineers (IEEE) Standard for Software Documentation—Standard 829, based on an internal template. The *IEEE Standards Association* is an organization with members working voluntarily to develop standards for various products. The IEEE defines the standards that are required for testing various applications. The contents of the IEEE standards are updated when the requirements change. The following two types of test plans are commonly used:

1. *Master Test Plan (MTP)*: The test lead prepares the MTP, depending on the functional specifications.
2. *Detailed Test Plan (DTP)*: The test analyst prepares the DTP, which consists of the main content of the test.

Purpose of a Test Plan

A penetration test plan is part of an overall security plan that sets the ground rules of the test. The test plan defines the following elements:

- *Test objective*: Specifies the objectives of the test plan
- *Scope of the testing effort*: Determines the scope of the penetration testing process
- *Limitations of resources and budget*: Stipulates the resources and budget required to perform the test process
- *Analysis and reviews*: Analyzes the penetration testing process and gives periodic reviews on the test process
- *Change control, communication, and coordination of key activities*: Details the change controls, communication, and key activities used in the penetration test process

The most important function of the penetration test plan is its ability to improve the test ground rules. The test ground rules formed during the planning phase address the following areas:

- The product configuration
- The environment within which to carry out the testing process
- Resources with which to perform penetration testing
- The product agenda

Building a Penetration Test Plan

The following four steps are essential for building a comprehensive test plan:

1. Setting up a test goal
2. Defining the objects to be tested
3. Hiring well-qualified penetration testers
4. Bounding the penetration analysis resources

Setting Up a Test Goal

For a successful penetration test, the following goals should be achieved:

- Define the number of errors or flaws present in the system
- Determine the level set of penetration test time
- Use unauthorized means to access the dummy target objects
- Violate and change the security policy
- Determine the proper usage of resources and money

Some systems are employed by multiple independent penetration testing teams to improve confidence in the test. Most penetration test processes focus on the design, implementation, and operational integrity of the security parameters to control flaws in the security interface.

Defining the Objects to Be Tested

Testers should focus on performing the penetration testing process on systems that require adherence to Trusted Computer Security Evaluation Criteria (TCSEC). Systems with these kinds of evaluation criteria are not designed to withstand hostile attack and penetration, which will always expose errors.

Testers that perform TCSEC evaluation at a high level are supplied with documentation and a collection of materials to support security testing. The collected security evidence will determine the penetration testing of a security system. The penetration testing must be done on a separate copy of the target of evaluation (TOE) in order to ensure noninterference with the actual users.

Hiring Well-Qualified Penetration Testers/Bounding the Penetration Analysis Resources

The penetration testing team should consist of well-qualified professionals. An organization should try to hire certified professionals with relevant experience.

Penetration analysis looks without any limitations for flaws present in a system. The major resource for penetration analysis is the penetration testing team. This team should have adequate knowledge about the target system they are going to test and spend time collecting security evidence related to the target system. The team should access the following resources:

- Compilers
- Editors
- Configuration management system
- Word processors
- Database management system

IEEE Standards

The following sections of standards are typical of those delineated by IEEE:

- *Test-plan identifier*: The **test-plan identifier** specifies the scope and purpose of a test along with the resources that are needed, activities involved, scheduling, etc. Mainly, it identifies the areas that need to be tested.

- *Introduction*: In this section, the overall introduction of the testing is specified. This may include the tools and software along with their standards and features. Various documents for reference, such as configurations, project plans, levels of testing, policies, legal liabilities, and various authorizations, are also specified.

- *Test items*: The test items need to be identified and specified. Once the test items are on hand, various other factors that involve testing should be listed, such as user guides, design plans, guides for installation, and so on. It is important for the tester to store a copy of all existing important files.

- *Features to be tested*: The tester needs to identify software features that need to be tested, as well as the test design and the design requirements.

- *Features not to be tested*: The software features that do not need to be tested are identified and the appropriate reason for not being tested is specified.

- *Approach*: This section describes the actual approach for overall testing. There are many features and combinations that need to be tested. The tester is required to give a detailed report of the approach, tools, and standards used for every level of testing. Specifying other factors such as testing resource availabilities, time management with deadlines, and comprehensiveness of the testing is also important.

- *Item pass/fail criteria*: The listed items that are selected for testing are tested and a test report is generated that specifies whether the item has passed or failed the test criteria.

- *Suspension criteria and resumption requirements*: The criteria to halt and restart the test are specified.

- *Test deliverables*: The test deliverables contain a detailed report of the various steps involved in identifying issues. This report could include the test plan, design, specifications, tools, criteria, configurations, case specifications, summary, etc.

- *Testing tasks*: The tester needs to identify the tasks and subtasks that are required to complete the process of testing.

- *Environmental needs*: The environmental needs could refer to the existing environment or could involve creating a new one along with the hardware and the software needed for testing. This also includes the tools needed, their source, and the resources required for the testing process.

- *Responsibilities*: The tester should identify a reliable and efficient team to handle the various tasks involved and to meet the goals efficiently within the specified deadlines.

- *Staffing and training needs*: The tester, after deciding on the team, should check the competency of the staff identified and decide whether training is required for the team to produce quality output.

- *Schedule*: The schedule should assure that all tasks are completed in such a way that deadlines are met with efficiency.

- *Risks and contingencies*: The team needs to identify the risks and legal liabilities that could arise while the testing process is in progress. There could also be factors such as delayed delivery of the product. The tester should be aware of all the risks and contingencies that might arise.

- *Approvals*: This section contains information on the personnel from whom the various approvals have been obtained to complete the testing.

Test-Plan Identifier

The test-plan identifier specifies the scope and purpose along with the resources that are needed, the activities involved, and the scheduling. It identifies the areas that need to be checked and the testing team that will perform the testing. The test planner should carefully select the required team so as to ensure the quality of work that is to be delivered. The required training should also be provided to the team, if necessary. The various aspects of the project should also be taken care of, such as the project agreement, the legal and financial issues involved, the time constraints, and any liabilities that may eventually arise. There are various levels in the process of testing. Therefore, it is important that each test-plan be assigned an identifier that is unique within the organization.

Test Deliverables

As part of its contractual obligations, a company specializing in security testing may need to provide a client with detailed accounts of all the penetration tests that were attempted (regardless of their success).

The test deliverables will change depending on the type of project. The *test deliverables* are documents that include a specification document, design document, test-plan document, user's manual, and installation manual. A realistic plan is based on the deliverables it produces.

There are two types of deliverables:

1. *Management deliverables*: These include project definitions and status reports, and are usually produced by the project manager. These deliverables ensure that the project is completed in a controlled manner.

2. *Business deliverables*: These are the outcomes of the project, also called business benefits, such as new system development, a new Web site, new services, or for example, increased security.

Test deliverables include the following elements:

- Management plan for managing the test team
- Plan for a common software/hardware platform for individual team members working on the project
- Problem statement
- Top-level design
- Initial task plan
- Initial schedule
- Project agreement document
- Requirements analysis document
- Software project management plan
- System design document

Penetration Test Planning Phases

The following phases are essential for penetration test planning:

1. *Defining the penetration test scope*: The scope of the penetration test specifies the areas to be tested. This makes sure that the team covers all the systems that need to be checked.

2. *Staffing*: At this stage of planning, the authorized person forms a team that performs the various activities involved in testing. The test utilizes various procedures and tools. The team is selected so that the results generated are accurate. The staff is given any required training.

3. *Developing the project plan*: This is an important part of the project, because it includes the critical aspects of the project. It contains details such as the need for the project, various hardware and software specifications, the agreement between the testers and the organization, the legal issues involved, deadlines, etc.

4. *Meeting the client*: The testing team is required to be very professional and efficient. This aspect of the testing team reflects on the expectations and the relationship between the team and the client. The quality of work that is delivered depends on the team's efficiency.

Defining the Scope

The project scope is based on the requirements of all stakeholders. There are various objectives that are to be defined in order to establish the scope of a project. The following objectives should be given a high priority:

- *Deliverables*: A list of the reports that are to be made available after the completion of the project
- *Functionality*: Verification of whether the system works as expected
- *Data definition*: A definition of the form that the results of testing will take
- *Technical structure*: The design of the project in the form of flow diagrams

The scope of the system is very much influenced by the changes incorporated during project development. Usually, the client does not understand the impact of the changes. The more changes the project is subject to, the more time and resources it uses. The effect of changes in requirements is to be discussed with the client. Often, a person from the client's company is continually updated on the progress of the project.

Time and project costs must be balanced with respect to the scope of the project. Changes that are beyond the scope need to be discarded. Other factors that are to be taken into consideration while defining the project scope are:

- Business process changes
- Technology changes
- Location changes
- Application changes

Project Scope

Features that the project is expected to exhibit as a part of the design specifications are to be tested. The features that are to be tested include the following areas:

- *Network security*: All network components need to be tested for security and secure configuration.
- *System-software security*: System-software vulnerabilities should be identified during the penetration test.
- *Client-side application security*: Client-side applications are to be checked for security and compliance with system requirements.
- *Client-side to server-side application communication security*: The transmission of data should be checked for security.
- *Server-side application security*: Applications on the Web servers and application servers should be checked for flaws that can be exploited.

- *Document security*: The organization should be advised to enhance security to protect important documents. Employees should destroy the documents that are no longer used but contain important details of the organization. The testing team should emphasize the use of shredders.
- *Inside accomplices*: The team should check for disgruntled employees who might release confidential data to the company's competitors.
- *Physical security*: The organization should restrict physical access to relevant departments only.
- *Intrusion detection/prevention systems*: The team should test any IDS or IPS.

When to Retest The testing team should retest an application if additional functionalities are to be tested. Automated tools are available to retest software. Retesting ensures that all additional functionalities are error free. The effect of changes in code can be noticed during the retest. The system should be retested for the following reasons:

- To find undiscovered bugs
- To identify the response of the system on:
  - A new operating system
  - New hardware such as firewalls, servers, routers, and wireless access points
  - Log files that have grown to the point that no free disk space is left
- To ensure that bugs are fixed
- To test individual modules
- To verify that a service patch rectifies a recently discovered security flaw
- When there is a change in the design and code
- When there are several input types to be tested

Staffing

Management

Responsibility and accountability for the tests conducted are necessary to complete the project on time. Management personnel are responsible for the following aspects of the project:

- The environment of the project
- Problem identification and correction
- Timely decisions and trade-offs between conflicting project goals

The following duties are important for good project management:

- *Effective leadership*: Leadership qualities help guide a team to progress toward the accomplishment of a specific goal. The following are some of the features of leadership:
  - Initiative
  - Accountability
  - Interaction with subordinates, superiors, and peers
  - Decisiveness
  - Listening and communicating
- *Facilitating teamwork*: Teams produce successful results when developed for the right reasons based on the right principles. The task at hand must be clearly defined and expressed. This includes understanding the project's purpose and the strategy for getting it done. The following factors are necessary for effective teamwork:
  - Commitment among team members
  - Self-assumed responsibility toward assigned tasks
  - Mutual trust among team members and management
  - Interaction and cooperation among team members

- *Managing resources*: Resources required for a penetration test project depend on the scope of the testing. Resources allocated for a project are defined and planned before the project's startup. Effective utilization of the available resources is an important characteristic of project management.

- *Proper planning*: Planning is vital to achieving goals. Strategic thinking is very important for planning. The following points make the importance of planning clear:

  - Planning ensures training needs are met

  - Proper planning will ensure deadlines are met

  - Planning makes the needs of the product/project clear

- *Maintaining progress card of the activities of a project*: Maintaining a progress card of the actions taken during the project helps management monitor the project at each stage. This will avoid any confusion at the later stages of the project and make reaching the goal easier.

- *Motivating staff*: The job of a project manager in the workplace is to get things done by motivating the employees. If jobs are assigned based on personnel abilities and the staff members are appreciated when their jobs turn out to be successful, it motivates the staff to strive more in their respective areas and ultimately enhances the quality of the project.

- *Managing risk*: At times, risks will appear while working on a project. Effective management of risks and finding a solution so that they will not affect the project is a critical characteristic of project management.

- *Defining project tasks/activities*: Defining project tasks/activities is a part of planning that helps define the requirements of the project.

Project Management Skills The following skills and experiences are essential for a project manager:

- Client presentations
- Project planning and administration
- Effective communication (oral and written)
- Leadership

The following skills and experiences are necessary for a policy examiner:

- Research and analysis
- Security industry standards (ISO 17799, GASSP)
- Threat analysis
- Principles of security management
- Business continuity and disaster-recovery standards

The following skills and experiences are necessary for a technical examiner:

- Client and server OS, NOS, UNIX, and Linux hardware devices
- Software and hardware configuration management
- Reported bugs and security flaws
- Network- and system-testing protocols and devices
- Physical plant security

Internal Employees

Internal employees play an important role in the penetration test. Their knowledge of the organization can be of great value to the penetration tester during the test. The testing team should make good use of the expertise of internal employees while carrying out the internal penetration test.

Internal employees can be used as targets if the penetration test is not announced to the staff of the organization being subjected to the test. Penetration testers can target internal employees and use social engineering to obtain valuable information related to the organization and information assets. This exercise should be carried out only with the involvement of top management and should be drafted in the agreement.

Test Teams

A licensed penetration tester heads the penetration testing project and is assisted by a group of experts, including the following people:

- Database and application expert
- Networking expert
- Ethical hacker
- Report and documentation writer

Tiger Team   A **tiger team** comprises a group of people mirroring details on the vulnerabilities present in the system, the attack methods, and the skills to defend against them. Through testing, the tiger team uncovers the flaws and vulnerabilities present in the system and thus secures the assets of an IT organization. Tiger teams are also known by other names such as red teams, ethical hackers, penetration testers, and intrusion testers.

The tiger team (Figure 4-1) is responsible for the following activities:

- Evaluating the network security level of the host system
- Testing the resources of an organization
- Preparing a report on vulnerabilities, threats, and attacks present, and submitting the report to the organization
- Generating a real attack without causing any damage to the system

Building the Tiger Team   The tiger team is made up of licensed penetration testers from various disciplines. The team consists of the following members:

- *Chief penetration tester*: The chief penetration tester heads the tiger team.
- *Database and application experts*: Database administrators help organize and store data. They are responsible for ensuring the performance of the system and help maintain the database. They help secure and maintain the performance management system. They are responsible for securing confidential data. Application experts are proficient in testing vulnerabilities in certain types of applications. There are often a number of application experts on a tiger team, each one with expert knowledge about certain applications.
- *Networking expert*: A networking expert has advanced networking knowledge.

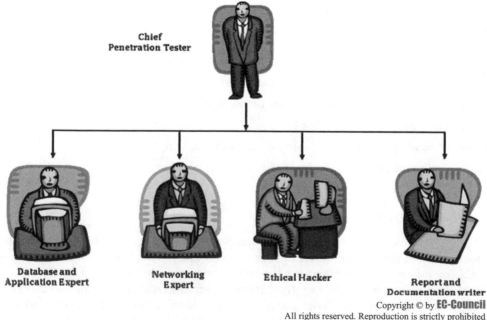

Figure 4-1   The test is headed by a chief penetration tester.

- *Ethical hacker*: The definition of an ethical hacker is very similar to a penetration tester. An ethical hacker is usually employed within the organization and can be trusted to attempt to penetrate networks and/or computer systems using the same methods as a hacker. When hacking is done by request and under a contract between an ethical hacker and an organization, it is legal. The most important point is that an ethical hacker has authorization to probe the target. The goal of the ethical hacker is to help the organization take preemptive measures against malicious attacks by initiating an attack on that organization, while staying within legal limits. This philosophy stems from the proven practice of trying to catch a thief by thinking like a thief.

- *Data analyst*: The data analyst is responsible for analyzing the data.

- *Project manager*: Project managers have control over the structure of the project team. The project team structure changes according to the project requirements.

- *Report and documentation writer*: The report and documentation writer develops manuals, project proposals, technical support documents, online help files, and product instructions.

Questions to Ask Before Hiring Consultants to the Tiger Team

- How much industry experience do they have? (The companies with whom they have worked and their demand in the market)

- How much technical experience do they have? (The technologies and platforms they have worked with)

- Do they have methodologies? (If yes, the attack methodologies and tools that they are familiar with)

- Who will ultimately do the work, and who is responsible for various tasks?

- What are their reputations and what certifications do they possess?

- How much will they cost the company?

- What is the final deliverable going to look like? Will the final report be delivered within the time constraints?

Developing the Project Plan

A project plan is a crucial part of project management. It specifies the goals and objectives, deadlines, resources required, approach, success factors, assumptions, and financial aspects. A well-developed project plan is said to have completed half of the actual task.

In the case of penetration testing, the plan begins by deciding if a white-box or a black-box testing technique will be used and speculates on usable exploits. A typical penetration testing project plan should involve the following:

- *Project definition*: It specifies the need for the project, gives a brief description of the project, and specifies what constitutes a successful outcome of the project.

- *Project goal*: It specifies the aim of the project and the reasons why the project is important.

- *Objectives*: These specify the set of objectives necessary to complete the project successfully.

- *Success factors*: These detail the advantages of the project and the aspects that lead to its success.

- *Assumptions*: This section describes the assumed details such as the strengths and weaknesses of the project, the opportunities for project extension, and the threats and hazards involved.

A sample project plan is illustrated in Figure 4-2.

Work Breakdown Structure

A **work breakdown structure** is a hierarchical tree structure that arranges the entire project in a well-organized fashion. It breaks the entire framework into sections and subsections, and distributes the divided work among all the employees. Work is divided in such a way that each task or set of tasks is a measurable quantity. Hence, a complex project is comprehended and partitioned in a way that each part is a well-defined package that involves a series of assignments.

Every assignment should have a definite work structure and a clear start and end. Every task must be deliverable in the sense that the work should be divided in a way that allows it to be delivered or submitted. For example, the work assigned to a person should have a starting and ending point, the maximum duration for its completion, the resources assigned to each task, and the task dependencies allotted and provided to the worker.

Test Plan Overview

Company Name	
Project Title	
Date	
Test Plan Created by	
Scope	
Description	

Figure 4-2 Project plans are essential for running a project efficiently.

Penetration Testing Schedule

The penetration testing schedule details the timing and duration of the various programs involved. It provides a thorough list of the tasks that are performed during penetration testing and specifies the allotted time for different tasks. Details, such as which task was done at what time and the status of the project after a stipulated duration, should be documented in a deliverable format.

Penetration Testing Project-Scheduling Tools

Using a project-scheduling tool will create efficient results. The following project-scheduling tools are useful for a variety of tasks:

- *Easy Schedule Maker*: An employee-scheduling tool that can be visually edited and maintains an unlimited number of employee schedules
- *FastTrack Schedule*: Provides a set of tools that can be used to plan efficiently, work swiftly, and achieve project goals
- *Gigaplan.net*: A Web-based tool that schedules work when all the workers are in place
- *ManagePro*: A tool that brings organization, planning, and execution together
- *Niku*: Helps to achieve high performance levels
- *OpenAir*: Improves utilization and cash flow by advancing billing and collections
- *PlanView*: A project portfolio management tool that helps reach project deadlines
- *Proj-Net*: Management tool can be used for all sizes of projects
- *Project Dashboard*: Supports different styles of project management and supports two-way integration with Microsoft Project

- *Project Office*: Provides Web-based tools for project investments. It creates, manages, and maintains the entire portfolio of an individual or an organization.
- *Time Disciple*: A project-scheduling tool used to minimize overheads, enhance productivity, and provide a cutting edge to a project
- *Xcolla*: A Web-based project-management tool that allows real-time information sharing between various team members
- *Gantt chart*: Tool used for creating a project schedule

The test-plan checklist in Figure 4-3 is a valuable tool for building a test plan.
Another useful tool for planning a penetration test, a simple flowchart, is shown in Figure 4-4.

Penetration Testing Hardware/Software Requirements

Penetration testing, like any other project, requires certain hardware and software resources. While conducting the tests, the following hardware will be required:

- Computer: A laptop or desktop computer is the basic entity required for penetration testing. The following should be installed:
  - Windows XP Virtual Server
  - Windows 2003 Virtual Server
  - Windows 2000 Virtual Server
  - Red Hat Linux 9
  - Wireless cards
  - High-capacity hard disk (preferably 160 GB or greater)
- Keyloggers
- Jamming devices

TEST PLAN CHECKLIST

Test Identifier	Yes	No
Is the scope of the project defined?		
Are all the test items identified?		
Are the items that are not to be tested identified?		
Are the Change Control Items identified and the members of the CCB defined?		
Are the features to be tested identified?		
Are the features that are not to be tested identified?		
Is the Test strategy identified and documented?		
Are the test criteria for security testing been documented?		
Are the entry criteria defined and documented?		
Are the exit criteria defined and documented?		
Is the list of deliverables documented?		
Is the test environment researched and documented?		

Figure 4-3 A test-plan checklist allows testers to make sure they have covered the necessary bases.

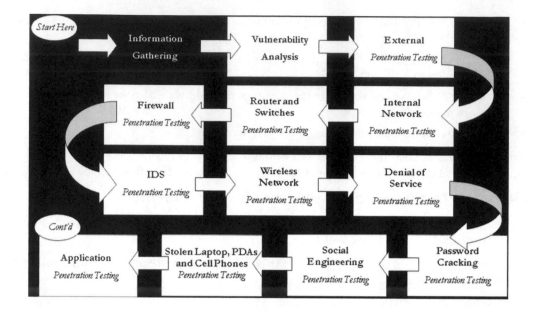

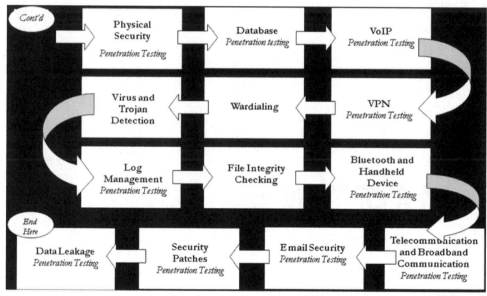

Figure 4-4 A simple flowchart will aid in organizing the sequence of events in a penetration test.

- Radio communication interceptors
- Telephone spying devices
- Wireless antennas

Certain software resources are also required for penetration testing. They are:

- Hacking Tools CD-ROM (Linux version)
- Hacking Tools CD-ROM (Windows version)
- Sniffing devices
- Penetration testing software (such as Core Impact)
- Vulnerability assessment tools

Meeting with the Client

The team should keep the client updated about the project. Any doubts and questions raised by the client should be clarified and answered, respectively. The following interactions with the client will be sure to keep the relationship on a secure footing:

- *Kickoff meeting*: A kickoff meeting is a meeting that officially marks the start of the implementation phase of the project. It is held in the initial stages of the project, after the groundwork for the project is done. The hardware and software resources required for the project, the development team, the project layout and design, the documentation template, and the cost limits and deadlines should all be ready when this meeting is held. The participants of this meeting should include the following people:

  - *Executive sponsor*: An executive sponsor is actually the client. Without the client, this meeting cannot be held, because the client is the one who sponsors the project. Any doubts can be clarified even at the last moment.

  - *Key stakeholders involved in the testing*: This team involves all the key players involved in penetration testing and also includes the managers, clients, CEO, and all those who are directly involved in the project.

  - *Tiger team conducting the assessment*: The most important element is the tiger team that is conducting the assessments and taking the responsibility for testing.

- *Status meetings*: The main agenda of these meetings is the status of the project. Issues such as how far the project has progressed, whether it will overshoot the deadline, and problems and solutions will be discussed. The progress of the work in terms of quantity and quality is also considered.

- *Deliverable template*: The project manager designs the template, which must be approved by higher authorities. The deliverable template is then given to the client so the client can get the look and feel of the documentation. The client's expectations would be known at this stage, and the client might give suggestions and make alterations to the template. After approval from both parties, the implementation process begins.

Tool: EC-Council's Vampire Box

Today's networks are becoming increasingly more complicated as new devices and technologies are incorporated into the modern work environment. Today, the functionality of a firewall is a required component of network security, as a new breed of sophisticated attacks is wreaking havoc on networks around the world.

Vampire Box unleashes Trojans, viruses, exploits, spyware, spam, malware and worms onto a network, as shown in Figure 4-5. If a firewall is updated and current, then it should block these attacks. Otherwise, the network security must be reassessed.

Vampire Box performs the following functions:

- Floods the network with Netbus, Back Orifice, Netcat, and other popular Trojans
- Attacks firewalls and antivirus systems with viruses and worms
- Floods the network with DoS packets and malformed TCP/IP packets
- Generates excess network traffic by flooding the wire with junk data
- Sends spyware and malicious programs (malware) onto the wire

Vampire Box does not require client software or modifications to the network. A user simply plugs it in and turns on the machine, and the system generates unwanted traffic. Vampire Box is updated automatically with new Trojans and viruses from a central Web site. The updates are seamless and automatic. Updates are performed weekly so that Vampire Box can keep up with the ever-changing virus and spyware variants.

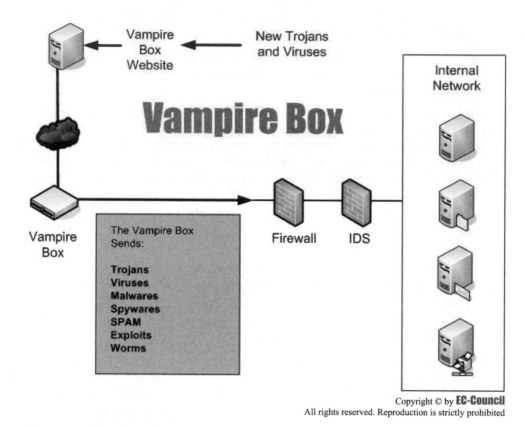

Figure 4-5   Vampire Box sends a number of viruses and other malicious programs to test a network's security.

Chapter Summary

- The IEEE standards give a list of the necessary elements for a penetration test.

- A kickoff meeting is a meeting where the project actually starts off. It is generally held in the initial stages of the project.

- A project plan is a crucial part of project management. It defines the project and specifies the goals and objectives, deadlines, resources required, approach, success factors, assumptions, and financial aspects.

- The test deliverables are documents that include a specification document, design document, test-plan document, user's manual, and installation manual.

- The scope of the penetration test specifies the areas to be tested.

- A penetration testing team should make good use of the expertise of internal employees while carrying out an internal penetration test.

- A work breakdown structure is a hierarchical tree structure that arranges the entire work of the project in a well-organized fashion. It breaks the entire framework into sections and subsections, and distributes this divided work among all the employees.

- The penetration test schedule consists of the timing and duration of the various programs involved.

## Chapter 5

Pre–Penetration Testing Checklist

Objectives

After completing this chapter, you should be able to:

- Create a pre–penetration testing checklist
- List the penetration testing requirements
- Find a lawyer that can assist the penetration team
- Prepare a nondisclosure agreement
- Prepare the tiger team
- Identify the different types of testing that will be carried out during the penetration test
- Identify necessary penetration testing personnel

Key Terms

External penetration testing   a type of penetration testing focused on the servers, infrastructure, and underlying software pertaining to the target

Internal penetration testing   a type of penetration testing performed from several network access points, including both logical and physical segments

Introduction to Pre–Penetration Testing Checklist

A pre–penetration testing checklist is an essential tool for all penetration testers. This checklist covers technical, personnel, contractual, and legal issues that must be taken care of before beginning the initial phases of a penetration test. Using it will ensure that the test runs smoothly and that all unforeseen events can be handled with relative ease. All licensed penetration testers should keep this list handy when starting a project. This chapter starts with the itemized checklist. A description of each item follows.

Checklist

1. Gather information about the client organization, including history and background.
2. If possible, identify the information security administrator of the client organization who will be helping with the penetration testing assignment.
3. Visit the client organization's premises to become familiar with the surroundings, parking, and facilities.
4. List the client organization's penetration testing requirements.
5. Obtain penetration testing permission from the company's stakeholders.
6. Obtain a detailed proposal of tests and services.
7. Identify the office space/location the team will be working in for this project.
8. Obtain temporary identification cards from the organization for the team that is involved in the process.
9. Identify who will be leading the penetration testing project (chief penetration tester).
10. If possible, obtain the previous penetration testing/vulnerability assessment reports from the client organization.
11. Prepare the rules of engagement that list the company's core competencies, limitations, and time scales.
12. Hire a lawyer who understands information technology and can handle the penetration testing legal documents.
13. Prepare the legal penetration testing document and have the lawyer vet it.
14. Prepare the nondisclosure agreement (NDA) and have the client sign it.
15. If possible, obtain liability insurance from a local insurance firm.
16. Identify the team's core competencies and limitations.
17. Allocate a budget for the penetration testing project.
18. Prepare a tiger team.
19. List the security tools that will be used for the penetration testing project.
20. List the hardware and software requirements for the penetration testing project.
21. Identify the client's security compliance requirements.
22. List the servers, workstations, desktops, and network devices that need to be tested.
23. Identity the type of testing that will be carried out: black-box or white-box testing.
24. Identity the type of testing that will be carried out: announced or unannounced.
25. Identify local equipment required for the penetration test.
26. Identify local manpower required for the penetration test.
27. List the contact details of key personnel of the client organization who will be in charge of the penetration testing project.
28. Obtain the emergency contact information for the client company.
29. List the tests that will not be carried out on the client network.
30. Identify the purpose of the test.
31. Identify the network topologies in which the test will be carried out.

32. Obtain special permission, if required, from local law enforcement.
33. List the known waivers/exemptions.
34. List the contractual constraints in the penetration testing agreement.
35. Identify the reporting time scales with the client organization.
36. Identify the list of penetration testers required for this project.
37. Negotiate the daily/hourly fee that will be charged for the penetration testing project.
38. Draft the timeline for the penetration testing project.
39. Draft a quote for the services that will be provided to the client organization.
40. Identify how the final penetration testing report will be delivered to the client organization.
41. Identify the reports to be delivered after the penetration test.

Step 1: Gather Information About Client Organization

Penetration testing is the process of assessing the security model of an organization. Before starting the project, a penetration tester should gather information about the company that is going to be tested, including the company history. Usually, large organizations provide official Web sites. The tester should use the company Web site as the main source of information. Some organizations release their details in newspapers or magazines, describing their growth and development. Gathering this type of information will give the tester an in-depth understanding of the company. The following history and background details will be helpful:

- Foundation of the company
- Objectives of the company
- Products released
- Assets of the company
- Employee details
- Stakeholders
- Potential business partners
- Clients of the company

Step 2: Identify Information Security Administrator of Client Organization Who Will Be Assisting

To make the penetration testing successful, testers must have an idea of the security-related issues of the organization. The information security administrator is the person who is responsible for the data and application security of the organization. He or she has intimate knowledge of the core parts of the security framework and is accountable for network and system updates and security on a day-to-day basis. Therefore, it is necessary to identify the administrator of the organization that is being tested. The security administrator can also assist testers in installing tools, testing the services, etc.

Step 3: Visit Client Organization's Premises

The tester should visit the client organization's premises. This should involve the basic facilities like parking areas and levels, restaurants, restrooms, elevators, clubs, swimming pools, and so on. The tester should check the entire physical infrastructure of the client organization. Visiting the premises will provide an idea of the physical security of the company.

The penetration tester should check the area where most employees utilize network equipment such as routers, switches, hubs, and so on. The following equipment areas should be checked individually:

- Examine the network equipment room where the routing setup is secured.
- Check the server room if it is different from the network equipment room.
- Inspect the area where the testing team will work.
- Determine whether the server and network rooms are provided with sufficient security.
- Choose a location to perform the testing process that is near the network equipment room.

Step 4: List Client Organization's Penetration Testing Requirements

In this step, the penetration tester gathers the requirements from the client organization. Requirements for a penetration test generally differ from one client to another. Penetration testing requirements depend on the following aspects:

- Nature and scope of work
- Critical nature of data
- Legal issues and regulations
- Business model

Client organizations may ask the penetration tester to perform some, or all, of the following types of testing:

- *External testing*: **External penetration testing** is the conventional approach to penetration testing. The testing is focused on the servers, infrastructure, and underlying software pertaining to the target. It may be performed with no prior knowledge of the site (black box) or with full disclosure of the topology and environment (white box).
- *Internal testing*: **Internal penetration testing** makes use of similar methods and is considered to be a more versatile view of security. Testing is performed from several network access points, including both logical and physical segments.
- *Black-box testing*: In order to simulate real-world attacks and minimize false positives, penetration testers can choose to undertake black-box testing (or a zero-knowledge attack, with no information or assistance from the client) and map the network while enumerating services, shared file systems, and operating systems discreetly.
- *White-box testing*: White-box testing takes place when the organization gives information about the target to a penetration tester. If the organization needs to assess its security against a specific kind of attack or a specific target, the organization can provide complete information about the attack or target to the penetration testers. The information provided can include network topology documents, asset inventory, and valuation information. Typically, an organization would opt for this when it wants a complete audit of its security.
- *Announced testing*: Announced testing is a type of testing that is performed after the testing team has provided a proper announcement to the organization before starting.
- *Unannounced testing*: Unannounced testing is a type of testing that is performed without a proper announcement to the organization. This type of testing is performed in secret.
- *Testing according to the number of IPs*: This involves testing the network based on the total number of IP addresses that the organization contains.
- *Physical-security/security-policy testing*: This is testing the physical security or security policy of a system.
- *Testing a particular server/service*: This type of testing targets a specific server or service.

Step 5: Obtain Penetration Testing Permission

Most companies have stakeholders who play a key role in the organization. A stakeholder is a person who is directly or indirectly involved in the functions of an organization and will be affected by any action the organization takes. Stakeholders can be: employees, directors, governments, shareholders, management, customers, investors, and the community. Company stakeholders must provide approval to help the penetration testers avoid future litigation.

Step 6: Obtain Detailed Proposal of Tests and Services

Client organizations should give detailed information about the nature and scope of the penetration test. The tester should ask the client to give a detailed proposal to perform this test. The following details should be included in the proposal:

- The number of IPs needed for testing
- The type of test

- The number of tests to be performed
- Whether there is an IDS system

Step 7: Identify Office Space/Location

Depending on the client organization's requirements, penetration testing can be a time-consuming process. The team should make sure that the space provided for them at the client's premises is comfortable, spacious, and airy. The location should have easy access to restrooms and the cafeteria, and should have restricted access for other employees of the client organization.

Step 8: Obtain Temporary Identification Cards from Organization for Team

After choosing the physical location at the client side, the team should request temporary identification cards for all testers who are going to be involved in the penetration testing process. The team members must use this access card to enter the premises. Each team member should receive his or her own identification card. This identification card will help the testing team avoid problems with the security guards, who usually work in shifts.

Step 9: Identify Chief Penetration Tester

The penetration testing team should have a mix of qualified professionals from different domains. The chief penetration tester will lead the project and be a point of contact for the client organization's management. The chief penetration tester plays a key role in delivering the project, handling issues related to testing, and maintaining the team.

Step 10: Ask Client Organization for Previous Penetration Testing/Vulnerability Assessment Reports

Organizations retain copies of penetration testing reports for future reference. The team should ask the client organization for previous penetration testing reports in order to give a clear idea of past problems. Most organizations will resist sharing their penetration testing report. If the organization provides the report, the team should check for the following:

- Compliance of the test
- Reasons to perform the test
- The previous penetration testing group
- When the test was carried out

Step 11: Prepare Rules of Engagement

- *Identify the core competencies of the client organization*: A core competency is something that a firm can do well and that meets the following three conditions specified by Hamel and Prahalad "*The CC of the Corporation*" from 1990:
  1. Provides customer benefits
  2. Is hard for competitors to imitate
  3. Can be leveraged widely in many products and markets
- *Identify the limitations specified by the client organization*: The rules of engagement should list points that limit the team's testing ability due to restrictions specified by the client organization.
- *List the time scale*: The time scale is the time it takes the organization to carry out its operation. Testers should be flexible about their timing so the testing process does not affect the organization.

Step 12: Hire a Lawyer

The team should hire a lawyer who understands technology and related matters. A legal document related to the penetration testing needs to be signed prior to initiation of the penetration testing assignment. A lawyer who understands information technology and the risks associated with penetration testing will be able to render professional services more efficiently.

Step 13: Prepare Legal Penetration Testing Document

After getting the legal document from the client organization, the team should study it with the help of a lawyer. Based on the document from the organization, the team prepares a penetration testing document and vets it with the lawyer. This document contains information related to legal aspects of testing and the scope of the project. The legal document mainly covers the following:

- Rules and regulations
- Terms and conditions
- Legal aspects of testing

Step 14: Prepare Nondisclosure Agreement (NDA)

A nondisclosure agreement (NDA), also known as a confidential disclosure agreement, is a legal contract that protects the organization's sensitive information. A typical NDA specifies the information that the penetration testing team is not allowed to disclose to other parties. As with all other documents, the testing team should consult a lawyer before giving the NDA to the client organization.

Step 15: Obtain Liability Insurance

The team should try to obtain liability insurance from a local insurance company in order to protect the team's interests if the client organization files a lawsuit. This could happen if the team causes damage to the organization during the course of penetration testing.

Step 16: Identify Team's Core Competencies and Limitations

Core competencies of a tester may include the following:

- *Network management*: Network management is the process of executing a set of functions required for controlling, planning, allocating, deploying, coordinating, and monitoring the resources of a network, including performing functions such as: initial network planning, frequency allocation, predetermined traffic routing to support load balancing, cryptographic-key distribution authorization, configuration management, fault management, security management, performance management, bandwidth management, and accounting management.
- *Program management*: Managing a program that is developed by programmers is another core competency for a tester.
- *Data administration*: Administrating the data is another core competency. As data are accessed by a large number of users, they are quite difficult to manage.
- *Risk management*: Managing risk is another core competency for a tester. One limitation of testing is configuration issues. Configurations vary from one system to another. The results of a test only reflect the security status for the testing period. Even minor administrative and architectural changes to the environment performed only moments after a penetration test can alter the system's security profile.
- *Technical knowledge of technologies*: For example, if the client has a Solaris server, the team must have at least one member who is proficient in Solaris.

Step 17: Allocate Budget for Penetration Testing Project

The team must prepare a budget for the entire process of penetration testing. The main purpose of this budget is to estimate the overall expenses required for the project. The budget estimates the amount of money necessary to run the project in the estimated time period. Penetration testing involves a lot of expenses that an organization has to bear. The following is a list of the expenses the budget may include:

- Traveling expenses
- Lodging expenses
- Food expenses
- Personnel expenses

Step 18: Prepare a Tiger Team

A tiger team is capable of performing a specialized task that tests the effectiveness of an organization. The tiger team is a team that plays a key role in the process of penetration testing. The tiger team is a combination of licensed penetration testers (LPTs), taken from different disciplines. A tiger team includes the following members:

- Oracle penetration tester
- Cisco penetration tester
- Database penetration tester
- Firewall penetration tester
- Report writers

Step 19: List Security Tools for Penetration Testing Project

Security tools play a major role in the penetration testing process. The following major tools are used in penetration testing projects, with examples included:

- *Port scanners*: Nmap, Firewalk, and SuperScan
- *Vulnerability scanners*: Nessus, Retina, SAINT, Whisker, X-Scan, and Metasploit
- *Application scanners*: AppScan and WebInspect
- *Firewall tools*: Firestarter and Fwlogwatch
- *Sniffers*: Wireshark, Kismet, and Tcpdump
- *Fingerprint/OS detection tools*: queso, siphon-v.666, and Winfingerprint
- *Hijacking tools*: pasvagg.pl and sw-mitm
- *HTML tools*: WebSnake
- *Intrusion detection system (IDS) tools*: AIDE, HostSentry, Logcheck, PortSentry, Snort, Swatch, and Tripwire
- *NetBIOS tools*: eum, nbnbs, and NetBIOS Auditing Tool
- *Network management/monitoring tools*: Analyzer, Cheops, ciscoconf, IP Watcher, IPAudit, iplog, NetSaint, and sting
- *NT-specific tools*: ELDump, NetViewX, and WsSes
- *Password tools*: ChkLock, MakePWL, and ZipPassword
- *Packet tools*: isic, Nemesis, NeoTrace, and SendIP
- *Phone tools*: THC-PBX and ToneLoc
- *Ping tools*: icmpquery, sping, NetPing, and VisualRoute
- *Promiscuous-mode detection tools*: CommView and Sentinel
- *Steganography tools*: Blindside, gifshuffle, Hide4PGP, JPHIDE and JPSEEK, SteganoGifPaletteOrder, Steganos, Stego, and wbStego
- *Cryptography tools*: PENS, ex-File, Cryptix, and LucentRegCrypto
- *DNS tools*: Whois, Nslookup, and Domain Information Groper (DIG)
- *Novell tools*
- *Remote tools*
- *Rootkits*
- *Network scanners*: THC-Amap, Xprobe2, CredDigger, and fping
- *Some miscellaneous tools*: Copernic, Genius, and ucd-snmp

Step 20: List Hardware and Software Requirements for Penetration Testing Project

This step explains the hardware and software requirements needed to perform the penetration testing. A highly configured system yields good results and finishes the project in less time. So the team should choose a highly configured system to finish the penetration testing process. The configuration mentioned below is mainly for laptop systems, as many organizations are using laptops as their personal computers. The following configuration aspects should be considered for every project:

- Ideal hardware configuration should contain the following:
  - An Intel Core Duo processor, the most secure and fastest processor that is leading the present generation
  - A 64-bit processor that runs with a frequency of 2.30–2.55 GHz
  - At least 2-GB RAM
  - Hard-disk storage capacity of at least 120 GB
- Software plays a key role in any system. Well-configured software includes the following:
  - Server software used in the penetration testing, including an IIS server, application server, and database server to store the records
  - Windows 2003 Server, Mac OS, and Linux operating systems

Step 21: Identify Client's Security Compliance Requirements

The following are the five major requirements of a client's security compliance:

1. *Administrative procedures*: This is a basic requirement of any company. Every company has an administration department that manages the entire organization. This administrative procedure is a key aspect of providing security to client organizations.
2. *Physical safeguards*: Every company should maintain physical safeguards such as providing security through access cards and having guards on duty.
3. *Technical security services*
4. *Technical security mechanisms*
5. *Standards*

Step 22: List Servers, Workstations, Desktops, and Network Devices to Be Tested

The following main types of servers may need to be tested:

- *IIS server*: This type of server should be tested, as it is used to store information and acts like a database for various applications.
- *Application server*: Application servers are mainly used to handle various applications on a network. Application servers are common to all platforms. The following are the two major types of application servers:
  - *Client application server*: This is a type of application server that is used to run various client-side applications.
  - *Web application server*: This type of server runs the server or Web-side applications on the network. The best example of a Web application server is Ariadne.
- *Windows server*: This is a server-side operating system developed by Microsoft. Windows 2000 and 2003 are the best versions of Windows servers.
- *UNIX/Linux server*: This is also a server-side operating system.

The testing team should make sure to test workstations and desktop machines as well.

Network devices play a major role in any organization. These devices connect various systems within the company. The following are some of the important network devices that need to be tested:

- *Routers*: Routers are more complicated than devices like repeaters and bridges. Routers use network-layer addresses and can have incorporated software that helps them identify which of multiple paths are possible between addresses and which path is best for the transmission of data.

- *Hubs*: A hub is a device that connects various devices to the network. Acting as a common connection point for devices in a network, a hub is commonly used to connect segments of a LAN. A hub contains multiple ports. When a packet arrives at one port, it is copied to the other ports so that all segments of the LAN can see it.

- *Switches*: A networking switch is the fundamental device in a wired or wireless LAN. It receives signals from each terminal on the network through Ethernet cables in a wired network and through radio waves in a wireless LAN. In both cases, the networking switch sends traffic across the LAN, permitting computers to communicate with each other and share resources.

- *Modems*: The term *modem* is formed from the terms *modulator* and *demodulator*. It is a device that converts digital signals into analog signals, and vice versa. The signals from the computer are in digital form, and the signals that are transferred over the telephone lines are in analog form. This conversion is done by the modem. Modulation is performed prior to sending the data, and demodulation is done after receiving the data. The modulator is the device that converts digital signals to analog signals by high-carrier frequency, and the demodulator is the device that converts the analog signal back to a digital signal using the same carrier frequency. These functions are integrated into this single device.

- *Network load balancers*: A network load balancer is a device used to balance or control the data load on a network. The basic function of a network load balancer is to distribute and control the maximum amount of data that a host or network device can handle. It is one of the most important parts of the network because overloading a single device can lead to system damage. Network load balancers are used commonly in both LANs and WANs.

- *Gateways*: A gateway is a device that is used to connect two different networks. A gateway device allows users to protect, share, store, and access data over a network.

- *Transceivers*: A transceiver is a network device that has both transmitters and receivers. The transmitter is used to transmit analog or digital signals, and the receiver is used to receive analog or digital signals. These transceivers are built into devices such as a NIC.

Step 23: Identity Type of Testing as Black Box or White Box

Black-Box Testing

The concept of black-box testing is based on the assumption that the tester has no prior knowledge or information about a system. In this sense, black-box testing simulates a true hacking attack, beginning with nothing but the organization's corporate name. From here, the ethical hacker gathers information about the network and the business from as many outside sources as possible. This can include publicly available information from sources such as Web sites and media publications.

In order to simulate real-world attacks and minimize false positives, penetration testers can choose to undertake black-box testing and map the network while enumerating services, shared file systems, and operating systems discreetly. Additionally, the penetration tester can undertake wardialing to detect listening modems and wardriving to discover vulnerable access points, if these activities legal and within the scope of the project.

White-Box Testing

If the organization needs to assess its security against a specific kind of attack or a specific target, the organization may provide information to the penetration testing team. The information provided can include network topology documents, asset inventory, and valuation information. Typically, an organization would opt for this when it wants a complete audit of its security.

In white-box testing, the testers can access the client's system design and implementation documentation, which may include listings of source code, manuals, and topological diagrams. This helps the ethical hacker adopt a structured, formal approach. The tester initially verifies the authenticity of the information provided as input for the network evaluation.

Step 24: Identify Type of Testing as Announced or Unannounced

Announced Testing

Testing that is carried out following a formal announcement is called announced testing. In this type of testing, the announcement is made to all the members of the organization, including all stakeholders.

- The following are some advantages of announced testing:
  - More efficient
  - Team oriented
- The following are some disadvantages of announced testing:
  - Lack of security
  - Less reliable results

Unannounced Testing

This type of testing is carried out without any prior announcement to the organization. This type of testing is done in secret.

- The following are some advantages of unannounced testing:
  - Strong security
  - Highly reliable
- The following are some disadvantages of unannounced testing:
  - Large impact
  - Less efficient
  - Requires a strict process

Step 25: Identify Local Equipment Required for Penetration Test

The list of local equipment required for performing the penetration testing process includes the following items:

- Category 5 (CAT5) taps
- Fiber taps/converter
- Access to the Internet, including the following types of access:
  - Filtered Internet access
  - Unfiltered Internet access
  - Uploads/downloads
- Separate office space allocation for the testing team
- Twenty-four hour power availability with a generator facility
- Refreshments, including access to the cafeteria

Step 26: Identify Local Personnel Required for Penetration Test

The list of local personnel required during the penetration testing process includes the following people:

- *Application administrator*: The main function of the application administrator is to control the applications that are available for users and groups.
- *Database administrator*: A database administrator performs the following functions:
  - Creating and testing database backups
  - Examining the integrity of the data
  - Checking the performance of the database
- *Network administrator*: The main function of the network administrator is to control and manage the hardware and software on a network.
- *Operating system administrator*: The main function of the operating system administrator is to create directories, manage operating system security, build backups, and restore the backups.

Step 27: List Contact Details of Key Personnel of Client Organization

In this step, the team needs to gather the contact details of key personnel who will be appointed as being in charge of the project for the client organization. The following details should be included in a list of key personnel contact information:

- Name of the personnel
- Department
- Role or designation
- Mobile number
- E-mail address
- Office number

Step 28: Obtain Emergency Contact Information for Client Company

The team also needs to gather the emergency contact information for key personnel.
  The following contacts should be located and informed during an emergency:

- Risk manager
- Database administrator
- Local security officer
- System administrator
- Network administrator
- Internet service provider

Emergency situations include fire, electrical breakdown, and network problems.
The contact details should include the following items:

- Mobile number
- E-mail address
- Office contact number

Step 29: List Tests Not to Be Carried Out on Client Network

The type of the tests to be conducted depends on the client organization. An e-commerce company may not allow a denial-of-service (DoS) test on its Web site, for instance.

Step 30: Identify Purpose of Test

The following are some of the possible purposes for a penetration test:

- To identify the threats facing an organization's information assets
- To identify the key vulnerabilities
- To safeguard the organization from failure
- To reduce an organization's IT security costs and provide a better return on IT security investment (ROSI) by identifying and resolving vulnerabilities and weaknesses
- To provide an organization with assurance—a thorough and comprehensive assessment of organizational security covering policy, procedure, design, and implementation
- To gain and maintain certification to an industry regulation (BS7799, HIPAA, etc.)
- To adopt best practices by conforming to legal and industry regulations

Step 31: Identify Network Topologies

The following network topologies can be used during the process of penetration testing:

- Bus
- Star

- Mesh
- Tree
- Ring

Step 32: Obtain Special Permission from Local Law Enforcement

Testers usually work on an intranet to test the network, but if the test is performed outside of a network, then special permission from local law enforcement may be required. The permission request should be in written form and should indicate the reasons, scope, and extent of the test being conducted. The tools that the penetration testers will be using must be documented. The results of the tests are to be kept confidential and are known only to the law enforcement agency and the security administration department.

Step 33: List Known Waivers/Exemptions

A waiver is the voluntary relinquishment or surrender of some known right or privilege. While a waiver is often in writing, sometimes a person's actions can act as a waiver. An example of a written waiver is a disclaimer, which becomes a waiver when accepted. Other names for waivers are exculpatory clauses, releases, and hold-harmless clauses.

Step 34: List Contractual Constraints in Penetration Testing Agreement

The team should check for service-level agreements in the project that may affect the scope of the test. Penetration testing involves risk. Both parties have to agree and sign documents defining the scope of the test.

Step 35: Identify Reporting Time Scales with Client Organization

The following reporting time scales identified by the client organization should be identified:

- *Normal time scale for project*: Specify the normal duration or time required for completing the project.
- *Local requested time scale for project*: Specify the local time scale the team requested to complete the project.
- *Distribution list of the project*: Specify the final distribution of the project.

Step 36: Identify List of Penetration Testers Required for Project

This list should include the following penetration testers required to complete the testing:

- *Database penetration testers*: A database penetration tester tests various databases used in the organization and checks for the following vulnerabilities:
  - SQL injection
  - Credit card threats
  - Extended stored procedures
  - Login threats
- *Firewall penetration testers*: A firewall penetration tester tests the vulnerabilities that can be exploited in a firewall. This tester should be an expert at bypassing firewalls using automated hacking tools.
- *Application penetration testers*: An application penetration tester knows the various vulnerabilities of Web applications and can use tools to remove such vulnerabilities that are found in various applications.

Step 37: Negotiate Daily/Hourly Fee

Based on the work to be performed by the team of testers, the chief penetration tester negotiates the fee, either hourly or daily.

Step 38: Draft Timeline for Project

Before starting any project, it is important to determine the timeline for completion. This timeline depends on the size of the project and the available resources. The penetration testing team should base the timeline on the size of the organization and the number of IPs that need to be tested. The client organization needs to define the goals of the testing so that the testing team can determine the timeline.

This timeline draft can be divided into the following three parts:

1. Starting time of the project
2. Project milestones
3. Project completion

Step 39: Draft Quote for Services

The penetration tester needs to prepare a quote that contains the details of services that will be provided to the client organization. The quote includes all the amenities that are required to perform the test.

Step 40: Identify How Final Penetration Testing Report Will Be Delivered

Preparing the final penetration testing report is of vital importance in a penetration testing assignment. This final report is prepared based on the penetration test performed on the organization. The report is not just meant for communicating facts, but also presents an expert opinion.

The goal of the report is to present all pertinent facts relating to the matter in an impartial and accurate manner, and to provide responsible, authoritative information to assist in making a determination whether to take corrective, remedial, or disciplinary action. While writing the report, related exhibits such as diagrams and pictures must be included.

As much as possible, the report should be written in the same order in which the facts were developed during the penetration test. The report should be written in such a way that it states the vulnerabilities, presents the results of the test, and sets forth the conclusions and recommendations.

The detailed report should contain the following items:

- *Vulnerabilities in the organization*: A pie graph or chart displaying the low-, medium-, and high-ranking vulnerabilities
- *Countermeasures to be taken to reduce those vulnerabilities*: Details countermeasures and remedies for the vulnerabilities found
- *Recommendations*: Provides best practices for the secure configuration of services and devices
- *Documentation of the results*: Contains detailed results of the penetration testing process
- *Final summary*: Provides a general overview of the testing process and the recommendations of the team

Step 41: Identify Reports to Be Delivered After Test

The following reports should be submitted to the client organization after the completion of the penetration testing process:

- *Network test reports*: Provides test reports on attacks over the network
- *Client-side test reports*: Provides test reports on attacks against end users
- *Web-application test reports*: Provides test reports on attacks against Web applications

Chapter Summary

- A penetration testing team should follow a checklist to prepare for the testing process before it begins.
- The testing team needs to assess the client site to make sure that all required resources are available.
- All aspects of the penetration testing process need to be spelled out before the test starts. This should be in the form of a written agreement.
- The team should consult a lawyer concerning any legal documents that are created or received prior to the testing process.

## Chapter 6

Information Gathering and Social Engineering Penetration Testing

Objectives

After completing this chapter, you should be able to:

- List the steps in the information-gathering process
- Define social engineering
- Crawl FTP sites and mirror pages
- Search the Internet for information about a target company
- Search Internet archive pages
- Conduct social engineering

Key Terms

Dumpster diving   the act of searching disposal areas for information that has not been properly destroyed

Information gathering   a process used to create a profile of a target organization or person

Revision numbers   numbers assigned to each successive revision of a product

Social networking Web sites   Web sites for contacting and connecting with friends, friends of friends, and relatives through scraps, instant messaging, and many other options

Vishing   a technique involving performing phishing over the phone, typically using Voice over IP (VoIP) technology

Introduction to Information Gathering and Social Engineering Penetration Testing

The main purpose of *information gathering* is to create a profile of a target organization or person. There are a number of ways to accumulate information regarding a target. An attacker can gather information by searching the Internet. Many companies reveal their activities, contact information, and history information on their Web sites. Conducting queries on the Web can reveal information about domain names and networks related to specific organizations. Valuable information can also be gathered from newspapers and other press releases, such as interviews given by the target company's employees. Contact information displayed in the ads and reports also provides useful information. Job Web sites provide valuable information regarding the technologies the organization uses, the needs of the organization, and contact information. Vital information can be gathered through interaction with target employees and public databases.

Social engineering is a form of information gathering in which the attacker attempts to manipulate individuals within the target organization to gain information about the company. This can be done over the phone, through e-mail, or even in person. Attackers may impersonate customers, clients, or service workers to gain entrance to a company's facilities and to access sensitive data.

Information-Gathering Steps

The following are some of the steps involved in information gathering:

1. Crawl the company's Web site and mirror the pages on a PC.
2. Crawl the company's FTP site and mirror the files on a PC.
3. Look up registered information in public databases.
4. List the products the company sells.
5. List the company's contact information, including e-mail addresses and telephone numbers.
6. List the company's distributors.
7. List the company's partners.
8. Search newsgroups, bulletin boards, and Web sites for information about the company.
9. Search trade association directories.
10. Research the popularity of the company's Web site.
11. Compare prices of products or services with a competitor.
12. Find the geographical location of the company.
13. Search Internet archive pages about the company.
14. Search similar or parallel domain name listings.
15. Search job posting sites for jobs the company has posted.
16. Browse social networking Web sites.
17. List key employees.
18. Investigate key personnel.
19. List employees' company and personal e-mail addresses.
20. Search for Web page posting patterns and revision numbers.
21. E-mail employees, disguised as a customer asking for a price quote.
22. Visit the company as a customer and extract privileged information.
23. Visit the company in person.
24. Use Web investigation tools to extract sensitive data about the company.
25. Use Intelius to conduct background checks on key company personnel.
26. Search eBay for the company's presence.
27. Use Domain Research Tool to investigate the company's domain.
28. Use the EDGAR database to research company information.
29. Use Google/Yahoo! Finance to search for press releases the company has issued.
30. Search company business reports and profiles at Hoover's.

31. Visit 411 and search for telephone numbers.
32. Search for U.K. telephone numbers at BT.
33. Retrieve the company's DNS record from publicly available servers.
34. Use GHDB to search for the company name.

Step 1: Crawl the Company's Web Site and Mirror the Pages on a PC

The following programs can be used to crawl Web sites and mirror the pages:

- *HTTrack*: This is a flexible open-source offline browser utility. It enables the user to download Web sites to a local directory from the Internet, building all directories recursively and downloading HTML, images, and files from the server to the user's computer. HTTrack organizes the relative link structure of the original site. The user can open a page of the mirrored Web site in his or her browser and can then browse the entire site through different links, similar to viewing the site online.
- *Webcrawl*: This is a program that enables users to download complete Web sites with their respective links in HTML documents.
- *cURL and Libcurl*: These are tools that work for Windows, Linux, UNIX, Amiga, and OS/2.
- *W3mir*: This is a Perl-based wide-ranging HTTP copying and mirroring tool.
- *WebCopier*: This is an offline browser that saves Web sites and stores them until the user is ready to view them.
- *FileDog*: This is an automated file transfer program. It downloads program updates, shareware, and freeware quickly.
- *BlackWidow*: This is a wide-ranging Internet tool. It can be used as a site ripper, offline browser, Web site scanner, site mapping tool, and site mirroring tool. BlackWidow is useful for scanning a site and creating a complete profile of the framework of the site, its files, its external links, and even its link errors.

Step 2: Crawl the Company's FTP Site and Mirror the Files on a PC

The following programs can be used to crawl FTP sites and mirror the files:

- *ftpcopy*: ftpcopy is an FTP client useful for copying files or directories from an FTP server. Its main function is to mirror FTP sites.
- *FTP Mirror Manager*: FTP Mirror Manager is used for managing the mirroring of numerous FTP servers. It includes a back-end module for configuration purposes, a front-end module in which a user's personal settings can be altered, and a cron job that can be scheduled by the back-end module.
- *GetRight*: GetRight is a tool that works with a Web browser for downloading files from the Internet. GetRight increases download speeds and helps in recovering downloads if an error occurs.
- *FTP Mirror Tracker*: FTP Mirror Tracker is a software package that supports clear, user-controlled redirection to neighboring anonymous FTP mirror sites that are copies of the original source. Redirection can be attained by directly making HTTP requests to FTP Mirror Tracker or through the use of a Web cache server.
- *Auto FTP Manager*: Auto FTP Manager is an advanced FTP client that allows a user to schedule and automate file transfers. Auto FTP Manager helps in establishing a connection to any FTP server and specifies rules that automate the file transfer process.

Step 3: Look Up Registered Information in Public Databases

The following tools can be used to find information about domains and IP addresses:

- *WHOIS*: WHOIS is an Internet utility used to search various domain databases for information related to domain names and IP addresses. All publicly available information about domain names can be extracted by this utility. WHOIS lookup provides the following information:
  - Details of the domain registrar
  - Domain owner name and contact details

- Name of the WHOIS database that stores the domain information
- *Sam Spade*: Sam Spade is a network query tool with the following integrated utilities:
  - *Nslookup*: Queries the Domain Name System (DNS)
  - *WHOIS*: Provides all the details of a domain name such as the name and contact details of the registrar, and the name and contact details of the domain name owner
  - *Traceroute*: Traces the route to the specified host
  - *Ping*: Sends an ICMP request to see if a host is alive
  - *SMTP verification utility*: Uses Simple Mail Transfer Protocol (SMTP) to verify the origin of e-mails
- *NetScanTools*: This set of tools includes those that are useful for network professionals. These include graphical versions of Ping, Traceroute, and Nslookup.
- *Whois.net*: Whois.net is a domain-based research service. It provides the following information:
  - Registrar name
  - Registrar WHOIS
  - Registrar home page
  - Registration creation date
  - Registration expiration date
- *WhereIsIP*: WhereIsIP is Internet software that is useful in finding out the geographic location of an IP address, domain name, ICQ contact, Web site, or e-mail sender.
- *Lokbox*: Lokbox is useful for extracting information on domain names and IP addresses. It provides the following details about a domain:
  - Registrant name
  - Name of the domain owner
  - Domain names that begin with a word specified
  - ISP of the hacker trying to break into a machine
- *ActiveWhois*: ActiveWhois is a simple network tool that is useful for extracting information about the owner of an IP address or Internet domain. The following details can be determined:
  - Country
  - Postal addresses of the owner
  - User of IP address and domains

Step 4: List the Products the Company Sells

The following steps can be taken to list the products sold by the company:

- Visit the company's Web site
- Request a product catalog
- Send an e-mail inquiry
- Request a discount if applicable
- Request a list of distributors and their retail channels
- Request an international contact for the company's products
- The following tools are helpful for listing the products of a company:
  - Internet Explorer browser
  - Google search
  - Telephone
  - Fax

Step 5: List the Company's Contact Information, Including E-Mail Addresses and Telephone Numbers

The following steps can be taken to list valuable contact information:

1. Visit the company's Web site for contact details
2. Use search engines, such as Google
3. Contact the company's distributors, retailers, and partners for business contacts in the company
4. Send an e-mail asking for product quotes, and record the contact information
5. Search Web sites such as phonedirectorysearch.com
6. Search the Yellow Pages
7. Contact the company's receptionist and ask for a contact person in one of the following departments:
   - Sales
   - Marketing
   - Customer service
   - Management
   - Technical support
   - Manufacturing

Step 6: List the Company's Distributors

The following techniques are useful for listing the company's distributors:

- *Sending an e-mail stating that the customer is from a particular location or country*: The company will respond with the distributor listing for that location. This allows the customer to approach the distributor at the correct location.
- *Searching the company's Web site for distributor information*: The distributors are typically listed in alphabetical order by country. This allows the user to quickly select the required location.
- *Using search engines like Google to find distributor information*: The user must type the necessary keywords in the search field to obtain the relevant information about distributors.
- *E-mail spider*: A tool such as e-mail spider can be used to extract e-mail addresses from the net. E-mail spider extracts the e-mail addresses that are targeted by using the Google and Yahoo! search engines. It detects numerous e-mail addresses in an hour, making the vulnerability scanning process easy.

Step 7: List the Company's Partners

The following techniques are useful for listing the company's partners:

- Send an e-mail asking to partner with the company in developing new technologies
- Identify the person who responds to the e-mail
- Look for partner information on the company's Web site; this is usually found under the press release or press room section
- Search for partner information on Google (search terms: "company name + partners + project + press release")

Step 8: Search Newsgroups, Bulletin Boards, and Web Sites for Information About the Company

The following places are useful for finding information about a company:

- *Focused search engines*: Details about the company can be found using Yahoo! or industry-focused search engines.
- *Bulletin boards and newsgroups*: Relevant information about the company can be obtained by searching through bulletin boards and newsgroups.

- *Negative Web sites*: In certain situations, users set up Web sites specifically to disparage a certain company. For example, if a company's Web site is www.jayscakes.com, then Web sites such as www.ihatejayscakes.com and www.jayscakessucks.com might exist.

Step 9: Search Trade Association Directories

Search for the company's information in the following trade association directories:

- *http://www.marketingsource.com/associations/information.html*
- *http://www.google.com/Top/Business/Associations/By_Industry/*
- *http://www.ipl.org/*

California Association Of Marriage And Family Therapists

Address:	7901 RAYTHEON RD SAN DIEGO, CA 92111-1606
Phone:	(858) 292-2638
FAX:	(858) 292-2666
Website:	www.camft.org
Email:	maryr@camft.org
Contact:	MRS. MARY RIEMERSMA, Executive Director
SIC Code:	8322
Profit Status:	Non-Profit
Year Founded:	1964
Members:	27500 Individuals
Staff Size:	17
Newsletter:	The Therapist - The Therapist (6/year)
Publications:	The Therapist--100 plus page bi-monthly magazine
Conventions:	One Annual Conference. Many Advanced Educational Series Workshops annually. Four regularly scheduled Board Meetings and various other meetings.
Description:	CAMFT (California Association of Marriage and Family Therapists) is a California nonprofit corporation made up of individuals (members) who choose to associate for common purposes.

Professional Businesswomen Of California

PO BOX 6657
SAN MATEO, CA, 94403-6657
Phone: (650) 548-2424 Fax: (650) 548-0840
Contact: MS. RUTH STERGIOU, Executive Director
URL: www.pbwc.org Email: pbwc@regdesk.com
Membership: 5000 SIC Code: 8699

Reach: State Staff Size: 5 Year Founded: 1989
Category: Activism - Women
Conventions: The 15th Annual Conference of the Professional BusinessWomen of California, Moscone Center, San Francisco
Newsletter: Yes, 4/year
Publications: Highlights, quarterly. Newsletter.

Special Olympics Florida

1105 CITRUS TOWER BLVD
CLERMONT, FL, 34711-1905
Phone: (352) 243-9536 Fax: (352) 243-9568
Contact: MR. MONTY CASTEVENS, President
URL: www.sofl.org Email: sofl1@aol.com
Membership: 19000 SIC Code: 8399

Reach: State Staff Size: 15 Year Founded: 1972
Category: Disabilities - Sports
Conventions: annual Leadership Conference
Publications: Special Edition, quarterly. Newsletter

Washington Public Employees Association

PO BOX 7159
OLYMPIA, WA, 98507-7159
Phone: (360) 943-1121 Fax: (360) 357-7627
Contact: MS. LESLIE LIDDLE, Executive Director
URL: www.WPEA.org Email: leslie@wpea.org
Membership: 5000 Individuals SIC Code: 8699

Reach: State Staff Size: 15
Category: Employees
Conventions: Monthly Executive Board Meetings, Monthly Membership Meetings, Annual Membership Meeting
Newsletter: WPEA Today (1/year)
Publications: Various unit newsletters

Figure 6-1   Trade association directories reveal valuable information about an organization.

Trade association directories provide the following information about a company, as shown in Figure 6-1:

- Organization's name and address
- Contact person and his or her designation
- Phone and fax numbers
- URL and e-mail addresses
- Description of services and membership statistics
- Information on publications and newsletters
- Meeting and convention information
- Nonprofit/for-profit status
- SIC code, industry category, year established, and staff size

Step 10: Research the Popularity of the Company's Web Site

There are many Web sites providing information to Internet viewers about Web site popularity. They provide complete reports about how many people are accessing a Web site daily.

The following are methods for checking the popularity of a company's Web site:

- Check for the link popularity of the company's Web site by checking the following Web sites:
  - *http://www.alexa.com/*
  - *http://www.marketleap.com/publinkpop/default.htm*
- Compare the company's Web site with a competitor's. Figure 6-2 compares the graphs of *www.google .com* and *www.yahoo.com.*
- Find the traffic graph of the Web site.
- Search the pages in a search engine index containing a link to the Web site of the company.

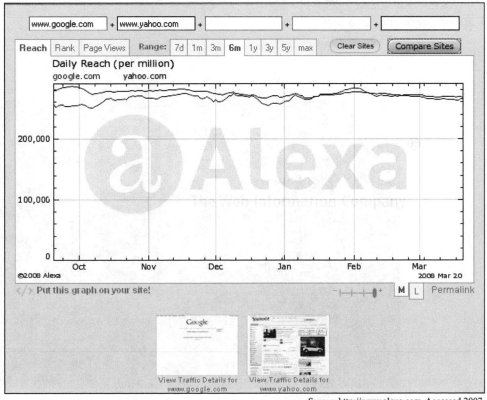

Source: http://www.alexa.com. Accessed 2007.

Figure 6-2   Alexa allows a user to compare Web site traffic.

Step 11: Compare Prices of Products or Services with a Competitor

Using a price comparison service allows a user to compare one company's prices of products or services with a competitor's prices. Price comparison service is provided by the following Web sites:

- *http://www1.dealtime.com/*
- *http://www.mysimon.com/*
- *http://www.kompass.com/*

Check for the following in the above Web sites:

- Merchant rating of the company
- Customer reviews
- List of the products and services the company provides

By referring to the above, the status of the company with its customers and merchants can be tracked.

Step 12: Find the Geographical Location of the Company

With the help of Google Maps, the geographical location of the company can be found, as shown in Figure 6-3. Check the neighboring companies and landmarks such as theaters, restaurants, etc. This service is also provided by the following Web sites:

- *http://www.WindowLiveLocal.com*
- *http://www.Wikimapia.com*
- *http://www.Palacepedia.com*

Step 13: Search Internet Archive Pages About the Company

Internet archive pages can reveal the following information:

- All changes made to the company's Web pages since the site's inception
- All major actions the target company has made
- Recently developed products

Figure 6-3   The geographical location of a company can reveal important information used in later social engineering attempts.

Source: http://www.archive.org. Accessed 2007.

Figure 6-4   Internet archive pages can reveal important company history.

- Press releases
- Former mistakes

The Web site *http://www.archive.org* reveals this information, as shown in Figure 6-4.

Step 14: Search Similar or Parallel Domain Name Listings

Try to search for information about an organization with domain names the organization may have used in the past. For example, if the company's domain is blitzkrieg.com, then it would be useful to search for the company name along with the following domain names:

- blitzkrieg.org
- blitzkrieg.net
- blitzkrieg.biz
- blitzkrieg.tv
- blitzkriegcom.com
- blitzkrieg_.com

The site *www.mydomainfriend.com* provides an automated tool that helps users easily generate a list of potential domain names for a Web site, as shown in Figure 6-5.

The procedure involves the following six steps:

1. Enter the primary domain name.

2. Enter the secondary domain name, if any.

3. Enter the optional domain name, if any.

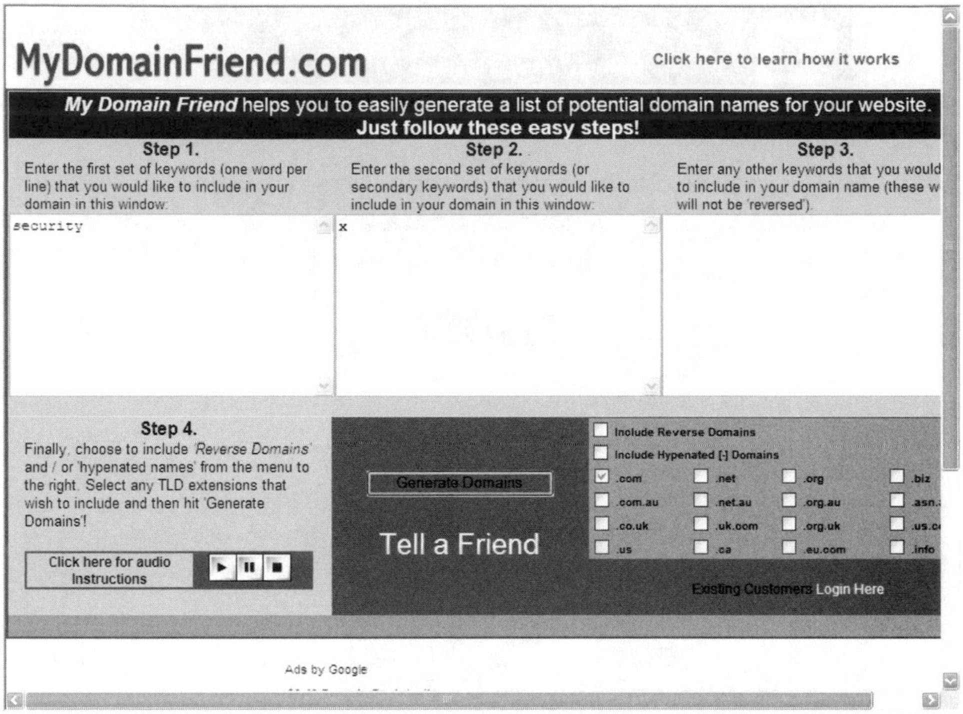

Source: http://www.mydomainfriend.com. Accessed 2007.

Figure 6-5 The site *www.mydomainfriend.com* is a useful tool for researching domain names.

4. Select whether to include reversed domain names and/or hyphenated names by checking the appropriate boxes.

5. Click **Generate Domains**. The results will be displayed in a new window.

6. Click **Search Now!** to instantly check the availability of that domain.

Step 15: Search Job Posting Sites for Jobs the Company Has Posted

Look for any opportunities that are available in the target company. Vacancies within a company can be found in leading newspapers, classifieds, and job search engines, as shown in Figure 6-6.

The fields or platforms in which the company is currently working can be determined from the requirements specified in any job listings. See if there are any requirements for system administrators, database operators, or security administrators. This will reveal the background of the working environment of the company.

For example, if the company requires a system administrator with some experience in Oracle, Cisco routers, or Checkpoint firewall, it clearly indicates that the organization uses those technologies.

Step 16: Browse Social Networking Web Sites

Today, there are several *social networking Web sites* available for contacting and connecting with friends, friends of friends, and relatives through scraps, instant messaging, and many other options. In such Web sites, profiles can be searched to find general information, as shown in Figure 6-7.

The following are methods for finding information on a social networking Web site:

- Search for information about the company on the following social networking Web sites:
  - *http://www.orkut.com*
  - *http://www.myspace.com*
  - *http://www.facebook.com*
  - *http://www.hi5.com*
  - *http://twitter.com*
- Search for communities related to a company and gather the personal e-mail addresses, phone numbers, and addresses of key personnel.

Figure 6-6   Job posting sites can reveal important information about a company's personnel.

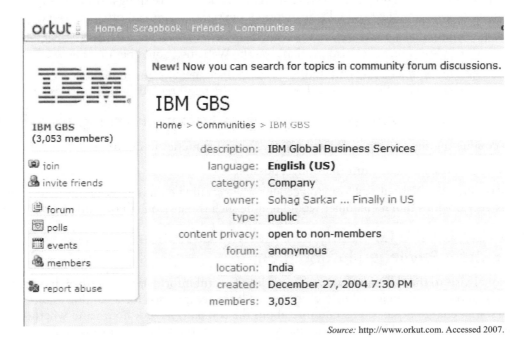

Figure 6-7   Companies often have communities on social networking sites.

Step 17: List Key Employees

It is always good to know the strengths of a company and all its employees. It is much easier, though, just to find out about the key personnel of the target organization. This is possible through posing as a customer and asking for a presentation.

Social engineering is the best tool for this step. Befriend some of the staff members and try to extract useful and sensitive information about the organization, such as details about the company's key personnel, future projects, human resources, and other confidential issues related to the organization. Also try to find out the contact information and telephone extensions.

Step 18: Investigate Key Personnel

Details about key personnel within an organization can be very helpful, especially for social engineering. Find the background of important employees and make a detailed study. This information might include the résumés of key employees such as the CEO, the president, the vice president, and managers. Résumés provide information such as the name, age, gender, and contact information, including home address, e-mail addresses, and phone numbers. They also provide the person's educational background, including college name, area of study, and year of graduation. A résumé also includes the person's total work experience, including the organizations for which he or she has worked and the projects on which he or she has worked. The background check should also include any promotions the person has received within a specific duration and the major achievements he or she has made in the organization. All this information can be gathered from Google, Yahoo!, or any job site search engine.

Step 19: List Employees' Company and Personal E-Mail Addresses

A list of employees' personal and company e-mail accounts provides greater flexibility when conducting an attack. If an employee's company e-mail address is known, then it may be possible to guess the employee's personal e-mail address by drawing clues from the company e-mail address and trying out Yahoo!, Hotmail, or Gmail accounts.

Step 20: Search for Web Page Posting Patterns and Revision Numbers

The following information can be useful for exploiting a company's Web site:

- *Copyright notices*: Copyrights are a way of protecting an author's original works. Permission has to be given by the copyright owner to reproduce, extend, or derive things from an original work without damaging or misusing the original framework. Copyright notices can often be found on the Web.
- *Revision numbers*: The **revision numbers** (numbers assigned to each successive revision of a product) of a company's products are also available on the Web and should be noted down.
- *Document numbers*: The names of important documents or the numbers that are assigned to them after each revision should be searched for on the Internet and recorded for future assessment.

Step 21: E-Mail Employee, Disguised as Customer Asking for Price Quote

When conducting the correspondence, keep the following tactics in mind:

- Try to extract as much information as possible.
- Avoid using a Yahoo! or Hotmail account when sending e-mail messages as a fake customer, because it is very obvious that a customer would handle such things from an official or business e-mail account.

Step 22: Visit the Company as Potential Customer and Extract Privileged Information

A personal visit to the company can result in a lot of useful information. Just drop in at the company's physical premises, and act as a potential new customer. Ask the receptionist for a catalog and if it is possible to talk to the person in charge of sales. Also inquire about the company's work hours and whether there are any branch offices. Try to acquire additional telephone numbers other than the ones mentioned on the official Web site.

Even the physical infrastructure of a company can provide information, so try to take photos of the exterior of the building and any important interior rooms you can get access to. This might be possible by visiting the restroom and then slowly and tactfully taking photos.

Step 23: Visit the Company in Person

Visit the company to gather general information such as the number of people working in the company and the names and phone numbers of the important people working there. Social engineering techniques can reveal other information about the company.

The following sources can also provide useful information:

- Ancillary staff such as security guards
- Agents standing outside the company gate who provide services to the company's staff
- Neighborhood merchants who deal with the company or its employees

Step 24: Use Web Investigation Tools to Extract Sensitive Data About the Company

Webinvestigator is a company that provides comprehensive online record searches in many categories, as shown in Figure 6-8. It systematically gathers information from database sources and data-center links to provide its members with investigation services.

The following categories and reports are available for searching:

- Online investigations:
  - *Background records*: Reports include addresses, relatives, phone numbers, properties, and judgments
  - *Criminal records*: Reports include case numbers, charges, offenses, arrests, filings, dispositions, and sentences
  - *Legal records*: Reports include property, liens, judgments, business records, and more
  - *SSN records*: Reports include Social Security number validations and death records
  - *Sex offenders*: Reports include registered addresses, aliases, case numbers, charges, and convictions
  - *Credit records*: Reports include credit history, credit worthiness, bankruptcies, and more
- Civil records:
  - *Birth records*: Reports include date, parents, and address
  - *Death records*: Reports include date, filings, name, age, and relatives
  - *Divorce records*: Reports include filing type, date, case number, location, name, age, and properties
  - *Marriage records*: Reports include location, name, age, and spouse

Figure 6-8   Webinvestigator provides online records for a variety of topics.

- *Property records*: Reports include owner, location, transfers, sales, descriptions, and tax info
- *Bankruptcy records*: Reports include date, case number, reason, legal files, and addresses
- People search:
  - *People search*: Reports include people location and missing people information
  - *Missing persons*: Reports include relatives, roommates, neighbors, aliases, and address history
- Reverse lookup:
  - *Reverse phone*: Reports include full addresses, names, contacts, and account history
  - *Reverse cell phone*: Reports include full addresses, names, contacts, and account history
  - *Reverse e-mail*: Reports include full addresses, names, contacts, and account history
  - *Reverse IP address*: Reports include hosting records, Web site owner records, and addresses
- Other records:
  - *Business records*: Reports include business addresses, UCC filings, court rulings, and more
  - *Non-U.S. records*: Reports include limited records for Canada and the UK

Step 25: Use Intelius to Conduct Background Checks on Key Company Personnel

Intelius can provide a background search on anyone, as shown in Figure 6-9. This detailed search includes the following information:

- Criminal check
- Bankruptcies
- Small claims
- Property information (if available)
- Neighbors (if available)
- Tax liens

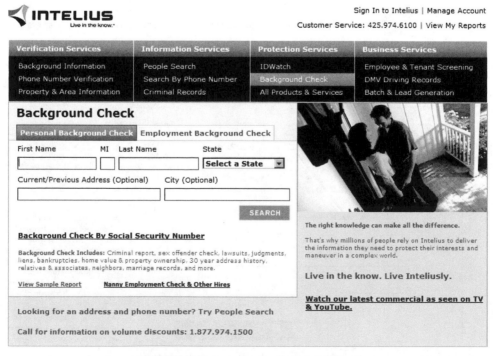

Figure 6-9 Intelius performs background searches on individuals.

- Judgments
- Licenses
- 20-year address history
- Mortgages

Step 26: Search eBay for the Company's Presence

Searching for product information can reveal a manufacturer's name, as shown in Figure 6-10. The manufacturer's details can be obtained with the help of different search engines on the Internet.

Step 27: Use Domain Research Tool to Investigate the Company's Domain

Domain Research Tool (DRT) is a tool used to find domains and is shown in Figure 6-11. It can autoappraise domains using user-specified formulas, send bulk automated offer e-mails, monitor important domains, and filter large domain lists and zone files.

DRT includes the following features:

- *Designed for bulk scanning*: Domain Research Tool was created to scan domains in bulk. This means that it can handle lists of up to 500,000 domains per scan cycle.

- *Powerful proxy support*: Scanning large lists cannot be done without utilizing proxy servers. DRT supports loading of up to 10,000 proxy servers for use during a scan. Throughout the scan, the proxy servers are rotated and poorly performing proxies are automatically disabled. DRT can also check the proxies to ensure that they are functional and nontransparent.

- *IDN support*: DRT supports international domain names (IDNs).

- *Typo generator*: DRT can instantly generate thousands of typos based on domain names and keyword phrases. This allows users to check the availability of domain names that are similar to an established domain name.

- *Portfolio management*: DRT includes a portfolio management feature designed to monitor and track the user's domain portfolio. Changes to domain WHOIS records, name servers, e-mails, IPs, site title, link popularity, overture score, and more are tracked and analyzed.

Figure 6-10 A company's presence on eBay can lead to important technical details and contact information.

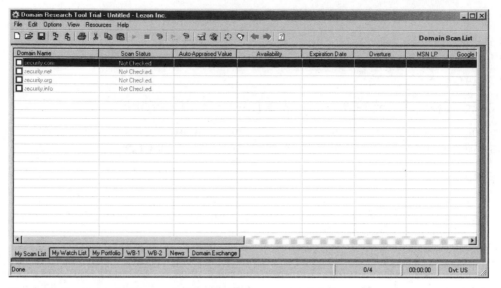

Figure 6-11   Domain Research Tool is used to research information on domain names.

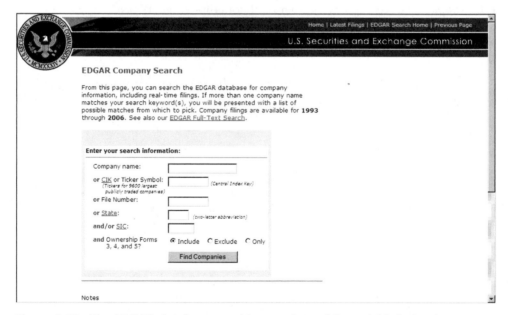

Figure 6-12   The EDGAR database provides a variety of financial information about a number of companies.

Step 28: Use the EDGAR Database to Research Company Information

The EDGAR database provides information on companies and real-time filings, as shown in Figure 6-12.

Step 29: Use Google/Yahoo! Finance to Search for Press Releases the Company Has Issued

Financial tools from Google and Yahoo! can be used to check on a company's financial situation, as shown in Figure 6-13. This will also reveal more information about partners associated with the company and its global presence.

Market summary

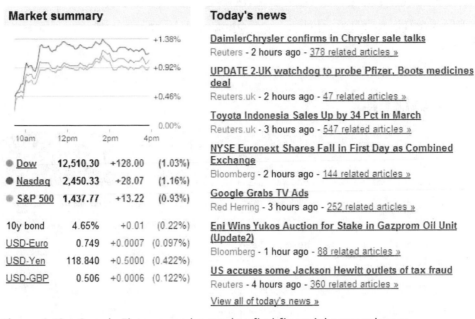

● Dow	12,510.30	+128.00	(1.03%)
● Nasdaq	2,450.33	+28.07	(1.16%)
● S&P 500	1,437.77	+13.22	(0.93%)
10y bond	4.65%	+0.01	(0.22%)
USD-Euro	0.749	+0.0007	(0.097%)
USD-Yen	118.840	+0.5000	(0.422%)
USD-GBP	0.506	+0.0006	(0.122%)

Today's news

DaimlerChrysler confirms in Chrysler sale talks
Reuters - 2 hours ago - 378 related articles »

UPDATE 2-UK watchdog to probe Pfizer, Boots medicines deal
Reuters.uk - 2 hours ago - 47 related articles »

Toyota Indonesia Sales Up by 34 Pct in March
Reuters.uk - 3 hours ago - 547 related articles »

NYSE Euronext Shares Fall in First Day as Combined Exchange
Bloomberg - 2 hours ago - 144 related articles »

Google Grabs TV Ads
Red Herring - 3 hours ago - 252 related articles »

Eni Wins Yukos Auction for Stake in Gazprom Oil Unit (Update2)
Bloomberg - 1 hour ago - 88 related articles »

US accuses some Jackson Hewitt outlets of tax fraud
Reuters - 4 hours ago - 360 related articles »

View all of today's news »

Figure 6-13   Google Finance can be used to find financial press releases.

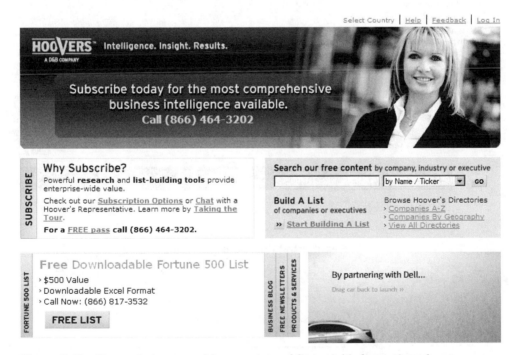

Figure 6-14   Hoover's, Inc., provides a variety of financial information about companies around the world.

Step 30: Search Company Business Reports and Profiles at Hoover's

Hoover's, Inc. (Figure 6-14), delivers company, industry, and market intelligence. Its database of 16.5 million companies, with in-depth coverage of 43,000 of the world's top business enterprises, can give useful information about a company's financial status.

Step 31: Visit 411 and Search for Telephone Numbers

The 411 Web site (Figure 6-15) reveals information on people and businesses.

Step 32: Search for U.K. Telephone Numbers at BT

The BT Web site (Figure 6-16) is helpful for finding the telephone numbers or addresses of individuals residing in the U.K.

Figure 6-15   The 411 Web site can provide phone numbers for individuals and companies.

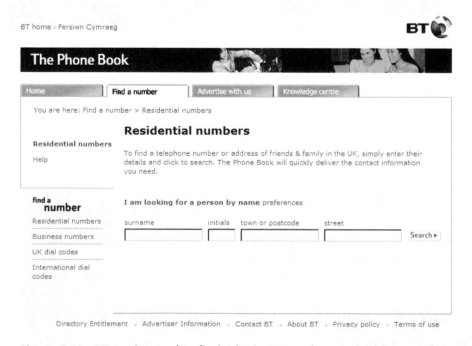

Figure 6-16   BT can be used to find telephone numbers and addresses of people based in the U.K.

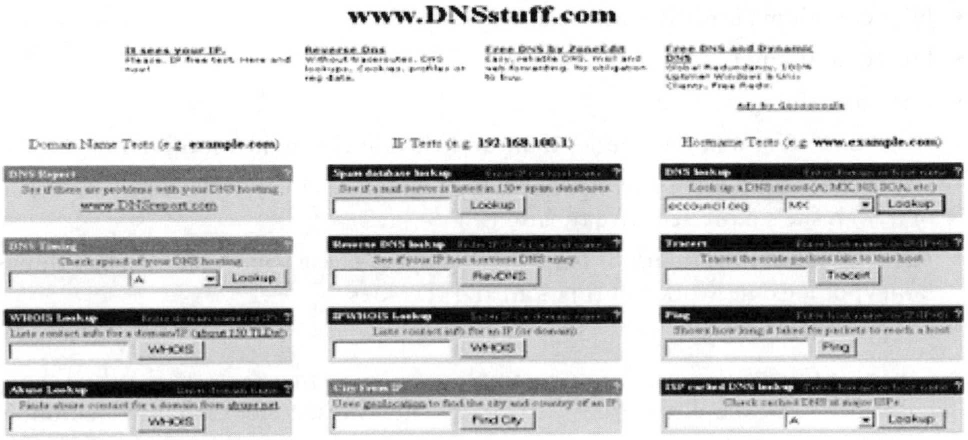

www.DNSstuff.com
Domain Name Tests (e.g. example.com)
IP Tests (e.g. 192.168.100.1)
Hostname Tests (e.g. www.example.com)
DNS Report
DNS Timing
WHOIS Lookup
Abuse Lookup
Spam database lookup
Reverse DNS lookup
IPWHOIS Lookup
City From IP
DNS lookup
Tracert
Ping
ISP cached DNS lookup
Lookup
WHOIS
Find City
RevDNS
Tracert
Ping

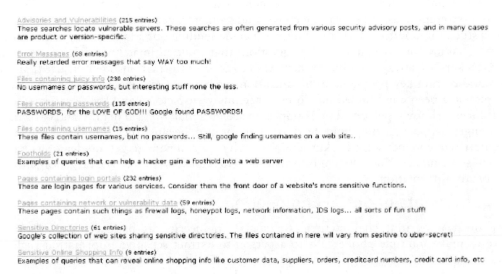

Figure 6-17 DNSstuff.com allows the user to gain information about IP addresses and a variety of other Web site information.

Step 33: Retrieve the Company's DNS Record from Publicly Available Servers

Using *www.DNSstuff.com* (Figure 6-17), it is possible to extract DNS information about IP addresses and mail server extensions and to perform DNS lookups, WHOIS lookups, and so on. It is possible to extract the entire range of IP addresses a company uses.

Step 34: Use GHDB to Search for the Company Name

The Google Hacking Database (GHDB) is a database of queries used by hackers to identify sensitive data on a Web site; see Figure 6-18. Users can go to *http://johnny.ihackstuff.com/ghdb.php*, search for the company name, and then use the following types of information that come up in the results:

- *Advisories and vulnerabilities*: These searches locate vulnerable servers. These searches are often generated from security advisory posts and in many cases, are product or version specific.
- Error messages.

Advisories and Vulnerabilities (215 entries)
These searches locate vulnerable servers. These searches are often generated from various security advisory posts, and in many cases are product or version-specific.
Error Messages (68 entries)
Really retarded error messages that say WAY too much!
Files containing juicy info (230 entries)
No usernames or passwords, but interesting stuff none the less.
Files containing passwords (135 entries)
PASSWORDS, for the LOVE OF GOD!!! Google found PASSWORDS!
Files containing usernames (15 entries)
These files contain usernames, but no passwords... Still, google finding usernames on a web site..
Footholds (21 entries)
Examples of queries that can help a hacker gain a foothold into a web server
Pages containing login portals (232 entries)
These are login pages for various services. Consider them the front door of a website's more sensitive functions.
Pages containing network or vulnerability data (59 entries)
These pages contain such things as firewall logs, honeypot logs, network information, IDS logs... all sorts of fun stuff!
Sensitive Directories (61 entries)
Google's collection of web sites sharing sensitive directories. The files contained in here will vary from sesitive to uber-secret!
Sensitive Online Shopping Info (9 entries)
Examples of queries that can reveal online shopping info like customer data, suppliers, orders, creditcard numbers, credit card info, etc

Figure 6-18 GHDB can be used to find queries that have proven useful to hackers in the past.

- Files containing sensitive information.
- Files containing passwords.
- Files containing usernames.
- *Footholds*: Examples of queries that can help a hacker gain a foothold into a Web server.
- *Pages containing login portals*: These are login pages for various services. Consider them the front door of a Web site's more sensitive functions.
- *Pages containing network or vulnerability data*: These pages contain such things as firewall logs, honeypot logs, network information, and IDS logs.
- Sensitive directories.
- *Sensitive financial information*: Examples of queries that can reveal online shopping information like customer data, suppliers, orders, credit card numbers, credit card information, etc.
- Vulnerable files.
- Vulnerable servers.
- Web server detection.

Social Engineering

The term *social engineering* is used to describe the various techniques used to trick people (employees, business partners, or customers) into voluntarily giving away personal information that would not normally be known to the general public. The approach varies according to the accessibility of the target. The first and most obvious method is simply a direct request, where an individual is asked to provide information directly. The following are common targets of social engineers:

- Receptionist and help desk personnel
- Technical support executives
- Vendors of target organization employees

The greatest tool of a social engineer is human nature. As part of human nature, people usually believe and trust others and derive fulfillment out of helping others who are in need. In order to get information, such as a phone number or a password, the attacker first establishes trust with an individual who has the information. On gaining this trust, the attacker can make a compelling request to the receptionist or the help desk person for some valuable information. Help desk persons and receptionists may give information readily if they think they are working to help a customer. The information could also be collected from the trash or it could be collected from a janitor.

Some social engineering tricks are telephone scams, hoaxes, and e-mail scams. Social engineers can pose as temporary employees or as cleaning crews, and gain entrance to a building and look for passwords written on notes stuck on monitors. Other techniques include sending out a fake survey with an offer of a cash reward or a prize, asking some seemingly subtle questions that could ultimately reveal some personal information.

Attackers are always looking for new ways to access information. They ensure that they know the surroundings and certain key people in an organization, such as security guards, receptionists, and help desk workers. People have been conditioned not to be exceedingly suspicious, and they correlate certain behaviors and appearances to known persons. For example, on seeing a man dressed in gray and carrying a bundle of mail and a messenger bag, people may hold the door open for him, because they think he is the mail carrier. A good social engineer will conduct some background research on a company to get an idea of its basic culture and may even obtain some names. These bits of information help attackers get into the target organization's systems and steal important information.

Requirements of Social Engineering

The most important characteristic for social engineering is patience. An effective social engineer may have to make multiple phone calls to a person to extract sensitive information such as his or her username and password.

Another key trait is confidence. An adequate level of confidence can be obtained by practicing with peers and rehearsing with the help of video recording devices to improve persuasion tactics. When persuading others, a social engineer should always maintain direct eye contact while speaking with them.

Along with confidence and patience, it is important to learn tactics to gain the trust of the target person. Social engineers often use the mirror technique and mimic the gestures that the target person is doing. For example, if the target person is smiling, the social engineer smiles back. If the target is nodding, he or she nods in agreement. This technique forges a connection and engenders trust.

Steps Preceding a Social Engineering Attempt

1. Print business cards of a bogus company.
2. Make sure an e-mail address is printed on the business card, for example, jdownes@insuranceusa.com.
3. Buy clothes that may be needed for the social engineering attacks—for example, a postal worker uniform.
4. Print bogus ID cards.
5. Set up a bogus Web site for the company on the business cards.
6. Register a new number for the mobile phone that will be used in the social engineering attack.

Dress Professionally

- Dress like a professional.
- Carry a briefcase.
- The attire should command respect.

Steps in Conducting a Social Engineering Penetration Test

- Step 1: Attempt social engineering techniques using the phone.
- Step 2: Attempt social engineering by vishing.
- Step 3: Attempt social engineering using e-mail.
- Step 4: Attempt social engineering by using traditional mail.
- Step 5: Attempt social engineering in person.
- Step 6: Attempt social engineering by dumpster diving.
- Step 7: Attempt social engineering using an insider accomplice.
- Step 8: Attempt social engineering using Web sites.
- Step 9: Attempt identity theft and phishing attacks.
- Step 10: Try to obtain satellite imagery and building blueprints.
- Step 11: Try to obtain an employee's details from social networking sites.
- Step 12: Use telephone monitoring devices to capture conversations.
- Step 13: Use video recording tools to capture images.
- Step 14: Use vehicle/asset tracking system to monitor motor vehicles.
- Step 15: Identify disgruntled employees and engage in conversation to extract sensitive information.
- Step 16: Document everything.

Step 1: Attempt Social Engineering Techniques Using the Phone

Call the company's help desk and ask questions to obtain sensitive information. Call the receptionist, engage in polite conversation, and extract contact information for the company. Be natural; rehearse many times before making the call. Have follow-up questions for every question. Record the conversation for reporting purposes.

Examples

"Hi, this is Jason, the VP of sales. I'm at the New York branch today, and I can't remember my password. The machine in my home office has that 'Remember password' feature set, so it's been months since I actually had to enter it. Can you tell me what it is or reset it or something? I really need to access this month's sales reports ASAP."

"Hi, this is Joanna at the Boston branch. I'm the new LAN administrator and my boss wants this done before he gets back from London. Do you know how I can:

- Configure our firewall to have the same policies as corporate?
- Download the latest DNS entries from the corporate DNS server to our local server?
- Run a transaction on a remote file and print server using a shell command?
- Back up the database to our off-site disaster recovery location?
- Locate the IP address of the main DNS server?
- Set up a backup dial-up connection to the corporate LAN?
- Connect this new network segment to the corporate intranet?"

Step 2: Attempt Social Engineering by Vishing

The *vishing* technique involves performing phishing over the phone, typically using Voice over IP technology. The main targets of this technique are financial institutions, government organizations, online sales, payment services, and so on.

This technique gathers the following information:

- PIN
- Payment card information
- Passport number
- Date of birth
- Bank account number
- Insurance number

Example

Pretend to be an employee of a bank, make a call to a person, and ask him or her to check his or her personal information like an account number, credit card number, debit card number, PIN, or password. Record these details and use this information for identity theft.

Step 3: Attempt Social Engineering Using E-Mail

A common social engineering method is to send e-mail posing as a system administrator. The e-mail asks the victim to send his or her password immediately. This e-mail is sent to multiple users to increase the chances that at least one person will respond.

The following steps can be used to perform social engineering through e-mail:

1. Track down users who use a single common password for various online accounts.
2. Send sweepstakes announcements to users and request that they provide their name, e-mail address, password, and mailing address through an online submission form.
3. Pose as a network administrator and send e-mails to users, asking them to provide their password.
4. Install pop-up windows on the network and ask users to enter their username and password.

Figure 6-19 gives two examples of e-mails that can be used to extract information from a target.

Step 4: Attempt Social Engineering by Using Traditional Mail

Social engineers may send snail mail to target company employees. These letters look so authentic that people fall for the scam. They may contain offers or packages to tempt the victims. They may ask the receiver to fill out certain personal information and send it back to the addressee.

For example, the attacker might send out a personal loan offer, requesting the victim to submit some vital information such as account numbers, e-mail addresses, Social Security numbers, bank statements, and so on through the mail.

Step 5: Attempt Social Engineering in Person

- Visit the physical facility and attempt social engineering techniques.
- Rehearse questions and answers.

Figure 6-19   E-mail can be used to gain valuable information such as passwords and usernames.

- Dress appropriately.
- Ask questions to obtain the following information:
  - Company policies
  - IT infrastructure

- Phone numbers
- Personal information

Examples

"Hi, I'm John Brown. I'm with external auditor Arthur Sanderson. We've been told by corporate to do a surprise inspection of your disaster recovery procedures. Your department has 10 minutes to show me how you would recover from a Web site crash."

"Hi, I'm Sharon. I'm a sales rep out of the New York office. I know this is short notice, but I have a group of prospective clients out in the car that I've been trying for months to get to outsource their security training needs to us.

They're located just a few miles away and I think that if I can give them a quick tour of our facilities, it should be enough to push them over the edge and get them to sign up.

They are particularly interested in what security precautions we've adopted. Seems someone hacked into their Web site a while back, which is one of the reasons they're considering our company."

"Hi, I'm with Aircon Express Services. We received a call that the computer room was getting too warm and need to check your HVAC system."

Using professional-sounding terms like HVAC (heating, ventilation, and air conditioning) may add just enough credibility to an intruder's masquerade to allow access to the targeted secured resource.

Step 6: Attempt Social Engineering by Dumpster Diving

The term *dumpster diving* is used to describe searching disposal areas for information that has not been properly destroyed. Trash cans contain sharp objects, caustic chemicals, rotten food, and other unhealthy and potentially dangerous items. Wear proper protective equipment while dumpster diving; latex surgical gloves underneath thick, heavy-duty work gloves are recommended.

Many organizations utilize hotel conference rooms or other unsecured facilities to conduct brainstorming sessions. Once the session is complete, no one considers wiping down the whiteboards used to record the output of the meeting.

To conduct dumpster diving, collect trashcans and paper bins. Trash can be looked at inside the office or outside the building. Look for the following items:

- Sensitive documents
- Customer contacts
- E-mail messages
- Purchase orders
- Appointments
- Schedules
- Envelope addresses
- Sticky notes

Step 7: Attempt Social Engineering Using an Insider Accomplice

The following personnel can perform the following tasks to act as insider accomplices in social engineering attempts:

- A developer building a Trojan horse or time bomb into a Web application (especially if the developer is a short-term consultant)
- A DBA adding some attacker-friendly stored procedures to the production database
- A Web master installing a backdoor or rootkit on the Web server
- A network engineer making an illicit copy of a production server's entire hard drive
- A system administrator forgetting to install an operating system security patch
- A value-added retailer (VAR) installing a firewall and leaving the manufacturer's default maintenance account active

- An engineer from the local utility company attaching a network sniffer to a LAN
- A member of the cleaning crew retrieving any useful-looking sticky note from the computer room's wastepaper bin

Gaining an Accomplice

Befriend someone inside the company and try to turn him or her into an accomplice to help gather sensitive information about the target company. This could be achieved through the following methods:

- Bribery
- Flattery
- Dating the person
- Exchanging information for movie tickets, sports tickets, etc.
- Handing out gifts such as cell phones

Step 8: Attempt Social Engineering Using Web Sites

Attempt to redirect employees using fake Web sites that look similar to genuine ones. Send an e-mail to employees and provide a link to the fake site. For example, provide the link *www.x1secure.com* (a fake site) that resembles *www.xsecure.com* (the genuine site).

Step 9: Attempt Identity Theft and Phishing Attacks

Gather the following information for identity theft:

- Complete name
- Postal address
- E-mail address
- Social Security number
- Date of birth
- Bank account details
- Credit card information

Step 10: Try to Obtain Satellite Imagery and Building Blueprints

This will help locate doors, windows, and exits at the premises. The building blueprints can be obtained from the land administration department.

Step 11: Try to Obtain Employee's Details from Social Networking Sites

The following steps can be used to gather details about an employee from social networking sites:

1. Gather the employee's details by visiting the following social networking sites:
   - Orkut (*www.orkut.com*)
   - Facebook (*www.facebook.com*)
   - Hi5 (*www.hi5.com*)
   - MySpace (*www.myspace.com*)
2. Visit the organization's communities on the social networking sites.
3. Visit the employee profiles available in the communities and get their name, contact details, e-mail address, postal address, and so on.
4. With these details, call the employees and gather their sensitive information like username, password, and so on.

Step 12: Use Telephone Monitoring Devices to Capture Conversations

Sensitive information can be obtained through recording phone calls without the other party's consent.

Step 13: Use Video Recording Tools to Capture Images

Recording tools can be used to capture screenshots of a victim's computer screen. This activity can provide the following valuable information:

- Passwords
- Credentials
- Personal information

Step 14: Use a Vehicle/Asset Tracking System to Monitor Motor Vehicles

Many devices exist that can track a vehicle through the use of global positioning technology.

Step 15: Identify Disgruntled Employees and Engage in Conversation to Extract Sensitive Information

Disgruntled employees can be identified through overheard conversations in the company's open areas. By be-friending a disgruntled employee, it is possible to obtain the following information:

- Company policies and IT infrastructure
- Workplace address and contact address
- Personal information
- Bank accounts and credit card numbers
- Organizational computer network details
- Organizational policies
- Organizational structure
- Organizational functions
- Details about future projects

Step 16: Document Everything

Document the following results and findings:

- Names and employee IDs
- Official e-mail IDs and passwords
- Personal e-mail IDs and passwords
- Social Security numbers and designations
- Workplace addresses and contact addresses
- Personal information
- Bank account numbers and credit card numbers
- Organizational computer network details
- Organizational policies
- Organizational structure
- Organizational functions
- Details about future projects

Chapter Summary

- Information gathering is used to create a profile of a target company or person.
- Social engineering is an attempt to manipulate individuals into revealing sensitive information.
- WHOIS is an Internet utility used to search various domain databases for information related to domain names and IP addresses.

- Listing a company's distributors can reveal valuable information about the company.
- Searching Internet archive pages can reveal important information.
- Many companies have communities on social networking sites.
- The DNS record of a company can be retrieved from public servers.
- The EDGAR database provides information on companies and real-time filings.
- The greatest tool of a social engineer is human nature.
- To conduct dumpster diving, a social engineer should collect trashcans and paper bins. Trash can be looked at inside the office or outside the building.
- Sensitive information can be obtained through recording phone calls without the other party's consent.
- Disgruntled employees can be identified through overheard conversations in the company's open areas.

## Chapter 7

Vulnerability Analysis

Objectives

After completing this chapter, you should be able to:

- List the steps in a vulnerability assessment
- Conduct a vulnerability assessment
- Classify vulnerabilities
- Use the various vulnerability assessment techniques
- List the phases of a vulnerability assessment
- Understand a vulnerability assessment report
- Create a timeline for a vulnerability assessment
- Name different vulnerability assessment tools

Key Terms

Active assessment   a type of vulnerability assessment that uses network scanners to scan the network to identify the hosts, services, and vulnerabilities present in that network

Automated scanning server   a self-management vulnerability assessment tool that protects networks, servers, databases, and various applications against vulnerabilities

Host-based assessment   a type of security check that involves carrying out a configuration-level check through the command line

Periodic vulnerability scanning   a process of scanning systems regularly to identify the security threats that may be present in an organization's systems and removing those threats after scanning

Vulnerability assessment   the process of recognizing, measuring, and prioritizing vulnerabilities in a system

Vulnerability assessment report   a report disclosing the risks that are detected after scanning a network

Introduction to Vulnerability Analysis

In today's world, organizations depend heavily on information technology. It is necessary for them to protect their vital information. This information can be related to the areas of finance, research and development, personnel, legality, and security. A vulnerability assessment is performed on these critical data to safeguard them.

The *vulnerability assessment* process involves recognizing, measuring, and prioritizing vulnerabilities in a system. It helps an organization know the threats and vulnerabilities of the system's infrastructure. Before starting a penetration test, it is essential to identify the vulnerabilities using a vulnerability scanner. Performing a vulnerability scan helps a penetration testing team evaluate whether or not the penetration test can be performed and identify areas to be targeted by a penetration test.

Vulnerability Assessment Steps

The following are the steps involved in a vulnerability assessment:

1. *Checking whether the target is alive*: Use the Internet Control Message Protocol (ICMP) to ping the target system and check whether the target is alive.

2. *Scanning the ports*: Check for open ports that can be attacked. Perform the scan in stealth mode for a particular period of time. Test the ports by sending them harmful information.

3. *Identifying the potential vulnerabilities and generating a report*: Use a network vulnerability scanner to identify the potential vulnerabilities and to obtain a report about these vulnerabilities.

4. *Classifying vulnerabilities and building responses*: Classify vulnerabilities and build responses accordingly. Many times, the response chosen for a vulnerability is nonactionable because of complexities and risks. The assessment process gives complete information about these issues, and this information is helpful during the risk management process.

5. *Classifying key assets and performing risk management*: The vulnerability assessment process classifies the key assets and makes a hierarchy of the key assets, which helps to drive the risk management process.

6. *Providing follow-up documentation/reports*: A vulnerability assessment provides follow-up documentation, reports, and additional consulting whenever required after the assessment process.

7. *Initiating an ongoing security effort*: A vulnerability assessment involves creating a plan to build an ongoing security effort.

Vulnerability Classification

The following are some of the classifications of vulnerabilities:

- *Misconfigurations*: Disabling security settings and features, due to lack of adequate knowledge about their functions, leads to vulnerabilities in network devices. Incorrect device configuration can also cause vulnerabilities.

- *Default installations*: Not changing the default settings when deploying software or hardware allows an attacker to easily guess the settings in order to break into the systems.

- *Buffer overflows*: Buffer overflows occur when a system's applications write content that is beyond the allocated buffer size.

- *Unpatched servers*: Hackers identify vulnerabilities in servers that are not patched and exploit them. Servers should be updated by applying patches.

- *Default passwords*: Default passwords are common to various operating systems and applications. During configuration, the passwords need to be changed. Passwords should be kept secret; failing to protect the confidentiality of a password allows an attacker to easily compromise a system.

- *Open services*: Open services are insecure and are open to attacks such as DoS.

- *Application flaws*: Applications should be secured using user validation and authorization. Applications pose security threats such as data tampering and unauthorized access to configuration stores. If applications are not secured, sensitive information may be lost or corrupted.

- *Operating systems flaws*: Due to vulnerabilities in operating systems, Trojans, worms, and viruses pose serious threats. Flaws lead to system crashes and instabilities.

- *Design flaws*: Design flaws can leave a piece of hardware or software open to attack if these flaws are discovered.

Types of Vulnerability Assessment

The following are the different types of vulnerability assessment techniques:

- *Active assessments*: **Active assessments** are a type of vulnerability assessment that uses network scanners to scan the network to identify the hosts, services, and vulnerabilities present in that network. Active network scanners have the capability to reduce the intrusiveness of the checks they perform.

- *Passive assessments*: Passive assessments sniff the traffic present on the network to identify the working systems, network services, applications, and vulnerabilities. Passive assessments also provide a list of the users who are currently using the network.

- *Host-based assessments*: **Host-based assessments** are a type of security check that involves carrying out a configuration-level check through the command line. These assessments check the security of a particular network or server. Host-based assessments are carried out through host-based scanners, which identify system vulnerabilities like incorrect registry and file permissions as well as software configuration errors. Many commercial and open-source scanning tools, such as SecurityExpressions, are used for host-based assessment.

- *Internal assessments*: An internal assessment involves scrutinizing the internal network to find exploits and vulnerabilities. The following are some of the possible steps in performing an internal assessment:

  - Specify the open ports and related services on network devices, servers, and systems.

  - Check for router configurations and firewall rule sets.

  - List the internal vulnerabilities of the operating system and server.

  - Scan for Trojans that may be present in the internal environment.

  - Check the patch levels on the organization's internal network devices, servers, and systems.

  - Check for the existence of malware, spyware, and virus activity and document them.

  - Evaluate the physical security.

  - Identify and review the remote management process and events.

  - Assess the file-sharing mechanisms (for example, NFS and SMB/CIFS shares).

  - Examine the antivirus implementation and events.

- *External assessments*: These types of assessments are based on external devices such as firewalls, routers, and servers. An external assessment estimates the threat of network security attacks external to the organization. It determines how secure the external network and firewall are. The following are some of the possible steps in performing an external assessment:

  - Determine the set of rules for firewall and router configurations for the external network.

  - Check whether external server devices and network devices are mapped.

  - Identify open ports and related services on the external network.

  - Examine patch levels on the server and external network devices.

  - Review detection systems such as IDS, firewalls, and application-layer protection systems.

  - Get information on DNS zones.

  - Scan the external network through a variety of proprietary tools available on the Internet.

  - Examine Web applications such as e-commerce and shopping cart software for vulnerabilities.

- *Application assessments*: An application assessment focuses on transactional Web applications, traditional client-server applications, and hybrid systems. It analyzes all elements of an application infrastructure, including how every element is deployed and how every element communicates with the client and server. Both commercial and open-source tools are used to perform such assessments.

Session Name:	R & D Section 6	Session ID:	13
File Name:	Session2_000413	Template:	Comprehensive
Comment:	Weekly Scan	Termination Status:	Finished

Scan Summary Information

Hosts Scanned:	3	Scan Start:	2000/04/13 18:15:20
Hosts Active:	3	Scan End:	2000/04/13 18:17:02
Hosts Inactive:	0	Elapsed:	00:01:42

Figure 7-1   Network assessments focus on possible attacks on network security.

- *Network assessments*: Network assessments determine the possible network security attacks that may occur on an organization's system, as shown in Figure 7-1. These assessments evaluate the organization's system for vulnerabilities that are related to the organization's network, such as missing patches, unnecessary services, weak authentication, and weak encryption. Network assessments are performed through firewall and network scanners such as Nessus. These scanners find open ports, recognize the services running on those ports, and find vulnerabilities associated with these services. These assessments help organizations determine how vulnerable systems are to Internet and intranet attacks and how an attacker can gain access to important information. A typical network assessment conducts the following tests on a network:
  - Checks the network topologies for inappropriate firewall configuration
  - Examines the router filtering rules
  - Identifies inappropriately configured database servers
  - Tests individual services and protocols such as HTTP, SNMP, and FTP
  - Reviews HTML source code for unnecessary information
  - Performs bounds checking on variables
- *Wireless network assessments*: In the past, wireless networks were built with weak and basically defective data encryption mechanisms. Now, wireless network standards have evolved, but many networks that were initially deployed are still active and ripe for attack. Wireless network assessments try to attack wireless authentication mechanisms and get unauthorized access. This type of assessment tests wireless networks and also identifies rogue wireless networks that may exist within an organization's perimeter. These assessments are performed on client-specified sites where wireless networks have been installed. They sniff wireless network traffic and try to crack encryption keys. If the network can be accessed, then other network access is tested.

Vulnerability Assessment Phases

The following are the three different phases of a vulnerability assessment:

1. Preassessment phase
2. Assessment phase
3. Postassessment phase

All phases consist of a sequence of tasks to meet specific objectives, as shown in Figure 7-2.

Preassessment Phase

During the preassessment phase, the following tasks are performed:

- *Defining the scope of the assessment*: This involves the following activities:
  - Recognizing serious vulnerabilities
  - Developing an assessment plan

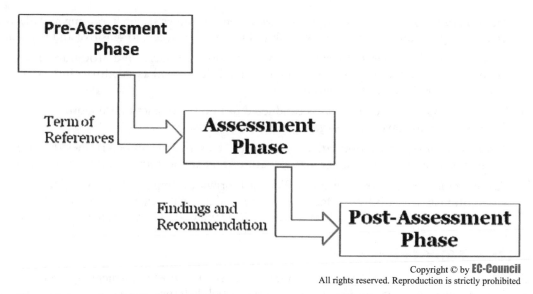

Figure 7-2   Vulnerability assessments take place in three phases.

- Specifying the elements of assessment
- Ranking key assets
- Improving knowledge and making security an essential part of the business strategy
- *Setting up information protection procedures*: The team must consider planning, scheduling, coordination, and logistics to set up information protection procedures.
- *Identifying and ranking critical assets*: This is the final phase of the preassessment task. The following objectives are completed during this phase:
  - Identifying critical assets
  - Ranking the critical assets
  - Using the results for the vulnerability assessment

Assessment Phase

The following tasks are performed during the assessment phase:

- *Examination of the network architecture*: This involves analyzing the information assurance features of the information network linked to the organization's systems. This analysis includes checking the network topology, network connectivity, communication protocols, and functioning of hardware and software components.
- *Evaluation of the threat environment*: Threats may come into the organization's network from individual persons or organizations. Good knowledge of the threat environment forms the basis of risk management. The assessment phase identifies these threats and possible trends.
- *Penetration testing*: Penetration testing is performed to discover vulnerabilities present in an organization's systems. Penetration testing includes processes such as setting up rules of engagement for the test, developing a test methodology, performing the test, and creating a final report.
- *Examination and evaluation of physical security*: Examination and evaluation of physical security involves checking the premises for physical security vulnerabilities. This type of assessment focuses on sites that are directly linked to critical facilities.
- *Carrying out a physical asset analysis*: The main purpose of this analysis is to check organizational systems and physical operational assets to find out whether vulnerabilities exist. This analysis checks for asset utilization, system redundancies, and crisis operating procedures.

- *Assessment of operations security*: This assessment examines security training and alertness programs as well as the procedures and methods employed for denying access to sensitive and nonsensitive information.
- *Observation of policies and procedures*: Observation of policies and procedures is important to develop a complete understanding of how a facility defends its critical assets through the development and implementation of policies and procedures.
- *Impact analysis*: Impact analysis is conducted to find the impact that unauthorized access to information systems may have on an organization's operations.
- *Assessment of infrastructure interdependencies*: This assessment determines the direct infrastructure connections among the different infrastructures that support an organization's vital services.
- *Carrying out a risk characterization*: This task provides support for prioritizing recommendations across all task areas. It first judges the recommendations for every task area and helps the organization determine the proper actions. It also provides a framework for reviewing vulnerabilities and threats.

Postassessment Phase

This phase is also known as the recommendation phase. The postassessment is based on the risk assessment. Risk characterization is categorized by key criteria, which help prioritize the list of recommendations.

In the postassessment phase, the following tasks are performed:

- Making the priority list for assessment recommendations
- Developing an action plan to implement the proposed recommendations
- Capturing lessons learned to improve the process in the future
- Conducting employee training

Comparing Approaches to Vulnerability Assessments

There are two types of vulnerability assessment solutions: product-based solutions and service-based solutions. Product-based solutions have the following characteristics:

- Installed on the organization's internal network and operated manually
- Installed on either a nonroutable or Internet-addressable portion of an organization's network
- Has some drawbacks, such as that it cannot deliver an outside view of the network flaws

Service-based solutions have the following characteristics:

- Offered by third parties, such as auditing firms or security consultant firms
- Some are hosted inside the network and others are hosted outside the network
- Has the drawback that hackers can audit the network from the outside

Characteristics of a Good Vulnerability Assessment Solution

A good vulnerability assessment solution has the following characteristics:

- Ensures correct outcomes by testing the network, network resources, ports, protocols, and operating systems
- Uses a well-organized inference-based approach for testing
- Automatically scans against constantly updated databases
- Creates brief, actionable, customizable reports, including reports of vulnerabilities by severity level and trend analysis
- Supports various networks
- Suggests proper remedies and workarounds for vulnerabilities
- Imitates the outside view of hackers

Vulnerability Assessment Considerations

Vulnerability assessments are the steps that are performed to detect and eliminate vulnerabilities from an organization's network. They include various levels of considerations.

The first point to be considered is the scope of the vulnerability assessment. The penetration testing agency has to work with the organization for more information on the following elements:

- Number of IP addresses to be scanned
- Specific departments to be tested

Once the testers have identified the area of the network to test, the next step is to decide how many people will be consulted for technical and nontechnical input. The number of members who will be taking part in the penetration testing activity will depend on the scope and nature of the vulnerability assessment.

Vulnerability Assessment Reports

The *vulnerability assessment report* discloses the risks that are detected after scanning the network. Tools such as Nessus, SAINT, and Retina are vulnerability scanners. These tools provide a comprehensive assessment report in a specified format. The report alerts the organization to possible attacks and suggests countermeasures.

The report provides details of the possible vulnerabilities with regard to the company's security policies. The vulnerabilities are categorized by severity into three levels: high, medium, and low risks.

High-risk vulnerabilities are those with the possibility of allowing unauthorized access into the network. These need to be rectified immediately, before the network is compromised. The report describes the kinds of attacks that are possible given the organization's set of operating systems, network components, and protocols.

Vulnerability reports cover the following elements:

- *Scan information*: This part of the report provides information such as the name of the scanning tool, its version, and the network ports that have to be scanned.
- *Target information*: This part of the report contains information about the target system's name and address.
- *Results*: This section provides a complete scanning report. It contains subtopics such as target, services, vulnerability, classification, and assessment.
- *Target*: This subtopic includes each host's detailed information. It contains the following information:
  - *<Node>*: Contains the name and address of the host
  - *<OS>*: Shows the operating system type
  - *<Date>*: Gives the date of the test
- *Services*: This subtopic defines the network services by their names and ports.
- *Vulnerability*: This subtopic describes the vulnerability by its name, category of attack, and service affected.
- *Classification*: This subtopic allows the system administrator to obtain additional information about the scanning such as origin of the scan.
- *Assessment*: This class provides information regarding the scanner's assessment of the vulnerability.

Timeline

The time taken for a vulnerability assessment will depend on the scope of the test, nature of the test, and number of penetration test personnel involved in the test. Problems may arise due to improper time management of any task. While scheduling a task, it is crucial to remember that there is no flexibility regarding time. Figure 7-3 shows a sample timeline. Time management includes the following processes:

- *Activity definition*: Activity definition involves identifying all the activities that have to take place during the assessment. Activity definition gives detailed information of the WBS (work breakdown structure) and supporting explanations.
- *Activity sequencing*: Activity sequencing involves reviewing the activities in the detailed WBS. This involves documentation of all the scheduled work and determining what tasks must be done before other tasks.

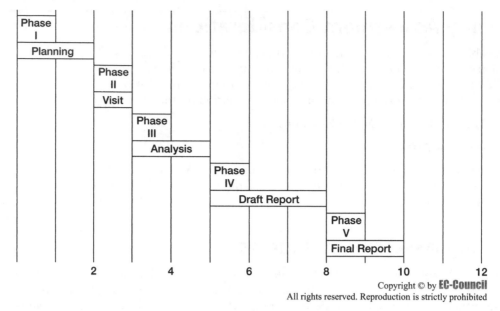

Figure 7-3   Timelines are useful graphic tools for scheduling
a vulnerability assessment.

- *Estimating the activity resources*: Estimating the quantities and types of resources for each activity is an important procedure. Resource availability is also checked during scheduling.

- *Estimating the duration of activities*: Estimating the duration for each activity is done in this step. Resource availability could affect the estimated duration.

- *Developing the schedule*: To determine the start and end date of each task, schedule development makes use of all the processes of time management.

Types of Reports

Vulnerability assessment reports are classified into two types:

1. *Security vulnerability report*: This is a combined report for all scanned servers that provides the following information:
   - Newly found vulnerabilities
   - Open ports and detected services
   - Suggestions for remediation
   - Links to patches

Figure 7-4 shows part of a sample security report.

2. *Security vulnerability summary*: This report is produced for every server after scanning. It gives a summary that includes the following elements:
   - Current security flaws
   - New security vulnerabilities detected
   - Resolved vulnerabilities

Figure 7-5 shows part of a sample security vulnerability summary.

Automated Scanning Server Reports

An *automated scanning server* is a self-management vulnerability assessment tool that protects the network, servers, databases, and various applications against vulnerabilities. This tool provides continuous and real-time security to the organization against vulnerabilities and threats.

Security Issues and Fixes: www.website.com

Type	Port	Issue and Fix
Vulnerability	smtp (25/tcp)	The remote sendmail server, according to its version number, may be vulnerable to a remote buffer overflow allowing remote users to gain root privileges. Sendmail versions from 5.79 to 8.12.8 are vulnerable. Solution : Upgrade to Sendmail ver 8.12.9 or greater or if you cannot upgrade, apply patches for 8.10-12 here: http://www.sendmail.org/patchps.html NOTE: manual patches do not change the version numbers. Vendors who have released patched versions of sendmail may still falsely show vulnerability. *** Nessus reports this vulnerability using only *** the banner of the remote SMTP server. Therefore, *** this might be a false positive. Risk factor : High CVE: CAN-2003-0161 BID: 7230 Other references : RHSA:RHSA-2003:120-01

Source: http://www.alertsite.com/security_vulnerability_report.html#www_website_com. Accessed 2007.

Figure 7-4   Security vulnerability reports are a combined report from all scanned servers.

New Vulnerabilities

Risk	Id	Service	Description
Severe	11837	ssh (22/tcp)	You are running a version of OpenSSH which is older than 3.7.1 CVE: CAN-2003-0682, CAN-2003-0693, CAN-2003-0695 BID: 8628 Other references : RHSA:RHSA-2003:279, SuSE:SUSE-SA:2003:039
Medium	12213	general/tcp	The remote host might be vulnerable to a sequence number approximation bug, which may allow an attacker to send spoofed RST packets to the remote host and close established connections. CVE: CAN-2004-0230 BID: 10183 Other references : OSVDB:4030, IAVA:2004-A-0007

Vulnerabilities no longer detected

Risk	Id	Service	Description
Severe	11837	ssh (22/tcp)	You are running a version of OpenSSH which is older than 3.7.1 CVE: CAN-2003-0682, CAN-2003-0693, CAN-2003-0695 BID: 8628 Other references : RHSA:RHSA-2003:279, SuSE:SUSE-SA:2003:039
Medium	12213	general/tcp	The remote host might be vulnerable to a sequence number approximation bug, which may allow an attacker to send spoofed RST packets to the remote host and close established connections. CVE: CAN-2004-0230 BID: 10183 Other references : OSVDB:4030, IAVA:2004-A-0007

Source: http://www.alertsite.com/security_vulnerability_summary.html. Accessed 2007.

Figure 7-5   Security vulnerability reports are developed for each server.

The two different types of scanning reports generated by an automated scanning server include:

1. *Standard report*: A standard report includes a complete analysis of the vulnerabilities found, using charts and graphs, as shown in Figure 7-6. It includes technical information about each detected vulnerability. Technical information includes a short summary, the impact analysis, and solutions for each vulnerability. A standard report helps system administrators or IT managers evaluate the network or server security level.

2. *Differential report*: A differential report provides information about changes since the previous scan. This report shows information about new vulnerabilities found. The graphical section of this report shows the changes in risk level over time. This report informs administrators about new issues that need to be dealt with.

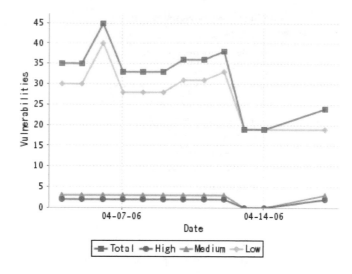

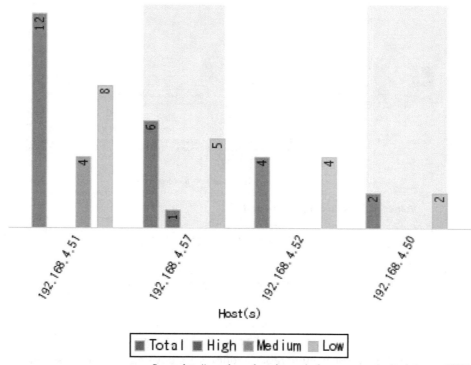

Source: http://www.beyondsecurity.com/avds_scanner_version.html. Accessed 2007.

Figure 7-6   Automated scanning servers can generate reports in graph form.

Periodic Vulnerability Scanning Report

Periodic vulnerability scanning is a process of scanning the systems regularly to identify the security threats that may be present in the organization's systems and removing the threats that may be identified after scanning. This process avoids the risks related to manual audits. Based on the results, a report will be generated that will determine the actions to be taken to eliminate or mitigate the vulnerabilities found during the process. Figure 7-7 shows part of a sample periodic vulnerability scanning report.

#	Service/Port	Synopsis	Type	Since	Issue status	Status modified	Action
1	ftp (21/tcp)	[view]	Security holes	25 September 2007 22:49	Acknowledged	07 March 2008 10:04	☐
2	ftp (21/tcp)	[view]	Security holes	25 September 2007 22:49	New	25 September 2007 22:49	☐
3	ftp (21/tcp)	[view]	Security holes	25 September 2007 22:49	New	25 September 2007 22:49	☐
4	ftp (21/tcp)	[view]	Security holes	25 September 2007 22:49	Acknowledged	01 November 2007 18:29	☐
5	domain (53/udp)	[view]	Security warnings	25 September 2007 22:49	New	25 September 2007 22:49	☐
6	domain (53/udp)	[view]	Security warnings	25 September 2007 22:49	New	25 September 2007 22:49	☐
7	imaps (993/tcp)	[view]	Security warnings	25 September 2007 22:49	New	25 September 2007 22:49	☐
8	imaps (993/tcp)	[view]	Security warnings	25 September 2007 22:49	Acknowledged	27 September 2007 04:58	☐

Source: http://www.watchmouse.com/en/seclog_demo.php?vdo=showIssues&vruleid=39306. Accessed 2007.

Figure 7-7 Periodic vulnerability scans are conducted on a regular basis.

Tools

Types of Vulnerability Assessment Tools

- *Host-based vulnerability assessment tools*: Host-based scanning tools are useful for servers that run various applications such as those that involve Web, critical file, database, directory, and remote access capabilities. These host-based scanners are able to detect high levels of vulnerabilities and provide the information required to eliminate those vulnerabilities. A host-based vulnerability assessment tool can find out what type of operating system is running on a particular host's computer and can detect its known vulnerabilities. It also examines general applications and services.

- *Application-layer vulnerability assessment tools*: Vulnerability assessment tools are designed to serve the needs of all kinds of operating system types and applications. These tools identify the various resources on a system that pose security threats. These vulnerabilities could be external DoS/DDoS threats, network data interception, or other application-layer vulnerabilities. Application-layer vulnerability assessment tools are typically directed toward Web servers or database servers.

- *Scope-of-assessment tools*: Scope-of-assessment tools provide assessment of security by testing for vulnerabilities in the applications and operating system of a network. These tools provide standard control and a reporting interface that allows users to select a suitable scan type. These tools generate a standard report of the vulnerabilities found during the scan. Some of the scope-of-assessment tools are designed to test a specific application or its type for vulnerability.

- *Depth assessment tools*: Depth assessment tools are used to identify previously unknown vulnerabilities in systems. Generally, these tools are used to identify vulnerabilities to an unstable degree of depth. Such types of tools include fuzzers that give arbitrary input to a system's interface. Many of these tools use a set of vulnerability signatures to test whether the product is resistant to a known vulnerability or not and then use variations of those signatures to find unknown vulnerabilities.

- *Active tools*: Active scanners perform vulnerability tests on the networks that use system resources. The main advantage of an active scanner is that the system administrator or IT manager has good control of the timing and degree of vulnerability scans. These scanners should not be used on critical systems because they use system resources, affecting the processing of other tasks.

- *Passive tools*: Passive scanners are those that do not affect system resources considerably, as they only observe system data and perform data processing on a separate analysis machine. A passive scanner first receives system data, which provides complete information on which processes are running, and then assesses that data against a set of rules.

- *Location/data examination*: Some of the location/data examination are:
  - *Network-based scanner*: Network-based scanners are those that have interaction only with the machine in which they reside and provide a report only to that same machine after scanning.
  - *Agent-based scanner*: Agent-based scanners reside on a single machine but have the ability to scan a number of machines on the network.
  - *Proxy scanner*: Proxy scanners are network-based scanners that have the ability to scan networks from any machine in the network.
  - *Cluster scanner*: Cluster scanners are similar to proxy scanners but have the ability to perform two or more scans on different machines simultaneously in the network.

Choosing a Vulnerability Assessment Tool

Vendor-designed vulnerability assessment tools can be used to test a host or application for vulnerabilities. There are several vulnerability assessment tools available, including port scanners, vulnerability scanners, and OS vulnerability assessment scanners. The right tools have to be chosen based on the test requirements. These tools are able to test from dozens to thousands of different vulnerabilities, depending on the product.

The selected tool should have a sound database of vulnerabilities and attack signatures that are updated frequently. The testing team should choose a tool that matches the organization's environment and personnel expertise. The team should also find out how many reports are produced, what information they contain, and whether the reports can be exported.

The following criteria should be followed at the time of using or purchasing any vulnerability assessment tool:

- *Types of vulnerabilities discovered*: The most important information at the time of evaluating any tool is to find out how many types of vulnerabilities it will discover.
- *Testing the capability of scanning*: The vulnerability assessment tool must have the capability to execute the entire selected test and must scan all the systems selected for scanning.
- *Ability to provide an accurate report*: The ability to prepare an accurate report is essential. Vulnerability reports should be short and clear and should provide methods for mitigating discovered vulnerabilities.
- *Functionality for writing own tests*: When a signature is not present for a recently found vulnerability, it is helpful if the vulnerability scanning tool allows user-developed tests to be used.
- *Ability to schedule tests*: It is important to be able to schedule tests, as it allows the test team to perform scanning when traffic on the network is light.

Vulnerability Assessment Tools Best Practices

The following are some best practices for using security assessment tools:

- Before using any vulnerability assessment tools, it is important to understand their function and to decide what information will be collected before starting the assessment.
- Security mechanisms are somewhat different depending on whether the testers are accessing the network from inside or outside the network, so they need to decide where to initiate the scan based on what information needs to be collected.
- Users should scan their systems frequently and regularly monitor them for vulnerabilities and exploits.

Vulnerability Assessment Tools

QualysGuard

QualysGuard's on-demand architecture enables organizations to perform vulnerability management without having to install or maintain any infrastructure. The fully automated system frees the security team from the task of running scans and maintaining security tools. QualysGuard (Figure 7-8) enables users to perform security audits as often as necessary, spot new vulnerabilities immediately, and proactively remediate them.

QUALYSGUARD VULNERABILITY MANAGEMENT LIFECYCLE

1. Discovery
2. Asset Prioritization
3. Assessment & Analysis
4. Remediation
5. Verification
6. Policy Compliance

Figure 7-8   QualysGuard allows users to perform scans whenever necessary.

Cycorp CycSecure

Cycorp CycSecure has the following features:

- *Automated network-state detection*: Cycorp CycSecure has the capacity to scan the network and build a model of it automatically. CycSecure keeps this model updated automatically.

- *Compound vulnerability analysis*: This scanner has the capability to detect compound vulnerabilities, which could typically go undetected because they involve attack methodologies with many steps that exploit different minor vulnerabilities present on many systems.

- *Identifies the most critical vulnerabilities*: The most critical vulnerabilities may not always be the ones that appear in isolation but instead may be those that are exploited in steps. CycSecure reports on the actions that can compromise the network and the consequences of those actions.

- *"What if" analysis*: CycSecure edits the network models to incorporate suggested changes to eliminate vulnerabilities. It then runs vulnerability analysis on the edited models so users can see the effects of planned changes to the network configuration. The "what if" analysis is done before performing time-consuming network changes.

- *Noninvasive and continuous assessment*: Because the attacks and analyses are carried out on a simulation of the network instead of the actual network, this scanner mitigates the risk of system damage, downtime, and bandwidth consumption.

eEye Retina Network Security Scanner

Retina is a vulnerability scanner that recognizes known vulnerabilities. The recognized vulnerabilities are sent for remediation based on the risk level or severity level. Retina can completely scan an entire Class C network in less than 15 minutes. It can identify vulnerabilities on a network and detect the types of operating systems, devices, and applications present on the network. Retina is a nonintrusive scanner that performs a simple scan on the target system's attributes, such as checking the system for the required files or versions of the files, and checking the registry for required values.

Initially, Retina performs the step of discovering assets, and then it performs an audit scan to locate vulnerabilities and configuration-related problems. It then suggests remediation to fix the vulnerabilities. The Retina Remediation Manager performs automated remediation of vulnerabilities and categorizes them based on their risk levels. Finally, a report of the vulnerability management process is generated. REM Security Management Console is used to enhance the reporting functionality. Thus, any organization can enhance its security.

eEye Retina includes the following features:

- Supports multiple platforms
- Regularly updates its database
- Customizable reporting
- Prioritization and automation
- Custom security audits

Foundstone Professional Scanner

Foundstone Professional Scanner includes the following features:

- The Foundstone engine is a vulnerability assessment and management scanner. The scanner manages and controls the vulnerability lifecycle.
- Foundstone solutions provide network security for the company's network.
- It maps the placement of wireless access points and load balancers in enterprise networks.
- It analyzes the vulnerabilities of the network, such as the misconfiguration of operating systems, network elements, commercial applications, databases, wireless devices, and Web applications.
- It has the ability to correlate the resources to critical events.
- It can identify the priority of the vulnerability based on resource value and security restrictions.
- It manipulates and reports vulnerabilities to evaluate and communicate costs/benefits and to measure improvement.

GFI LANguard

GFI LANguard is a security-auditing tool that identifies network vulnerabilities and suggests ways of fixing them. GFI LANguard scans the network, based on the IP address or range of IP addresses specified, and alerts users about the vulnerabilities encountered on the target system.

Security issues encountered on the target system can be handled with operating system functionalities and the built-in features offered by GFI LANguard. For instance, disabling the unnecessary ports, closing shares, and installing necessary hotfixes and patches prior to exploitation can overcome security issues encountered on the target network.

The scanning engine acquires hardware and software information (service pack levels, installed applications, potential vulnerable devices, etc.) during the scanning process.

GFI LANguard includes the following functions:

- Allows users to perform security audits on both Windows-based and Linux-based target systems
- Identifies known vulnerabilities such as those involving CGI, DNS, FTP, SMTP, and RPC
- Enumerates OS configuration, security updates, and installed applications
- Categorizes security vulnerabilities on the basis of high, medium, and low risk levels
- Generates reports
- Supports multithreading, SNMP auditing, and Microsoft SQL auditing

ISS Internet Scanner

The ISS Internet Scanner identifies security flaws in enterprise networks. The scanner can identify more than 1,300 network elements such as wireless access points, firewalls, servers, and desktops. The scanner identifies the configurations of the devices and the missing patches in the operating systems. It identifies the vulnerabilities that could be exploited.

ISS Internet Scanner includes the following features:

- *Asset identification*: The scanner identifies devices using TCP stack fingerprinting and an integrated NMAP asset database on the network.
- *Intelligent scanning*: The scanner identifies the speed of the target operating system and runs tests automatically with varying speeds to find vulnerabilities on different systems.
- *Common policies*: The scanner gives an option to choose among 20 predefined scans. The policies are from the SANS and X-Force Catastrophic Risk Index policies.
- *Review scans*: Using the ISS real-time display option, the scans in progress can be viewed to identify vulnerabilities.
- *Catalog of vulnerabilities*: The scanner catalog provides vulnerability details, including the possible cause of the flaws.
- *Reporting*: The scanner produces an easy-to-view report of vulnerabilities that can be customized for each department in the organization. The scanner contains more than 70 predefined report formats.

SAINT

SAINT is an acronym for Security Administrator's Integrated Network Tool. SAINT identifies any weaknesses present on a network in a nonintrusive manner. It collects information about the versions of the operating system and also the open ports on the network. The graphical user interface of SAINT enables access to SAINT's data management and allows users to schedule scans.

Symantec NetRecon

Symantec NetRecon provides a step-by-step approach to uncovering vulnerabilities using a unique root cause and path analysis. The scanner learns the methods of vulnerability detection. It develops a strategy based on previous test results.

The security administrator can customize the tool's reports for a diverse range of users, both technical and executive. Reports can be generated in Microsoft Word, Microsoft Excel, and HTML.

NetRecon Scanner includes the following features:

- Can test the whole network for security vulnerabilities and can suggest recommendations on how to fix them
- Scans multiple operating systems including UNIX, Linux, Windows 2000, and NetWare
- Stays current with the latest security updates
- Can display scan progress with a graphical view that could reveal the causes of vulnerabilities

Shadow Security Scanner

Shadow Security Scanner can audit more than 2,000 vulnerabilities in UNIX, Windows, and Linux systems as well as router devices and other network devices. As a network vulnerability scanner, Shadow Security Scanner helps get direct access to the network's core. It can perform multiple network scans simultaneously with considerable speed. The scanner can save all its scanning sessions in various formats such as HTML, XML, CHM, PDF, and RTF.

Shadow Database Scanner

This scanner provides risk management, database management, and analysis of SQL servers. It was developed to provide secure and reliable detection of a large number of security system weaknesses. Once the system is scanned, the data are used to detect areas in the server that are prone to vulnerabilities. Shadow Database Scanner then suggests solutions for eliminating the vulnerabilities.

Nessus

Nessus is a popular vulnerability scanning tool. It detects and identifies software bugs in computers. It is an open-source tool that determines security threats. Nessus contains some specific measures to minimize the chance of a system crash. The two parts of this tool are a server (nessusd) and a client (nessus). The central client manages the entire network and controls all the servers at remote stations.

Nessus uses the following steps when scanning:

1. Data gathering
2. Host identification
3. Port scanning
4. Plug-in selection
5. Reporting of data

The user can create a domain group and account to obtain detailed information from a Windows-based host. After completing this task, the user gets access, not only to registry key settings but also to the service-pack patch levels, Internet Explorer vulnerabilities, and services running on the host.

Nessus is a client-server application. The nessusd server runs on a UNIX system, keeps track of all the different vulnerability tests, and performs the actual scan. It has its own user database and secure authentication methods so that remote users using the Nessus client can log in, configure a vulnerability scan, and set it on its way. To enable users to write their own security tests, NASL (Nessus Attack Scripting Language) is included in the Nessus software package.

Microsoft Baseline Security Analyzer (MBSA)

The Microsoft Baseline Security Analyzer (MBSA) is a device that can determine which significant updates exist on a target computer as well as which security updates are needed, as shown in Figure 7-9. MBSA can target the local computer, a remote computer, a particular list of computers, a series of IP addresses, or all the computers in a chosen domain. The tool will scrutinize computers for a revision status based on a downloaded XML catalog file and will generate a report to a file or on the screen.

MBSA allows the user to scan for common security misconfiguration faults on target computers. After a computer is assessed, other tools must be used to install the missing service packs and updates.

SPIKE Proxy

SPIKE Proxy (Figure 7-10) is a tool used to find application-level vulnerabilities in Web applications. It functions as an HTTP and HTTPS proxy and provides low-level access to the Web developer or Web application for the entire Web application interface, while also providing automated tools and techniques for discovering common problems. These tools can perform the following tasks:

- Automated SQL-injection detection
- Web site crawling (guaranteed not to crawl sites other than the one being tested)
- Login-form brute forcing
- Automated overflow detection
- Automated directory traversal detection

Foundstone's ScanLine

ScanLine (Figure 7-11) is a command-line port scanner for all Windows platforms. It can perform traditional ICMP pinging and optional additional ICMP time-stamp scanning. It can show host response times and number of hops, and it can do TCP scanning, simple UDP scanning, banner grabbing, and hostname resolving. It can handle large numbers and ranges of IP addresses easily.

Source: http://www.microsoft.com/technet/security/tools/mbsavisio.mspx. Accessed 2007.

Figure 7-9 Microsoft Baseline Security Analyzer determines if security updates are needed.

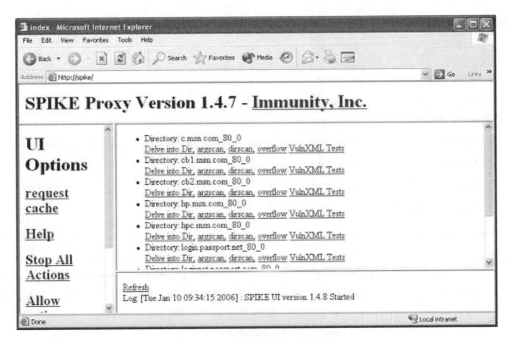

Figure 7-10   SPIKE Proxy functions as an HTTP or HTTPS proxy.

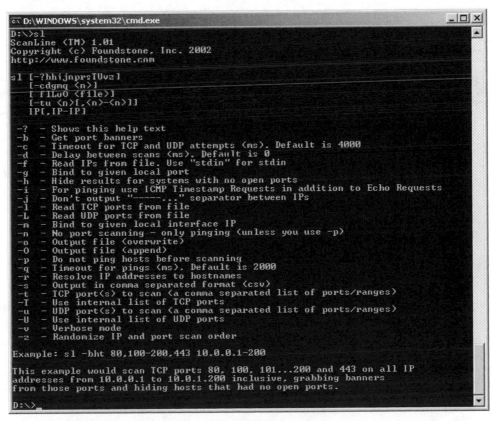

Figure 7-11   ScanLine is a command-line port scanner.

Cerberus Internet Scanner

Cerberus Internet Scanner (CIS) scans remote hosts for vulnerabilities. This tool is designed to help administrators find and fix the security holes present in their computer systems.

It includes the following features:

- All the security scans are embedded in DLLs so that they can be updated without having to rebuild the executable.
- It can be run in command-line mode, in the background, which aids in scanning many machines at once.
- It generates easy-to-read HTML-based reports.
- It is multithreaded, so it is quick to execute.

Other Vulnerability Tools

- *Nmap*: Nmap is an open-source utility for network exploration and security auditing.
- *Winfingerprint*: Winfingerprint is an administrative network resource scanner that allows the user to scan machines on a LAN and returns various details about each host.
- *Security Auditor's Research Assistant (SARA)*: The Security Auditor's Research Assistant (SARA) is a third-generation network security analysis tool that performs the following functions:
  - Integrates the national vulnerability database
  - Performs SQL injection tests
  - Performs exhaustive XSS tests
  - Adapts to many firewalled environments
  - Supports remote self-scan and API facilities

Chapter Summary

- The vulnerability assessment process involves recognizing, measuring, and prioritizing vulnerabilities in a system.
- A vulnerability assessment provides follow-up documentation, reports, and additional consulting whenever required after the assessment process.
- Hackers identify vulnerabilities in servers that are not patched and exploit them.
- Active assessments are a type of vulnerability assessment that uses network scanners to scan the network and to identify the hosts, services, and vulnerabilities present in that network.
- Network assessments determine the possible network security attacks that may be launched against an organization's system.
- The three different phases of a vulnerability assessment are the preassessment, assessment, and postassessment phases.
- Vulnerabilities are categorized by severity into three levels: high, medium, and low risks.
- The time taken for a vulnerability assessment depends on the scope of the test, nature of the test, and number of penetration test personnel involved in the test.
- Host-based scanning tools are useful for servers that run various applications such as those that involve Web, critical file, database, directory, and remote access capabilities.

## Chapter 8

External Penetration Testing

Objectives

After completing this chapter, you should be able to:

- Conduct an external penetration test
- Create topological network maps
- Identify the physical location of target servers
- Conduct a variety of port scans on a target network
- Firewalk on a router's gateway
- Locate the DNS record of a domain
- Examine cookies generated by a server
- Examine hidden fields
- Grab the banners of a variety of servers
- Check for ICMP responses
- Test for a variety of ports

Key Terms

AfriNIC (African Network Information Center)   the RIR (see definition of ARIN) (see definition of ARIN) for Africa

APNIC (Asia and Pacific Network Information Centre)   the RIR that manages the distribution and registration of numeric Internet resources in the Asia Pacific region

ARIN (American Registry for Internet Numbers)   one of five Regional Internet Registries (RIRs); provides Internet resource allocations, registration services, and coordination activities that support the operation of the Internet in North America

connect() command   a high-level system call used to establish a connection

Cookies   text stored on a computer that allows Web sites to authenticate user identity, speed up transactions, monitor user behavior, and personalize presentations

Firewalking   a method for collecting information pertaining to a remote network that is secured by firewalls

IPv6 (Internet Protocol version 6)   a network-layer protocol used for packet-switched networks

LACNIC (Latin American and Caribbean Internet Addresses Registry)   the RIR for the Latin American and Caribbean regions

RIPE NCC (Réseaux IP Européens Network Coordination Centre)   the RIR that provides Internet resource allocations, registration services, and coordination activities that support the operation of the Internet in Europe

Session hijacking   the process of overtaking a valid session by generating an authentication session ID

Stealth ports   ports that do not generate any kind of acknowledgment from a machine

Telnet   a network-based TCP/IP client-server protocol that facilitates an interactive TCP connection to services on the network host

Topological map   a map of a network's external IT infrastructure

Introduction to External Penetration Testing

External penetration testing evaluates the strengths and weaknesses of an organization's internal and external architecture by using the Internet. Finding such flaws enables the organization to defend itself against intruders. This type of testing differs from internal penetration testing, because it is conducted from outside a network, while internal testing is conducted from within a network. The main objective of external penetration testing is to identify existing vulnerabilities that can be exploited from outside of a network. Doing this helps the system administrator identify vulnerabilities and keep them from being exploited.

External penetration testing is a process of determining the following:

- Security flaws of client systems
- Strengths of client systems

External penetration testing is performed during a predetermined evaluation period and should include the following tasks:

- Collecting available information regarding externally accessible configurations
- Analyzing and identifying the services and topologies of external client networks
- Scanning the ports and services of client Internet services that are prone to attack

The main aim of external penetration testing is to provide the client with the ability to foresee external attacks. It also emphasizes practical means of minimizing the risks related to information systems and networks. Implementing this approach enhances the security of the client's networked resources and aids in mitigating the costs and uncertainties that arise from possible external attacks. Penetration testing offers solutions for securing important online business operations. The process not only secures business Web sites, it also makes their services more attractive to clients who are looking for a secure way to conduct business online.

Steps for Conducting External Penetration Testing

1. Inventory company's external infrastructure.
2. Create topological map of the network.
3. Identify the IP addresses of the targets.
4. Locate the traffic routes that go to the Web servers.
5. Trace the TCP traffic path to the destination.
6. Trace the UDP traffic path to the destination.
7. Identify the physical location of the target servers.
8. Examine the use of IPv6 at the remote location.
9. Look up the the domain registry for IP information.
10. Find IP block information about the target.
11. Locate the ISP servicing the client.

12. List open ports.
13. List closed ports.
14. List suspicious ports that may be stealth ports.
15. Port scan every port on the target's network.
16. Use SYN scan on the target and analyze the response.
17. Use connect scan on the target and analyze the response.
18. Use Xmas scan on the target and analyze the response.
19. Use FIN scan on the target and analyze the response.
20. Use null scan on the target and analyze the response.
21. Firewalk the router's gateway.
22. Examine TCP sequence number prediction.
23. Examine the use of standard and nonstandard protocols.
24. Examine IP ID sequence number prediction.
25. Examine the system uptime of the target.
26. Examine the operating systems used by different targets.
27. Examine the patches applied to the operating system.
28. Locate the DNS record of the domain and attempt DNS hijacking.
29. Download applications from the company's Web site and reverse engineer the binary code.
30. List programming languages and application software used to create various programs on the target server.
31. Look for errors and custom Web pages.
32. Guess different subdomain names and analyze different responses.
33. Hijack sessions.
34. Examine cookies generated by the server.
35. Examine the access controls used by the Web {application/server}.
36. Brute-force URL injections and session tokens.
37. Check for directory consistency and page-naming syntax of the Web pages.
38. Look for sensitive information in the Web page source code.
39. Attempt URL encoding on the Web pages.
40. Try buffer overflow attempts in input fields.
41. Look for invalid ranges in input fields.
42. Attempt escape-character injection.
43. Try cross-site scripting (XSS) techniques.
44. Record and replay the traffic to the target Web server and note the response.
45. Try various SQL-injection techniques.
46. Examine hidden fields.
47. Examine Server-Side Includes (SSI).
48. Examine e-commerce and payment gateways handled by the Web server.
49. Examine welcome, error, and debug messages.
50. Probe the server through SMTP mail bouncing.
51. Grab the banners of HTTP servers.
52. Grab the banners of SMTP servers.
53. Grab the banners of POP3 servers.
54. Grab the banners of FTP servers.

55. Identify the Web extensions used on the server.

56. Try to use an HTTPS tunnel to encapsulate traffic.

57. OS fingerprint target servers.

58. Check for ICMP responses (Type 3 port unreachable).

59. Check for ICMP responses (Type 8 echo request).

60. Check for ICMP responses (Type 13 time-stamp request).

61. Check for ICMP responses (Type 15 information request).

62. Check for ICMP responses (Type 17 subnet address mask request).

63. Check for ICMP responses from broadcast address.

64. Port scan DNS servers (TCP/UDP 53).

65. Port scan TFTP servers (port 69).

66. Test for NTP ports (port 123).

67. Test for SNMP ports (ports 161 and 162).

68. Test for Telnet ports (port 23).

69. Test for LDAP ports (port 389).

70. Test for NetBIOS ports (ports 135–139 and 445).

71. Test for SQL server ports (ports 1433 and 1434).

72. Test for Citrix ports (port 1495).

73. Test for Oracle ports (port 1521).

74. Test for NFS ports (port 2049).

75. Test for Compaq, HP Inside Manager ports (ports 2301 and 2381).

76. Test for remote desktop ports (port 3389).

77. Test for Sybase ports (port 5000).

78. Test for SIP ports (port 5060).

79. Test for VNC ports (ports 5800 and 5900).

80. Test for X11 ports (port 6000).

81. Test for JetDirect ports (port 9100).

82. Port scan FTP data (port 20).

83. Port scan Web servers (port 80).

84. Port scan SSL servers (port 443).

85. Port scan Kerberos and Active Directory (TCP/UDP 88).

86. Port scan SSH servers (port 22).

Step 1: Inventory Company's External Infrastructure

In this process, the external resources of the target's network are identified. The team must identify the locations of all servers, including those that are located at other sites. The team should create drawings that show network cabling and server locations. Drawings should include both the physical location and the persons responsible for each server. Figure 8-1 shows an example drawing.

Step 2: Create Topological Map of the Network

A *topological map* is essentially a map of a network's external IT infrastructure. To create a topological map of the network, the testing team should first create a topological diagram of the external IT infrastructure (Figure 8-2). The drawing must contain the following items:

- Servers
- ISP connections

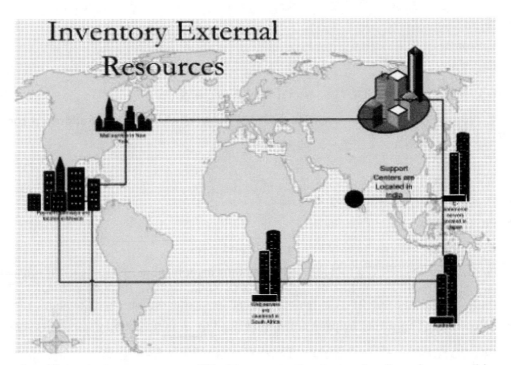

Figure 8-1 An inventory map will help a penetration tester visualize where possible vulnerabilities may be.

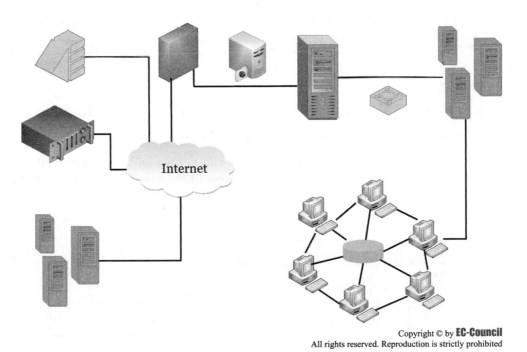

Figure 8-2 A topological diagram of the external IT infrastructure gives a graphic representation of a company's network infrastructure.

- Infrastructure used
- Customers
- Partners

Step 3: Identify IP Addresses of the Targets

The IP addresses of the target network must be identified. This includes addresses for the following types of servers:

- Mail servers
- Web servers
- Domain Name System (DNS) servers
- Proxy servers

The following tools can be used to identify IP addresses:

- *NeoTrace*: NeoTrace is a tool for identifying information about Internet sites. It is useful for tracing any computer present on the Internet by entering an e-mail address, IP address, or URL. The display shows the route between the user and the remote site, encompassing the intermediate nodes and their registrant data.
- *ip2country*: This utility helps in converting IP addresses into country names, as shown in Figure 8-3.

Step 4: Locate Traffic Routes That Go to Web Servers

The network topological map can be checked manually by logging into individual devices present on the network and by using built-in system commands, such as tracert (Windows) or traceroute (UNIX). These commands are useful for depicting the path followed by an ICMP request as it traverses the network (hopping from device to device) to its ultimate destination.

Traceroute is a tool that traces a packet from a computer to an Internet host. It shows the number of hops the packet requires to reach the host and the time required for each hop. Traceroute is useful for identifying the maximum possible delay that occurs. Traceroute utilities function by transmitting packets with low time-to-live (TTL) fields. The TTL value indicates the number of hops the packet is permitted before it is returned. When the TTL value is too low, the packet cannot reach its destination, so the last host returns the packet and identifies itself. Intermediate hosts are identified by sending a series of packets and incrementing the TTL value with each successive packet.

Steps 5 and 6: Trace TCP and UDP Traffic Paths to Destination

The following tools are useful for tracing TCP and UDP traffic:

- *pathChirp*: an active probing scheme for bandwidth estimation based on packet dispersion. The advantage of pathChirp is that it overcomes system I/O bandwidth limitations on high-speed networks.

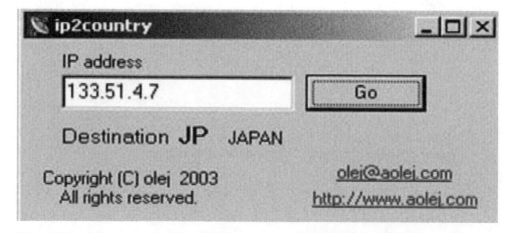

Figure 8-3   ip2country can identify the country of origin of an IP address.

pathChirp employs a packet tailgating technique where small packets with no TTL limit immediately follow large packets with TTL = *m*.

- *Pathrate*: a tool that estimates a path's capacity. It is based on packet pair/train dispersion.

- *Pathload*: a tool that estimates a path's available bandwidth. It is based on a one-way delay trend of regular streams. The tool reports a range of available bandwidth.

- *Tulip*: a tool that analyzes reordering, loss, and major queuing events by leveraging properly implemented and less-exploited router features. Tulip identifies points of reordering and loss in terms of hops. Tulip's accuracy is validated by using end-to-end internal consistency measurements.

- *Netperf*: a yardstick to measure the performance of various types of networking. It is useful for unidirectional throughput. It consists of facilities for CPU utilization measurement and end-to-end latency. The basic purpose of this tool is to focus on bulk data transfer and request/response performance using either TCP or UDP and the BSD sockets interface.

Step 7: Identify Physical Locations of Target Servers

NeoTrace can display the physical locations of servers on a geographical map, as shown in Figure 8-4.

Step 8: Examine Use of IPv6 at Remote Location

IPv6 (Internet Protocol version 6) is a network-layer protocol used for packet-switched networks. It is an upgrade of the IPv4 protocol. In this step, the target servers are checked for the presence of IPv6. The following goals were behind the creation of IPv6:

- To address the problems of IPv4

- To allow persistent mobile computing and information sharing on an international scale

- To allow communication with every device that is connected to a network

Most applications that are compatible with IPv4 are also compatible with IPv6. The applications that are not compatible with IPv6 but are compatible with IPv4 are SQL and SNMP. IPv6 is useful for implementing geographic and regional addressing, where organizations have common prefixes based on the region where they are located and the provider through whom they are connecting. IPv6 also enforces security by using IPSec for host-level end-to-end security. The IPv6 protocol cannot broadcast packets to the network. For accomplishing one-to-many communications, IPv6 uses multicast addressing.

Figure 8-4 NeoTrace uses a map to trace the physical locations of online computers.

The 46Bouncer tool can aid in IPv6 examination. 46Bouncer accepts TCP/UDP connections in IPv4/6 and sends them to an application in IPv6/4. Thus, it functions as a proxy between the IPv4 and IPv6 worlds.

Step 9: Look Up Domain Registry for IP Information

The following steps are necessary to look up domain registries:

1. *Locate DNS servers*: DNS servers translate hostnames to IP addresses. This process is performed through the use of records that hold a zone database file that stores hostnames and their respective IP addresses. DNS servers have the capability of caching results for a specific time period so that when the same request appears again, the server can directly retrieve the information from the cache without having to look in the zone files.

2. *Look for primary and secondary servers*: Primary DNS servers have main authority over the database records of a particular zone, i.e., they have the master copy of data or records of a particular zone. The secondary DNS servers maintain a copy of these records and synchronize with a primary server.

The following tools are useful for looking up domain registries:

- *All-Nettools.com*: Provides free online network tools including SmartWhois, Traceroute, and Ping
- *Completewhois*: WHOIS engine providing information on domain ownership and IP addresses
- *DNS Report*: Provides a comprehensive report of name-server records
- *DNSstuff*: Offers network tools such as WHOIS, DNS lookup, Traceroute, Ping, and spam database lookup

Step 10: Find IP Block Information About Target

Locating the IP block of a company is necessary in penetration testing. An IP block of any company can be traced by making use of the following tools:

- *Sam Spade*: Sam Spade is a network query tool that has the following integrated utilities:
  - *Nslookup*: This utility provides DNS details.
  - *WHOIS lookup*: WHOIS lookup provides all the details of a domain name.
  - *Traceroute*: This utility traces the route to the DNS server and provides details about all the intermediate gateways between the DNS and a specified computer connected to the system.
  - *SMTP verification utility*: Simple Mail Transfer Protocol (SMTP) verifies the origin of e-mails.
- ***ARIN (American Registry for Internet Numbers) database***: ARIN is an online database that maintains IP addresses and their corresponding records. ARIN assigns IP addresses and maintains the IP address records for the North American region. The Internet Assigned Numbers Authority (IANA) has allotted the following IP address blocks to ARIN: 63.0.0.0–76.255.255.255, 199.0.0.0–199.255.255.255, 204.0.0.0–209.255.255.255, and 216.0.0.0–216.255.255.255. ARIN monitors all of the IP addresses belonging to these IP address blocks. It allows users to find information about registration of IP blocks through ARIN's WHOIS service. The ARIN lookup tool accepts domain names or IP addresses as inputs, and gives the following information about the domain names:
  - Domain owner name
  - Contact details of domain owner
  - IP address range
  - Name of domain name servers

The following organizations handle this task for other parts of the world:

- ***AfriNIC (African Network Information Center)***: The Regional Internet Registry (RIR) for Africa
- ***APNIC (Asia and Pacific Network Information Centre)***: The RIR that manages the distribution and registration of numeric Internet resources in the Asia Pacific region
- ***LACNIC (Latin American and Caribbean Internet Addresses Registry)***: The RIR for the Latin American and Caribbean regions
- ***RIPE NCC (Réseaux IP Européens Network Coordination Centre)***: The RIR that provides Internet resource allocations, registration services, and coordination activities that support the operation of the Internet in Europe

Step 11: Locate ISP Servicing the Client

The following information is uncovered when the ISP is located:

- *Name of the ISP*: The penetration tester needs to find the name and address of the ISP who is providing Internet services to the client.

- *Pricing plans*: Most ISPs have different pricing plans for their provided services. They offer various service packages at different prices.

- *Services provided*: ISPs offer different kinds of services in different packages. A penetration tester should track down information about all the kinds of service packages that are being offered by the specific ISP. It should learn about the services as well as the value-added services that are being provided. These services may include:

  - Dial-up access
  - DSL/ISDN dedicated access
  - Multiunit high-speed Internet solutions for apartments and condos
  - Domain name services
  - Web hosting
  - Photo albums

A penetration tester should learn about other companies that fall under the same IP block. The penetration tester can call the ISP and ask for the default equipment (hardware such as modem, etc.) delivered when signing up for a plan similar to the one used by the target company.

Step 12: List Open Ports

Table 8-1 shows a list of port numbers and their uses.

Port Number	Use
0	Reserved
1	TCP port service multiplexes
2	Management Utility
3	Compression Process
4	Unassigned
5	Remote Job Entry
6	Unassigned
7	Echo
8	Unassigned
10/12/14	Unassigned
17	Quote of the Day
20	File Transfer (Default Data)
21	File Transfer (Control)
22	SSH Remote Login Protocol
23	Telnet
24	Any Private Mail System
25	Simple Mail Transfer
27	NSW User System FE
31	MSG Authentication
43	WHOIS
44	MPM FLAGS Protocol

Table 8-1   These are common port numbers with the different applications for which they are used   (*continues*)

Port Number	Use
48	Digital Audit Daemon
49	Login Host Protocol (TACACS)
50	Remote Mail Checking Protocol
52	XNS Time Protocol
55	ISI Graphics Language
61	NI MAIL
62	ACA Services
71	Remote Job Service
76	Distributed External Object Store
80	World Wide Web HTTP
86	Micro Focus COBOL
88	Kerberos
93	Device Control Protocol
143	Internet Message Access Protocol
146	ISO-IP0
153	SGMP
156	SQL Service
161	SNMP
162	SNMPTRAP
177	X Display Manager Control Protocol
178	NextStep Window Server
180	Intergraph
190	Gateway Access Control Protocol
194	Internet Relay Chat Protocol
197	Directory Location Service
200	IBM System Resource Controller
201	AppleTalk Routing Maintenance
246	Display Systems Protocol
260	Openport
282	Cable Port A/X
361	Semantix
418	Hyper-G
458	Apple QuickTime
569	Microsoft Rome
595	CAB Protocol
601	Reliable Syslog Service
700	Extensible Provisioning Protocol
729	IBM NetView DM/6000 Server/Client
828	itm-mcell-s
912	APEX relay-relay service
996	VSInet
999	Puprouter

Table 8-1 These are common port numbers with the different applications for which they are used (*continued*)

The following tools are useful for port scanning:

- *SuperScan*: scans target systems based on a specified IP address. It includes the following features:
  - Supports unlimited IP ranges, i.e., individual IPs (192.168.0.1), IP ranges (192.168.0.1–192.168.0.70), and CIDR format ranges (192.168.0.1/24)
  - Improves host detection using multiple ICMP methods (ping)
  - Supports TCP scanning with the connect and SYN methods
  - Supports UDP scanning with the data and data + ICMP methods
  - Performs ping, traceroute, and WHOIS tool functions
  - Displays banner information (OS information) and provides enumeration capabilities
  - Generates automated HTML reports
- *Nmap (Network Mapper)*: a tool used to search networks to find the state of ports and the services running on those ports. The following are the port states Nmap identifies:
  - *Open*: An open port on a host indicates that the port is listening and will respond to connection requests. Once the port is found to be open, Nmap can identify the services running on it. Attackers can illegitimately access these services.
  - *Closed*: Certain ports are closed, even though the host is alive. A response from these ports indicates that the host is up. Access to these ports can be restricted using firewalls or filters to secure them from unauthorized access.
  - *Filtered*: Information on filtered ports cannot be accessed, even if they are in an open state. Packet filtering devices, such as firewalls, prevent port scanning on these ports.
  - *Unfiltered*: The ACK scan type result identifies if a probed port is filtered or unfiltered, but it does not differentiate between open and closed ports. The Window, SYN, and FIN scan types identify open and closed ports.
  - *Open\filtered*: When there is a delay in response to a probe packet, Nmap interprets it as the port being filtered. The UDP, IP, NULL, FIN, and Xmas scans identify the ports that are open and filtered.
  - *Closed\filtered*: If Nmap cannot determine whether the port is closed or filtered, it categorizes the port as closed and filtered. The idle scan option of Nmap results in identifying such ports.
- *NetScanTools Pro*: (Figure 8-5) can be used to research IP addresses, hostnames, domain names, e-mail addresses, and URLs automatically or with manual tools. NetScanTools Pro includes the following features:
  - *Information-gathering tools*: Includes DNS checking and testing tools with query utility options, tools for tracing domain names and IP addresses, tools for using NetBIOS to show hidden shares that can be used to attack viruses and worms, tools for tracing e-mail address validity, port-mapping tools, etc.
  - *Security-testing solutions*: can show connected IP devices on a LAN using ARP, even those that are protected by firewalls; can check for unauthorized or unintentionally installed services or open listening ports on IPv4-connected computers.

Step 13: List Closed Ports

Once a port is closed, any request made to that port will result in an acknowledgment from the machine that the port is closed.

The following port-scanning tools will list closed ports:

- *Firewalk*: **Firewalking** is a method that collects information pertaining to a remote network that is secured by firewalls. The Firewalk tool determines whether a packet can pass through an attacker's host to a particular destination that is using packet-filtering devices. This method also helps find open ports on a gateway.
- *HackerShield*: This is a security and vulnerability-scanning tool. It checks and automatically updates potential problems with security checks. It can also repair and reverse the changes made.
- *HostScan*: This is a network-scanning tool that conducts a port scan through which it searches for open ports on the network.
- *Nessus*: Nessus is a popular vulnerability-scanning tool used to determine the vulnerabilities in a system.

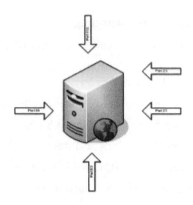

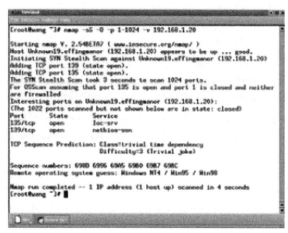

Figure 8-5 NetScanTools Pro comes with a number of different scanning capabilities.

- *Netcat*: This is a UNIX-based utility that can read and write data across network connections, using the TCP or UDP protocol.
- *Netcop*: This is a spyware detection and removal application. It offers security and protects the network environment of its users.
- *Nmap*: Nmap is mostly used for port scanning. It can be executed at the command line or run through a GUI.

Step 14: List Suspicious Ports That May Be Stealth Ports

A penetration tester should look out for stealth ports; *stealth ports* will not generate any kind of acknowledgment from the target machine. This lack of acknowledgment will typically cause the requesting machine to wait until its own internal time-out mechanism gives up waiting for a reply.

Step 15: Port Scan Every Port on Target's Network

The process of port scanning starts when a tester sends a ping message to the target host. The received message can fall under one of these categories:

- Open ports
- Closed ports
- Blocked ports

Testers must examine open ports that are vulnerable with respect to security and stability issues. Port scanning is often the first tool an intruder uses for hacking a system. The intruder uses the information gathered from port scanning for compromising system security.

Step 16: Use SYN Scan on the Target and Analyze Response

A SYN scan, also called a stealth scan, involves an incomplete TCP three-way handshake. The host sends a SYN packet to the target. This identifies whether there is an open port listening on the target host. If there is an open port, it responds with a SYN/ACK. Once this acknowledgment is received, the host terminates the connections by sending an RST. This practice is often referred to as half-open scanning, as a full TCP connection is not established. Many systems do not log the attempt and discard it as a communications error.

From the TCP SYN scan, the state of ports (open, closed, or filtered) can be distinctly identified. The filtered state is recognized by an ICMP unreachable error of type 3, code 1, 2, 3, 9, 10, or 13.

Step 17: Use Connect Scan on the Target and Analyze Response

This is a default scan option in Nmap for users with no root privileges. When Nmap issues the connect() command, the operating system initiates a connection. The **connect() command** is a high-level system call used to establish a connection. It is available with the Berkeley API. The connect() scan allows a complete connection to be made with the target. An IDS mechanism can detect this scan from the logs that are created when a system is connection-scanned. The scan can be performed simultaneously on various ports, increasing the scan speed. Ports that are listening can be connected to. Connection requests to closed ports return an error message that the port is unreachable. A connect() scan has the following disadvantages:

- The connect() scan is not as effective as the SYN, in that it does not send raw packets.
- Every connect() request is logged in the machine. Therefore, system scans are not concealed.

Step 18: Use Xmas Scan on the Target and Analyze Response

Xmas scans exploit the ability of the TCP RFC 793 that differentiates open and closed ports. The TCP RFC 793 standard states that a probe packet that does not contain an RST flag, when sent to the target host, results in sending an RST if the port is closed.

The following example of an Xmas scan show how the process works:

- *Xmas scan directed at an open port*:

```
192.5.5.92:4031  -----------FIN/URG/PSH----------->192.5.5.110:23

192.5.5.92:4031  <----------NO RESPONSE------------192.5.5.110:23
```

- *Xmas scan directed at a closed port*:

```
192.5.5.92:4031  -----------FIN/URG/PSH----------->192.5.5.110:23

192.5.5.92:4031<-------------RST/ACK--------------192.5.5.110:23
```

In the example, the control flags of the initial TCP packet are set to FIN, URG, and PSH by the Xmas scan. These packets, when sent to an open port on a system whose TCP/IP implementation is built according to RFC 793, will not obtain any response from the host. If the port is closed, the remote host will reply with an RST/ACK.

Step 19: Use FIN Scan on the Target and Analyze Response

FIN scan exploits the ability of the TCP RFC 793 that differentiates open and closed ports. A FIN scan is initialized by setting only the FIN flag of the TCP packet. Except for the initialization of packets, the FIN scan works on the same principles as the Xmas scan, and the process of identifying open and closed ports is also similar to an Xmas scan.

The following example shows how a FIN scan works:

- *FIN scan directed at an open port*:

```
192.5.5.92:4031  -----------FIN---------------->192.5.5.110:23

192.5.5.92:4031  <----------NO RESPONSE----------192.5.5.110:23
```

- *FIN scan directed at a closed port*:

```
192.5.5.92:4031 -------------FIN----------------192.5.5.110:23

192.5.5.92:4031<-------------RST/ACK------------192.5.5.110:23
```

Step 20: Use Null Scan on the Target and Analyze Response

The null scan does not set any TCP control flags. The null scan is an example of stealth scanning and can be used to identify an OS. The following example shows how a null scan works:

- *Null scan directed at an open port*:

```
192.5.5.92:4031 -----------NO FLAGS SET---------->192.5.5.110:23

192.5.5.92:4031 <----------NO RESPONSE------------192.5.5.110:23
```

- *Null scan directed at a closed port*:

```
192.5.5.92:4031 -------------NO FLAGS SET--------192.5.5.110:23

192.5.5.92:4031<-------------RST/ACK-------------192.5.5.110:23
```

Step 21: Firewalk Router's Gateway

Firewalking is a method that collects information pertaining to a remote network that is secured by firewalls. It uses traceroute-like analysis to determine whether a packet can pass through an attacker's host to a particular destination that is using packet-filtering devices. In this step, the tester firewalks the router's gateway.

Step 22: Examine TCP Sequence Number Prediction

The Nmap tool can predict the TCP sequence number and use the details to target hosts. It can then use this information to perform session hijacking or to identify the services running on remote hosts.

Nmap's -O option is used to identify the sequence number. The -O option initiates the TCP/IP fingerprinting routines, which actually identify which operating system the target host is running and its version.

Step 23: Examine Use of Standard and Nonstandard Protocols

Using unknown protocols affects intrusion detection systems. Many IDS cannot identify vulnerabilities in unknown protocols. Therefore, if a network is using a nonstandard protocol that the IDS does not know about, the IDS will be unable to detect vulnerabilities related to that protocol.

Step 24: Examine IP ID Sequence Number Prediction

Predicting IP ID sequence numbers can be accomplished by using the following techniques:

- *Traffic analysis*: Sequential IP ID numbers expose the number of packets sent by a host over a given period. This can be used to estimate Web site traffic, determine when people log on, and other information.
- *Host alias detection*: Sometimes, a single host will have multiple IP addresses or Ethernet interfaces. It is possible to determine which IPs match a given host by looking for similar IP ID sequence numbers.
- *Load balancer demultiplexing*: This is almost the reverse of the above technique. Large sites often use load-balancing equipment so that a single address maps to a small farm of servers. By noting the IP ID values, a user can often determine how many machines are behind the load balancer and which one the user is connected to.

Hping2 is a tool that sends custom ICMP/UDP/TCP packets to the target system to gather information about the target. In the following example, the "id" value in the Hping2 report displays the details of the load balancer that beta.search.microsoft.com handles at 207.46.197.115:

```
hping2 -c 10 -i 1 -p 80 -S beta.search.microsoft.com
```

```
HPING beta.search.microsoft.com. (eth0 207.46.197.115): S set, 40 headers + 0 data bytes

        46 bytes from 207.46.197.115: flags=SA seq=0 ttl=56 id=57645
        win=16616 rtt=21.2 ms

        46 bytes from 207.46.197.115: flags=SA seq=1 ttl=56 id=57650
        win=16616 rtt=21.4 ms

        46 ms bytes from 207.46.197.115: flags=RA seq=2 ttl=56 id=18574
        win=0 rtt=21.3

        46 ms bytes from 207.46.197.115: flags=RA seq=3 ttl=56 id=18587
        win=0 rtt=21.1

        46 ms bytes from 207.46.197.115: flags=RA seq=4 ttl=56 id=18588
        win=0 rtt=21.2

        46 bytes from 207.46.197.115: flags=SA seq=5 ttl=56 id=57741
        win=16616 rtt=21.2 ms

        46 bytes from 207.46.197.115: flags=RA seq=6 ttl=56 id=18589
        win=0 rtt=21.2 ms

        46 bytes from 207.46.197.115: flags=SA seq=7 ttl=56 id=57742
        win=16616 rtt=21.7 ms

        46 bytes from 207.46.197.115: flags=SA seq=8 ttl=56 id=57743
        win=16616 rtt=21.6 ms

        46 bytes from 207.46.197.115: flags=SA seq=9 ttl=56 id=57744
        win=16616 rtt=21.3 ms

        --- beta.search.microsoft.com. hping statistic ---

        10 packets transmitted, 10 packets received, 0% packet loss round-trip
        min/avg/max = 21.1/21.3/21.7 ms
```

Step 25: Examine the System Uptime of the Target

The penetration tester should find the following information:

- When was the last time the server rebooted?
- When was the last time the server crashed?
- What is the uptime of the server?

The following tools are used to find and analyze the system uptime of a server:

- Netcraft
- Uptime

Step 26: Examine Operating Systems Used by Different Targets

The tester should examine the operating systems used by different targets by using the following methods:

- Using banner-grabbing techniques to identify a remote OS
- Looking for honeypots, packet crafters, and banner fakers

The following tools can help identify the operating system of a target machine:

- *Nmap*: Nmap can scan a target system and identify the operating system. The options available to identify the OS are:
  - O: Enable OS detection
  - osscan-limit: Limit OS detection to promising targets
  - osscan-guess: Guess OS more aggressively
- *Telnet*: **Telnet** is a network-based TCP/IP client-server protocol. With it, a user can initiate an interactive TCP connection on a network host. With telnet, a penetration tester can connect to a host and see the banner, which typically shows operating system information.
- *Netcat*: Netcat is a UNIX-based utility that can read and write data across network connections, using the TCP or UDP protocols. It is a reliable network debugging and exploration tool.

Step 27: Examine Patches Applied to Operating System

The penetration tester should take the following steps:

1. Examine the patches applied to the operating system.
2. List the dates patches were applied to the server.
3. Look for version number and OS level.

Step 28: Locate DNS Record of Domain and Attempt DNS Hijacking

The penetration tester should locate the domain vendor responsible for the DNS of the target server. Information about the vendor can be collected using different tools, such as www.DNSstuff.com and Sam Spade. These tools provide the required information, which can then be used for DNS hijacking.

Step 29: Download Applications from Company's Web Site and Reverse Engineer Binary Code

The penetration tester should download the following types of applications from the remote Web sites:

- *Java programs*: These programs run in the Java Runtime Environment (JRE).
- *Executable programs*: These are executable programs that can be run directly on systems.
- *Flash programs*: These are interactive programs run in the Flash player.

Reverse engineering the binary code is a process of getting back to the original source code of the program by using different disassembling and decompiling tools. It is equally important to look into the following factors:

- *Programmer's name*: The name of the programmer who wrote it
- *Comments*: The comments the programmer has provided at the various steps of the program so as to keep the user informed of the actual operations that are carried out by the program
- *Sensitive information*: Sensitive information could be, for example, how much memory the program occupies or the other resources it uses
- *Programming style*: The programming style is the way in which the program is written and the different functions it uses

The following tools can be used to reverse engineer binary code:

- *IDA Pro*: This tool is used as a disassembler in manual binary code analysis.
- *Flash Saver*: Flash Saver is an efficient Flash download tool that can help the user save Flash files from a Web page. The user can then use other tools to decompile the Flash file.
- *REC Decompiler*: REC (Reverse Engineering Compiler) is a portable reverse engineering compiler/decompiler. It reads an executable file and tries to produce a C-like representation of the code and data that was used to build the executable file.

Step 30: List Programming Languages and Application Software Used to Create Various Programs on Target Server

In order to accomplish this, it is necessary to check for in-house and commercial applications, and identify the programming languages that were used to create desktop and Web applications. The following are some of the languages used:

- *C*: C is a highly portable language that is relatively small and contains few hardware-specific elements. It includes no input/output statements or memory management techniques. Functions to address these tasks are available in the extensive C standard library. C has the following advantages:
  - Source code is highly portable
  - Machine code is efficient
  - C compilers are available for all current systems

- *AWK*: The AWK utility interprets a special-purpose programming language that makes it possible to handle simple data-reformatting jobs with just a few lines of code. AWK helps users do the following:
  - Manage small, personal databases
  - Generate reports
  - Validate data
  - Generate indexes and carry out various documentation activities

- *C++*: C++ is a superset of the C language that incorporates features of object-oriented programming.

- *JavaScript*: JavaScript was developed as a complement to HTML. Programs written in JavaScript can be directly linked into HTML files.

- *C#*: C# is an object-oriented language designed in a robust way to give the optimum mix of simplicity, expressiveness, and performance. C# is influenced by OOP languages such as Java, Visual Basic, and C++.

- *Perl*: Perl is a stable, cross-platform programming language. It is used for mission-critical projects in the public and private sectors. Perl is open-source software, licensed under the GNU General Public License (GPL).

- *COBOL*: COBOL was created for developing business, typically file-oriented, applications. It was not designed for writing systems programs.

- *PHP*: PHP is a programming language that helps in the development of Web-based applications. It is a cross-platform, server-side, HTML-embedded scripting language.

- *Java*: This is an object-oriented programming language that is designed to be platform independent.

- *Python*: Python is a dynamic object-oriented programming language that can be used for many kinds of software development.

- *J++*: This is a Microsoft proprietary Java version. It does not support some of the Java standard libraries, such as RMI and JNI.

- *Ruby*: This is an interpreted scripting language that provides many features for processing text files and performing system management tasks. It is extensible and portable. Ruby has a simple syntax and has exception-handling features.

- *J#*: J# is a transitional programming language for programmers of Sun's Java and Microsoft's J++ languages. The J# programming language can work with the Java byte code, as well as source code. It uses the same general syntax as Java, but with different APIs.

- *Tcl*: Tcl is a scripting language that is easy to learn. It is mostly used for scripted applications, GUIs, rapid prototyping, and testing. It has a very simple syntax.

- *PowerBuilder*: PowerBuilder is a fourth-generation language that aids rapid application development (RAD). It is similar to Visual Basic, but focuses on data manipulations and data handling. It is commonly used by the financial sectors of companies.

- *Visual Basic*: This is an event-driven programming language that has a large user base in business programming. It is derived from BASIC; allows access to databases using DAO, RDO, or ADO; and allows for the creation of ActiveX controls and objects.
- *VBScript*: This is an active scripting language derived from Visual Basic.

Step 31: Look for Errors and Custom Web Pages

In this step, a penetration tester enters various URL strings into a browser and observes how the server responds to them. There is the possibility that the server will throw an error message. These error messages could show up in custom Web pages.

Step 32: Guess Different Subdomain Names and Analyze Responses

Initially, the penetration tester needs to acquire or gather all the possible relevant information about the main domain that a particular organization uses. When information gathering is complete, the tester can look into the subdomains that the organization uses. There could be a possibility that all the subdomain names that exist under the main domain are not being used. The penetration tester should attempt to guess the subdomain names relevant to the organization. A company named Xsecurity, for example, could have the following easily guessed subdomains:

- sales.xsecurity.com
- marketing.xsecurity.com
- internal.xsecurity.com
- intranet.xsecurity.com
- devl.xsecurity.com
- test.xsecurity.com
- backup.xsecurity.com
- partner.xsecurity.com
- beta.xsecurity.com
- secret.xsecurity.com
- preview.xsecurity.com
- temp.xsecurity.com

Step 33: Hijack Sessions

Session hijacking is the process of overtaking a valid session by generating an authentication session ID. An attacker steals the session ID and takes control of the ongoing session. The attacker gains complete access to all of the user's data after hijacking is done successfully. Sessions can be hijacked by IP spoofing, which is when an attacker impersonates an authentic user and inserts source-routed IP packets into an active communication between two nodes on a network. This type of attack requires the attacker to execute a denial-of-service attack against the endpoint to prevent it from answering.

Step 34: Examine Cookies Generated by the Server

Client-side cookies are useful for verifying the identity of a user by storing CFID and CFTOKEN. *Cookies* stored on the computer's hard drive maintain text that allow Web sites to authenticate a user's identity, speed up transactions, monitor the user's behavior, and personalize presentations. Unauthorized users can also access cookies. An attacker can examine a cookie to determine its purpose and to gather the information stored in it.

Step 35: Examine the Access Controls Used by the Web Server

Penetration testers should look for login pages and identify the authentication method the Web server uses. The following types of authentication will reveal information about Web servers:

- *Form authentication*: Form authentication is a cookie-based authentication system in which the usernames and passwords are stored in databases. This authentication support makes it easy for a Web developer to add personalized Web pages or password-protected areas. This functionality helps in multiple areas across various enterprise applications.

- *Windows authentication*: Windows authentication provides a default authentication provider for ASP. NET. It can be configured so that Windows domain users are automatically logged in. The following different kinds of Windows authentication options are available:
  - Windows authentication provider
  - Anonymous authentication
  - Digest authentication
  - Basic authentication

- *Biometrics authentication*: This authentication is a verification of the user's identity by means of a physical trait or behavioral characteristic that cannot easily be changed, such as a fingerprint.

- *Secret-question authentication*: Secret-question authentication uses a piece of information or a question to prove identity for access. These questions should be those that are easily recollected by the user. There could be multiple secret questions asked to protect highly sensitive areas.

- *Session-based authentication*: To use session-based authentication, Web clients must use a browser that supports cookies. There are two selections for enabling session-based authentication: single-server and multiserver selections. The single-server option causes the server to generate a cookie that is honored only by the server that generated it, while the multiserver option generates a cookie that allows single sign-on (SSO) with any server that shares the Web SSO configuration document.

- *Digital certificates*: Digital certificates are electronic files that are issued by a trusted third party that is a certified authority (CA). The certificate or the signature that is issued by this authority confirms the user's identity and cannot be forged or replicated. These signatures keep data safe from unauthorized access.

Step 36: Brute-Force URL Injections and Session Tokens

A brute-force attack employs the trial-and-error method to acquire access. Some Web applications contain user IDs and other sensitive information in a URL. This information is contained in the form of parameters in the query component of the URL (the fields that occur after the ? symbol in a URL). A brute-force tool can also help a penetration tester find a legitimate session ID that is present in the URL. A session ID is an identification string that links Web pages to a user. Attackers try to embed different combinations of these session IDs into a valid URL and gain illegal access.

As a brute-force tool uses the trial-and-error method, the attackers inject these session ID strings into the URL and examine the response.

Brute-force strings are injected into the following URL fields:

- Sessions
- Forms
- User
- ID
- Login
- Access

Step 37: Check Directory Consistency and Page-Naming Syntax of Web Pages

A well-designed Web application is one that enables the user to access the application with ease and a very high level of comfort. A typical Web application consists of the following easily found elements:

- *Logical directory structure*: A directory is a container of files that, in turn, contains all the data related to or regarding the application. The framework of the directory is generally designed so that the user finds it easy to search for files and data within the directory.

- *Filenames based on naming conventions*: For consistency, a Web site should employ a naming convention that makes it easy to tell what the purpose of each file is.

- *Repository for images*: There is usually a separate section for every application wherein various images, PDFs, and other related documents are stored.

- *Repository for sensitive information*: Another section to store all the confidential and sensitive information must be created for all applications.

- *Structured links and pages*: The linking of different files, documents, and pages should be correct and well formatted.

- *Site outline*: A site outline or a site map is always a part of a well-designed Web application. This shows the way the pages are arranged in that particular site, as shown in Figure 8-6.

Step 38: Look for Sensitive Information in Web Page Source Code

The next step for external penetration testing is to look for sensitive information in the Web page source code. The HTML source code might reveal the following information:

- *Developer information*: The name, background, and details of the person or team who developed the Web application

- *Login information*: The necessary login details, such as usernames, could be embedded in the source code

- *Revision numbers*: HTML documents often contain revision numbers, indicating which revision the current version is

- *Dates*: Dates such as installation dates, revised dates, and other important dates that are associated with the application

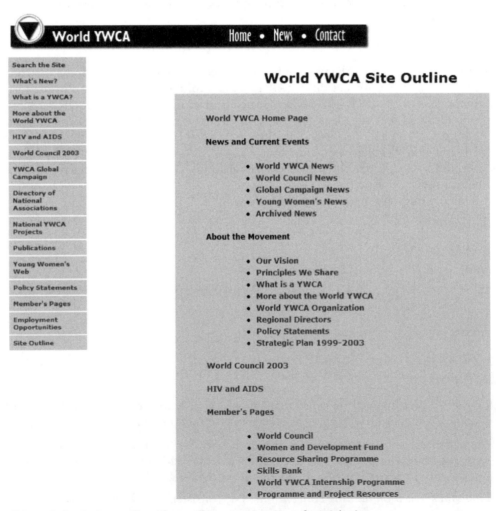

Figure 8-6 A site outline shows the organization of a Web site.

Step 39: Attempt URL Encoding on the Web Pages

To provide worldwide interoperability, uniform encoding of URLs is a must. There are many URL-encoding converters that convert encoded URL into unencoded URL, and unencoded URL into the encoded URL format. URLs convert each non-ASCII character (special symbols) into its equivalent hexadecimal value, prefixed by a % symbol. Penetration testers should try to access Web sites using various URL encoding strategies. There are a number of attacks based on URL encoding techniques.

Step 40: Try Buffer Overflow Attempts in Input Fields

A buffer overflow occurs when a process tries to accommodate more data in the buffer than is allocated for that buffer. As a result, the neighboring memory locations are overwritten with this extra data. An attacker could insert code into this data that can trigger the execution of harmful programs or cause a program to operate in an undesired fashion. In this step, penetration testers attempt buffer overflows by inputting large amounts of data into forms and examining the response. The following tools can be used to initiate a buffer overflow:

- *NTOMax*: This is a server stress-testing tool. This scriptable tool accepts text file inputs and conducts a series of tests over these inputs. The main task of this tool is to find buffer overflows in the server.
- *Hailstorm*: This tool tests for vulnerabilities in compliance with individual customer-specific security policies, as well as for common vulnerabilities.

Step 41: Look for Invalid Ranges in Input Fields

A Web designer may decide to use some of the built-in validation capabilities of a client-side language (such as HTML, JavaScript, or VBScript) to make sure that an input value is not longer (or shorter) than expected. This will ensure that the written code is accepted and the desired output is generated.

A penetration tester should try a random selection of input values or a large range of numbers as input values for testing purposes, and observe the response the server generates.

Step 42: Attempt Escape-Character Injection

Some operating systems will execute system-level commands if they are embedded in an application's data input stream. This occurs when the hidden data is enclosed within escape characters. The application may permit the command to escape up to the process that is currently running the application. The receiving process then attempts to execute the system command using its own system privileges.

Step 43: Try Cross-Site Scripting (XSS) Techniques

Penetration testers should look for cross-site scripting (XSS) vulnerabilities in Web applications. XSS techniques allow attackers to insert malicious code into Web pages and applications.

Step 44: Record and Replay Traffic to Target Web Server and Note Response

Penetration testers can log the responses from servers while recording and replaying the traffic to the target Web servers. A recording session will record everything done during it, including keystrokes, scrolling, and clicking links. The tester can then replay the entire session at any time with the click of a button. When replaying a session, the penetration tester can look for anomalies. The following tools can be used to record and replay traffic:

- *Cruise Control*: is Internet Explorer software that is used for logging and replaying browser sessions. This software can automatically log into Web sites and can store all information required to navigate to a particular place on a Web site.
- *WebLOAD*: is a scalability and integrity-testing solution for Web applications. WebLOAD can exactly imitate what Internet users do and can predict the real life demands on Web applications. It can report the limitations and the weak links in an application prior to deployment.

Step 45: Try Various SQL-Injection Techniques

SQL-injection attacks are attacks in which malicious code is injected into SQL queries. SQL injection attacks can exploit vulnerabilities in the following:

- *Form fields*: Form fields are Web page elements used to gather information.
- *URLs*: Uniform Resource Locators (URLs) are addresses of Web pages.

- *Login screens*: Login screens are used by Web pages and applications to authenticate users.
- *Guestbooks*: Web users use guestbooks to give their opinion on any subject.

The penetration tester can check whether the system is secure against SQL injection attacks by attempting to inject malicious SQL code.

Step 46: Examine Hidden Fields

Hidden fields in Web pages may provide important information. These hidden fields may become a source for compromising sensitive information. For example, hidden fields in Web pages could reveal the following information:

- Price
- Username
- Password
- Encryption used
- Web page behaviors

A penetration tester can check the hidden fields in Web pages and find any possibility of compromised vital information.

Step 47: Examine Server-Side Includes (SSI)

Server-Side Includes (SSI) are placeholders (or markers) in an HTML document that the Web server will dynamically replace with data just before sending the requested document to a browser. The following is an example:

```
<HTML>
<HEAD><TITLE>Show SSI at work</TITLE></HEAD>
<BODY>
<P>Lots of really Interesting stuff to read</P>
<!--#Include file = "copywrite.Inc"-->
</BODY>
</HTML>
```

SSI creates the following potential security risks:

- *Server overloads*: In a shared-server configuration, parsing of SSI-enabled files by Web servers can create a considerable load on servers because the server parses all files, whether the SSI directives are included or not.
- *Risks related to CGI scripts*: SSI files can execute any file containing CGI scripts or programs, which pose a greater server security risk. The danger with an include command comes when an intruder is able to manipulate a Web page into including a file that would otherwise not be available.

The following steps can be taken to secure SSI files:

1. Enable suexec utility.
2. SSI-enabled files should have extensions other than .html or .htm, as these extensions pose greater security risks in a shared-server environment. Administrators should use extensions such as .shtml, which allows for efficient security management.
3. Servers can be configured to disable the running of scripts and programs from SSI files.

Step 48: Examine E-Commerce and Payment Gateways Handled by Web Server

Electronic commerce (e-commerce) refers to the conducting of business on the Internet. This can include buying or selling goods and services over the Internet. A payment gateway is a facility made by a billing processor so that credit card information can be collected and passed over the Internet. A payment gateway could be called the digital equivalent of a credit card processing terminal. There are many payment gateways available; the most popular include Authorize.Net, USA ePay, and Verisign.

To ensure the server is secured for performing e-commerce business and payments and to find any chances of vulnerability, the penetration tester has to look out for the following:

- E-commerce gateways built in-house
- Outsourced e-commerce gateways
- How payments are handled
- Confirmation e-mails
- Minimum order amount
- Account and merchant ID

Step 49: Examine Welcome, Error, and Debug Messages

It is the duty of the penetration tester to check the following Web messages:

- *Web application welcome message*: The welcome messages that appear on the Web pages have to be examined.
- *Web application error messages*: These error messages are displayed when, for example, a wrong password is provided.
- *Web application intrusion warning messages*: These messages are displayed when the Web server detects an intrusion attempt. These messages can give important information about the security structure of Web servers.
- *Web application debugging messages*: A debugging message is displayed when an application is run in debugging mode. Debugging messages give information about the presence of any bugs in applications and problems in application flow.
- *Web application site maintenance messages*: Site maintenance messages are routine messages displayed at regularly specified intervals. These messages remind administrators about the scheduled maintenance of Web sites.

Step 50: Probe the Server by SMTP Mail Bouncing

SMTP mail bouncing indicates that the intended recipient does not exist on that server. Bounced mail carries information about the SMTP server such as server name, version, and various services running on the server, as shown in Figure 8-7.

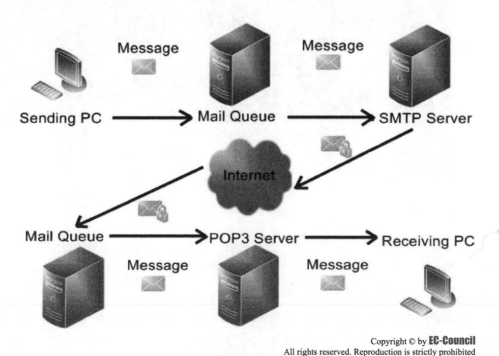

Figure 8-7   Bounced mail carries information about the SMTP server.

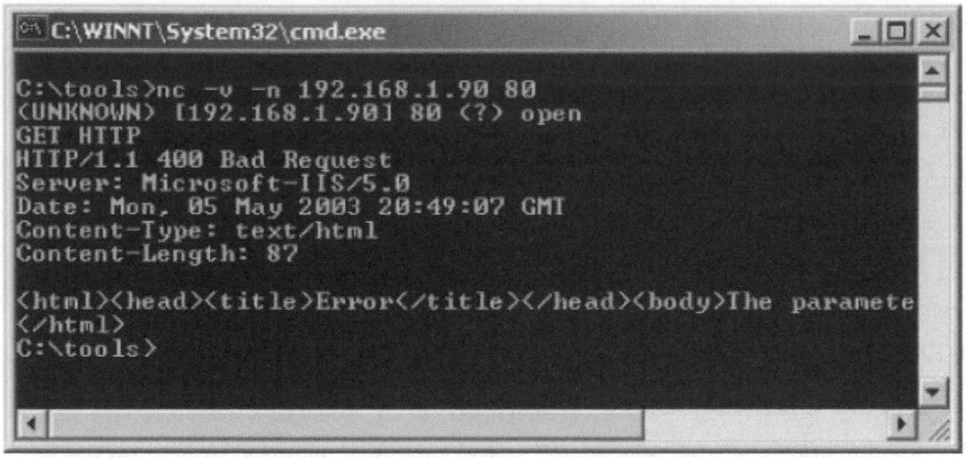

Figure 8-8   Httprint can be used to capture the banners of HTTP servers.

Figure 8-9   GNIT NT Vulnerability Scanner can be used to capture the banners
of POP3 servers.

Step 51: Grab the Banners of HTTP Servers

Httprint is a Web server fingerprinting tool that captures the banners of HTTP servers, as shown in Figure 8-8.

Step 52: Grab the Banners of SMTP Servers

GNIT NT Vulnerability Scanner can be used to capture banner messages from an SMTP server.

Step 53: Grab the Banners of POP3 Servers

GNIT NT Vulnerability Scanner can be used to capture the banners of POP3 servers, as shown in Figure 8-9.

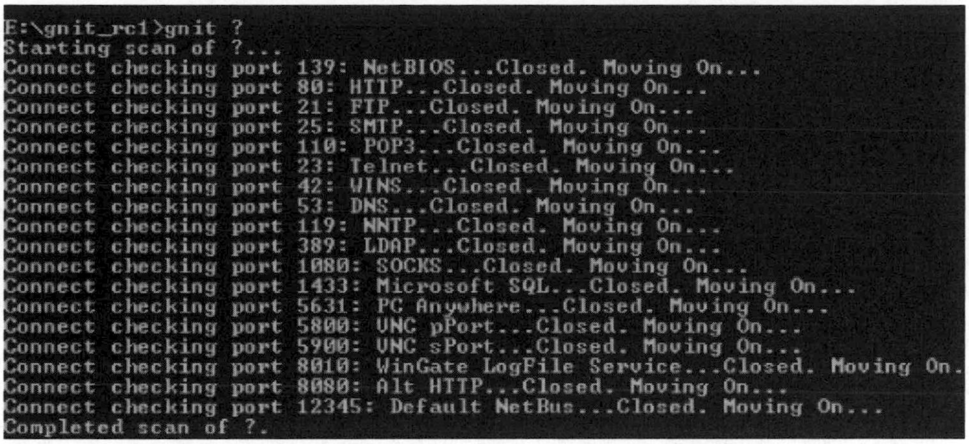

Figure 8-10 GNIT can be used to perform a variety of functions.

Step 54: Grab the Banners of FTP Servers

Netcat can be used to grab the banners of FTP servers. In the simplest usage, **nc <host> <port>** creates a TCP connection to the given port on the given target host. The standard input is then sent to the host, and anything that comes back across the connection is sent to the standard output. This continues indefinitely, until the network side of the connection shuts down.

Step 55: Identify Web Extensions Used on Server

GNIT NT Vulnerability Scanner can be used to perform a number of different functions, as shown in Figure 8-10. It allows the penetration tester to identify which Web extensions the server is using.

Step 56: Try to Use HTTPS Tunnel to Encapsulate Traffic

Penetration testers can use the freeware tunneling software HTTP Tunnel to try to encapsulate all P2P traffic as HTTP and forward it to the corporate network's default gateway over port 80.

Step 57: OS Fingerprint Target Servers

This step identifies an OS using only ICMP packets. The following tools can be used to conduct an OS fingerprint:

- NetScanTools Pro (Figure 8-11)
- Nmap

Step 58: Check for ICMP Responses (Type 3 Port Unreachable)

SYN scan is the default and most popular scan option. It can be performed quickly, scanning thousands of ports per second on a fast network not hampered by intrusive firewalls. A port is marked as filtered if an ICMP unreachable error (type 3, code 1, 2, 3, 9, 10, or 13) is received.

If, according to the information in the gateway's routing tables, the network specified in the Internet destination field of a datagram is unreachable (i.e., the distance to the network is infinity), the gateway may send a destination-unreachable message to the Internet source host of the datagram.

Step 59: Check for ICMP Responses (Type 8 Echo Request)

An echo request is an ICMP message that sends a packet of data to the host and expects those data to be sent in return in an echo reply. The host must respond to all echo requests with an echo reply containing the exact data received in the request message.

Step 60: Check for ICMP Reponses (Type 13 Time-Stamp Request)

The penetration tester should check to see if and how a server responds to a time-stamp request message.

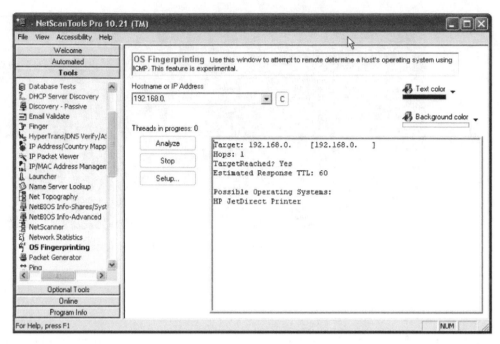

Figure 8-11 NetscanTools Pro can be used to create an OS fingerprint.

Step 61: Check for ICMP Responses (Type 15 Information Request)

Checking for ICMP responses enables a host to learn the network part of an IP address on its subnet by sending a message with the source address in the IP header filled and all zeros in the destination address field. The replying IP module should send the reply with the addresses fully specified. This message is a way for a host to find out the number of the network it is on.

The identifier and sequence number may be used by the echo sender to aid in matching the replies with the requests. For example, the identifier might be used like a port in TCP or UDP to identify a session, and the sequence number might be incremented on each request sent. The destination returns these same values in the reply, as shown in Figure 8-12.

```
Information Request or Information Reply Message

   0                   1                   2                   3
   0 1 2 3 4 5 6 7 8 9 0 1 2 3 4 5 6 7 8 9 0 1 2 3 4 5 6 7 8 9 0 1
  +-+-+-+-+-+-+-+-+-+-+-+-+-+-+-+-+-+-+-+-+-+-+-+-+-+-+-+-+-+-+-+-+
  |     Type      |     Code      |          Checksum             |
  +-+-+-+-+-+-+-+-+-+-+-+-+-+-+-+-+-+-+-+-+-+-+-+-+-+-+-+-+-+-+-+-+
  |           Identifier          |        Sequence Number        |
  +-+-+-+-+-+-+-+-+-+-+-+-+-+-+-+-+-+-+-+-+-+-+-+-+-+-+-+-+-+-+-+-+

IP Fields:

Addresses

     The address of the source in a information request message will be
     the destination of the information reply message.  To form a
     information reply message, the source and destination addresses
     are simply reversed, the type code changed to 16, and the checksum
     recomputed.
```

Figure 8-12 An ICMP reply allows a host to find the number of the network it is on.

Step 62: Check for ICMP Responses (Type 17 Subnet Address Mask Request)

Requests for the correct subnet mask can reveal useful information to penetration testers, as shown in Figure 8-13.

Step 63: Check for ICMP Responses from Broadcast Address

This step reveals the broadcast address in use on the client's subnet. Penetration testers should check for a broadcast IP address by setting the net and subnet (if used) fields to all ones, and then checking if the address is all ones.

Step 64: Port Scan DNS Servers (TCP/UDP 53)

Penetration testers can use Nmap to scan for DNS servers on TCP/UDP port 53. A UDP scan is activated with the -sU option. It can be combined with a TCP scan type, such as SYN scan (-sS), to check both protocols during the same run. The UDP scan works by sending an empty (no data) UDP header to every targeted port, as shown in Figure 8-14.

Step 65: Port Scan TFTP Servers (Port 69)

By default, TFTP servers listen on UDP port 69. Penetration testers can use the PortQry tool to troubleshoot TCP/IP connectivity issues. This utility reports the port status of target TCP and UDP ports on a local computer or on a remote computer. A command similar to the following one should be entered:

The output in Figure 8-15 will be received.

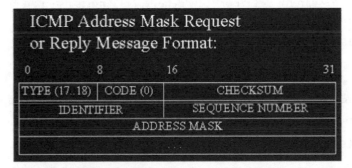

Figure 8-13 Requests for the correct subnet mask can reveal useful information.

```
C:\WINNT\System32\cmd.exe                                           _|□|x|

C:\nmap-3.81>nmap.exe -sS 192.168.1.107 -p 21,22,25,53,80,161,443

Nmap for Windows v3.81
Original version (WinPCap is required) : http://www.insecure.org/nmap
This version (works without WinPCap)   : http://packetstuff.com
Compiled with Packet Sniffer SDK v2.3  : http://microolap.com/pssdk


Starting nmap 3.81 ( http://www.insecure.org/nmap ) at 2006-04-16 11:49 Eastern
Daylight Time
Interesting ports on W2KLAB (192.168.1.107):
PORT     STATE  SERVICE
21/tcp   open   ftp
22/tcp   closed ssh
25/tcp   open   smtp
53/tcp   closed domain
80/tcp   open   http
161/tcp  closed snmp
443/tcp  open   https
MAC Address: 00:0C:29:B0:16:54 (VMware)

Nmap finished: 1 IP address (1 host up) scanned in 0.922 seconds
```

Figure 8-14 DNS servers can be port scanned with Nmap.

```
Querying target system called:

myserver.example.com

Attempting to resolve name to IP address...


Name resolved to 169.254.23.4

querying...

UDP port 69 (tftp service): LISTENING or FILTERED

Sending TFTP query to UDP port 69...

UDP port 69 is LISTENING
```

Figure 8-15   PortQry can be used to scan for TFTP servers.

Step 66: Test for NTP Ports (Port 123)

Nmap can be used to scan for NTP ports. By default, NTP ports listen on port 123. Penetration testers can use the following command to find the NTP service on the network:

```
nmap -sU -p 123 x.x.x.x
```

Step 67: Test for SNMP Ports (Ports 161 and 162)

By default, SNMP listens on ports 161 and 162. Nmap can be used to locate the SNMP service on the network. Penetration testers can use the following commands to find the SNMP service on the network:

```
nmap -sU -p 161 x.x.x.x

nmap -sU -p 162 x.x.x.x
```

Step 68: Test for Telnet Ports (Port 23)

Nmap can be used to scan for telnet ports. By default, telnet listens on port 23.

Step 69: Test for LDAP Ports (Port 389)

PortQry can send an LDAP query by using both TCP and UDP and interpret an LDAP server's response to that query correctly. PortQry parses, formats, and then returns the response from the LDAP server to the user. For example, the penetration tester will receive the output in Figure 8-16 if the following command is entered:

```
portqry -n myserver -p udp -e 389
```

Step 70: Test for NetBIOS Ports (Ports 135–139 and 445)

The default ports used by NetBIOS service are 135, 136, 137, 138, 139, and 445. Nmap can be used to scan for open NetBIOS ports. NAT (NetBIOS Auditing Tool) can also be used to scan for open NetBIOS ports.

Step 71: Test for SQL Server Ports (Ports 1433 and 1434)

By default, SQL servers listen on ports 1433 and 1434. A network scanner can be used to identify open SQL server ports.

```
UDP port 389 (unknown service): LISTENING or FILTERED
Sending LDAP query to UDP port 389...

LDAP query response:

currentdate: 12/13/2003 05:42:40 (unadjusted GMT)
subschemaSubentry: CN=Aggregate,CN=Schema,CN=Configuration,DC=domain,DC=example,DC=com
dsServiceName: CN=NTDS Settings,CN=myserver,CN=Servers,CN=Default-First-Site-Name,CN=Sites,CN=Configura
namingContexts: DC=domain,DC=example,DC=com
defaultNamingContext: DC=domain,DC=example,DC=com
schemaNamingContext: CN=Schema,CN=Configuration,DC=domain,DC=example,DC=com
configurationNamingContext: CN=Configuration,DC=domain,DC=example,DC=com
rootDomainNamingContext: DC=domain,DC=example,DC=com
supportedControl: 1.2.840.113556.1.4.319
supportedLDAPVersion: 3
supportedLDAPPolicies: MaxPoolThreads
highestCommittedUSN: 4269431
supportedSASLMechanisms: GSSAPI
dnsHostName: myserver.domain.example.com
ldapServiceName: domain.example.com:myserver$@domain.EXAMPLE.COM
serverName: CN=myserver,CN=Servers,CN=Default-First-Site-Name,CN=Sites,CN=Configuration,DC=domain,DC=ex
supportedCapabilities: 1.2.840.113556.1.4.800
isSynchronized: TRUE
isGlobalCatalogReady: TRUE
domainFunctionality: 0
forestFunctionality: 0
domainControllerFunctionality: 2

======== End of LDAP query response ========

UDP port 389 is LISTENING
```

Figure 8-16   PortQry can be used to test for LDAP ports.

Step 72: Test for Citrix Ports (Port 1495)

Citrix is a server solution that enables Mac and UNIX users to access Windows programs using Microsoft Terminal Services software. All processing is done on the server, so the user experience is similar to that of a mainframe terminal session, but with the Windows 2000 environment. By default, Citrix listens on port 1495. Penetration testers can scan for the service using a network port scanner.

Step 73: Test for Oracle Ports (Port 1521)

Oracle uses port 1521 for networking services. Penetration testers can use a port scanner such as Nmap to scan for services on port 1521.

Step 74: Test for NFS Ports (Port 2049)

Network File System (NFS) is a network file system protocol, originally developed by Sun Microsystems in 1984, that allows a user on a client computer to access files over a network as easily as if the network devices were attached to its local disks. NFS, like many other protocols, builds on the Open Network Computing Remote Procedure Call (ONC RPC) system.

Penetration testers can use Nmap to conduct an RPC scan to discover NFS ports. By default, NFS listens on port 2049. The following command detects NFS ports:

```
nmap -v -sR -p 2049 x.x.x.x
```

Step 75: Test for Compaq, HP Inside Manager Ports (Ports 2301 and 2381)

By default, HP-UX is installed with the autostart feature enabled. A daemon listens on port 2301 and only starts the System Management Homepage on port 2381 when requested; the daemon then stops it again after a timeout period. Port 2301 is used for the Compaq Insight Management Web Agents. Port 2381 is also the Compaq HTTPS port.

Step 76: Test for Remote Desktop Ports (Port 3389)

Port 3389 is typically blocked to enhance network security. Remote desktop connections use port 3389, so a network port scanner can be used to scan for port 3389. Penetration testers can use the following command to detect the remote desktop service:

```
nmap -sT -p 3389 X.X.X.X
```

Step 77: Test for Sybase Ports (Port 5000)

By default, Sybase listens on port 5000. Penetration testers can use a network scanner to detect the service. They can use the following command:

```
nmap -sT -p 5000 x.x.x.x
```

Step 78: Test for SIP Ports (Port 5060)

Session Initiation Protocol (SIP) is an application-layer control (signaling) protocol for creating, modifying, and terminating sessions with one or more participants. These sessions include Internet telephone calls, multimedia distribution, and multimedia conferences.

SIP clients use TCP or UDP, typically using port 5060, to connect to SIP servers and other SIP endpoints. SIP is primarily used in setting up and tearing down voice or video calls. However, it can be used in any application where session initiation is a requirement. These include event subscription and notification, terminal mobility, and so on.

SIP can be regarded as the enabler protocol for telephony and voice over IP (VoIP) services. By default, SIP listens on port 5060. Penetration testers can run a port scan on the network to find whether any VoIP service is running.

Step 79: Test for VNC Ports (Ports 5800 and 5900)

Virtual Network Computing (VNC) is a graphical desktop sharing system that uses the RFB (Remote Frame Buffer) protocol to remotely control another computer. It transmits the keyboard and mouse events from one computer to another, relaying the graphical screen updates back in the other direction, over a network.

VNC is platform independent. A VNC viewer on any operating system can usually connect to a VNC server on any other operating system. There are clients and servers for almost all GUI operating systems, as well as for Java. Multiple clients may connect to a VNC server at the same time. Popular uses for this technology include remote technical support and accessing files on a work computer from a home computer.

VNC works on port 5900 by default. The Java Viewer works on port 5800. Penetration testers can scan for these default ports using a network scanner.

Step 80: Test for X11 Ports (Port 6000)

The X Window System (commonly X11 or X) is a networking and display protocol that provides windowing on bitmap displays. It provides the standard toolkit and protocol to build graphical user interfaces (GUIs) on UNIX, UNIX-like operating systems, and OpenVMS, and is supported by almost all other modern operating systems.

X provides the basic framework, or primitives, for building GUI environments: drawing and moving windows on the screen and interacting with a mouse and/or keyboard. X does not mandate the user interface; individual client programs handle this. As such, the visual styling of X-based environments varies greatly; different programs may present radically different interfaces.

X features network transparency. The machine where application programs (the client applications) run can differ from the user's local machine (the display server).

By default, the X server listens on port 6000 for incoming connections. Penetration testers can scan for port 6000 using Nmap.

Step 81: Test for JetDirect Ports (Port 9100)

Penetration testers can scan for JetDirect ports (port 9100) with Nmap. HP printers use this port for the JetDirect protocol.

Step 82: Port Scan FTP Data (Port 20)

In PORT mode, the FTP server always sends data from TCP port 20. Penetration testers can use Nmap to scan the network for open FTP ports.

Step 83: Port Scan Web Servers (Port 80)

This scan determines TCP and UDP ports that use port 80 for transporting HTTP data from a Web server, as shown in Figure 8-17.

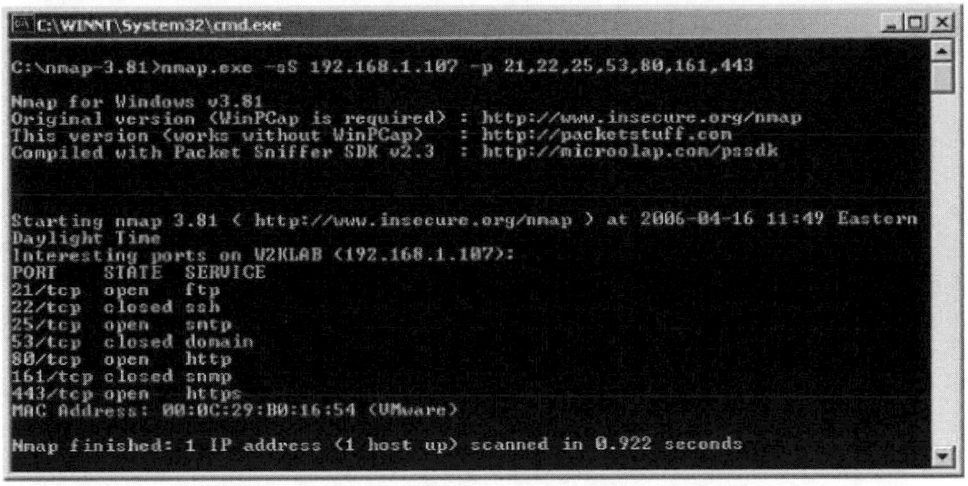

Figure 8-17   Nmap can be used to scan for port 80 on Web servers.

Step 84: Port Scan SSL Servers (Port 443)

The -sV scan option in Nmap identifies SSL services. Penetration testers can use the following command:

```
nmap -F -sV x.x.x.x
```

Step 85: Port Scan Kerberos-Active Directory (Port TCP/UDP 88)

Kerberos-Active Directory uses port 88 as its default port. Penetration testers can port scan the network for services listening on port 88.

Step 86: Port Scan SSH Servers (Port 22)

By default, SSH servers listen on port 22. Penetration testers can use Nmap to identify the service with the following command:

```
nmap -sS -p 22 x.x.x.x
```

Chapter Summary

- External penetration testing evaluates the strengths and weaknesses of an organization's internal and external architecture by using the Internet.
- To create a topological map of a network, a topological diagram of the external IT infrastructure must be constructed.
- NeoTrace can be used to trace any computer present on the Internet by entering an e-mail address, IP address, or URL.
- The DNS server translates hostnames to IP addresses.
- Once a port is closed, any request made to a machine via the closed port will result in an acknowledgment from the machine that the port is closed.
- From a TCP SYN scan, the state of ports (open, closed, and filtered) can be distinctly identified.
- Using unknown protocols affects some intrusion detection systems because these systems are unable to detect vulnerabilities in these protocols.
- Sensitive information can be revealed by analyzing HTML source code.

## Chapter 9

Internal Network Penetration Testing

Objectives

After completing this chapter, you should be able to:

- Conduct internal network penetration testing
- Map an internal network
- Port-scan individual machines
- Plant viruses, Trojans, and rootkits on a target machine
- Hide sensitive information
- Capture a variety of traffic
- Use Wireshark
- Poison a victim's proxy server
- Hijack a variety of sessions

Key Terms

Internal network penetration testing a type of penetration testing that focuses on the security weaknesses and strengths of an organization's computers and devices from within the company

MAC flooding a computer network enumeration and footprinting technique (attack) that involves the spoofing of a network interface's unique MAC address

Man-in-the-middle attack an attack that intercepts network traffic flowing between the application and the victim system

Null sessions unauthenticated connections to a Windows NT or 2000 system

Packet sniffing the process of listening (with software) to a raw network device for packets that are of interest

Password sniffing the process of gathering passwords and user information by using sniffing tools

Port scanning a scanning process that determines the open ports on a machine

Rootkit a collection of tools that enables an attacker to hide the fact that he or she has gained administrative privileges

Introduction to Internal Network Penetration Testing

Internal network penetration testing involves testing the security weaknesses and strengths of an organization's computers and devices from within the company. It includes checking the site location and connecting to the internal network. It is mainly performed to check for known vulnerabilities that could be exploited.

Internal penetration testing is carried out from within an organization. It uses almost the same tools and methods as external penetration testing to test the internal network. The difference is that external penetration testing is conducted from outside an organization, so it generally focuses on unknown vulnerabilities. Internal penetration testing highlights the following elements of an organization's network:

- Protocol and network infrastructure vulnerabilities
- Server operating system and application vulnerabilities
- Internal controls and procedures
- Unsuitable user privileges
- Internal "intrawalls" separating subnetworks

The following scenarios need to be addressed when conducting an internal penetration test:

- What if an employee with knowledge of the IT infrastructure penetrates the network?
- What if a hacker breaks into the internal networks that house employees' PCs and databases, and steals sensitive information?
- What if a casual guest or visitor walks into the company and steals data from an isolated machine?

Steps for Internal Network Penetration Testing

The following steps should be carried out when conducting internal network penetration testing:

1. Map the internal network.
2. Scan the network for live hosts.
3. Port-scan individual machines.
4. Try to gain access using known vulnerabilities.
5. Attempt to establish null sessions.
6. Enumerate users/identify domains on the network.
7. Sniff the network using Wireshark.
8. Sniff POP3/FTP/telnet passwords.
9. Sniff e-mail messages.
10. Attempt replay attacks.
11. Attempt ARP poisoning.
12. Attempt MAC flooding.
13. Conduct man-in-the-middle attacks.
14. Attempt DNS poisoning.
15. Try logging in to a console machine.
16. Boot the PC using an alternate OS and steal the SAM file.
17. Bypass the OS to obtain information.
18. Reset the administrator password.
19. Attempt to plant a software keylogger to steal passwords.
20. Attempt to plant a hardware keylogger to steal passwords.
21. Attempt to plant spyware on the target machine.
22. Attempt to plant a Trojan on the target machine.
23. Attempt to bypass antivirus software installed on the target machine.

24. Attempt to send a virus using the target machine.
25. Attempt to plant rootkits on the target machine.
26. Hide sensitive data on target machines.
27. Hide hacking tools and other data on target machines.
28. Use various steganography techniques to hide files on target machines.
29. Escalate user privileges.
30. Capture POP3 traffic.
31. Capture SMTP traffic.
32. Capture IMAP e-mail traffic.
33. Capture the communications between FTP client and FTP server.
34. Capture HTTP traffic.
35. Capture RDP traffic.
36. Capture VoIP traffic.
37. Run Wireshark with the filter -ip.src == ip_address.
38. Run Wireshark with the filter -ip.dst == ip_address.
39. Run Wireshark with the filter -tcp.dstport == port_no.
40. Run Wireshark with the filter -ip.addr == ip_address.
41. Spoof the MAC address.
42. Poison the victim's IE proxy server.
43. Attempt session hijacking on telnet traffic.
44. Attempt session hijacking on FTP traffic.
45. Attempt session hijacking on HTTP traffic.
46. Document everything.

Step 1: Map the Internal Network

The first step a penetration tester should follow is to map the internal network by identifying the following components:

- *Number of subnets*: A subnet is a set of networked computers with the same IP routing prefix. Subnets are established to divide a network into smaller parts for efficiency.
- *Number of hosts*: The number of hosts shows the penetration tester how many computers need to be involved in the test.
- *Operating systems running on each host*: The penetration tester should check which operating systems are running on each host to help plan for testing OS-specific vulnerabilities.

Step 2: Scan the Network for Live Hosts

The penetration tester should check for live hosts on the network using the following tools:

- *Angry IP Scanner*: Angry IP Scanner is a small but fast IP scanner that can scan IPs in any range and allows the user to ping each IP address to check whether or not it is alive. It verifies an IP address, scans ports, and determines the hostname related to an IP address. This tool employs different threads for each scanned address to reduce scanning speed. It shows NetBIOS information such as host computer name, MAC address, and currently logged-in user.
- *Network Scanner*: Network Scanner is a multithreaded IP, SNMP, and NetBIOS scanner with a user-friendly interface. Computer security analysts and system administrators use this tool for scanning the network. It is used to accomplish the following tasks:
  - Ping computers
  - Scan for listening TCP ports

- Display types of resources that are shared on the network
- Permit the mounting of shared resources as network drives
- Browse those resources using Windows Explorer
- Filter the results list
- Check for user-defined ports
- Resolve hostname and autodetect local IP ranges

Step 3: Port-Scan Individual Machines

The next step the penetration tester should perform is to port-scan the individual machines. *Port scanning* determines the open ports on a machine. It also determines the various services running on the host system. Each service is identified by its port number. Such ports are referred to as well-known ports (as defined by IANA).

Port-scanning software, in its most basic form, simply sends out a request to connect to the target computer on each port sequentially and makes a note of which ports respond or seem open to more in-depth probing. A port scan is a method used by penetration testers to determine what ports are open or in use on a system or network. By using various tools, a penetration tester can send data to TCP or UDP ports one at a time. Based on the response received, the port scan utility can determine if that port is in use. Using this information, the penetration tester can then focus the attack on the ports that are open and try to exploit any weaknesses to gain access. A port scan will return the following responses:

- *Open ports*: The target host system sends a reply signifying that a service exists with the valid port number.
- *Closed ports*: These responses signify that the connection to a port is refused.
- *Blocked ports*: These indicate a no-reply message from the host.

Once the open ports on a network have been discovered, the necessity for those ports to be accessible from outside the network can be determined. If it is not necessary for those ports to be open, they should be shut down or blocked.

The following well-known ports should be scanned:

- 21: FTP
- 23: Telnet
- 25: SMTP
- 53: DNS
- 80: HTTP
- 110: POP3
- 137: NetBIOS

Step 4: Try to Gain Access Using Known Vulnerabilities

In this stage of internal testing, vulnerability research is conducted on the internal systems to identify software vulnerabilities. Systems are exploited based on these vulnerabilities.

After determining the open ports through a port scan, the penetration tester can begin work determining vulnerabilities present on the services used by those ports.

The goal of running a vulnerability scanner is to identify devices on the network that are open to known vulnerabilities. Different scanners accomplish this goal through different means. Some work better than others.

The following commercial vulnerability-scanning packages are highly rated:

- *Nessus*: This vulnerability scanner checks for software security bugs. It identifies live hosts, gathers operating system information, performs port scanning and vulnerability scanning, and grabs banners to attempt to exploit known software vulnerabilities.
- *Retina*: Retina identifies software vulnerabilities and other existing vulnerabilities on the network, finds common security holes in the network, and determines protocols running on the ports.
- *GFI LANguard Network Security Scanner*: This tool can be used to scan the network for missing security patches and service packs, open shares, open ports, unused user accounts, and so on.

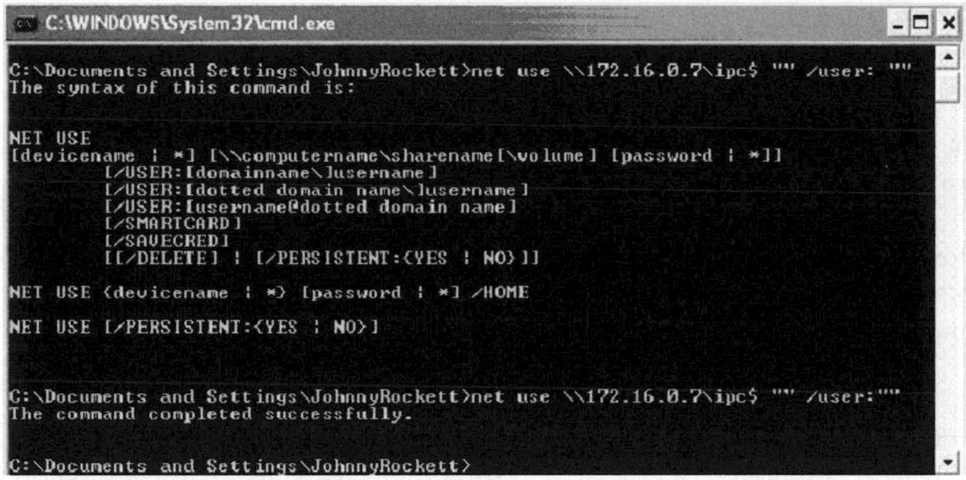

Figure 9-1 Null sessions can be used to gain a great deal of information about Windows NT and 2000 systems.

Step 5: Attempt to Establish Null Sessions

Null sessions are unauthenticated connections to a Windows NT or 2000 system. The following command can be used to establish a null session:

```
net use \\192.168.6.8\IPC$ "" /u:""
```

The preceding syntax connects to the hidden interprocess communications share (IPC$) at IP address 192.168.6.8 as the built-in anonymous user (/u:"") with a null ("") password. If successful, the penetration tester now has an open channel over which to attempt various techniques that can be used to gather as much information as possible from the target, i.e., network information, shares, users, groups, registry keys, and so on. See Figure 9-1.

Step 6: Enumerate Users/Identify Domains

Based on the established null session, the penetration tester can extract the following information:

- User accounts on the target system
- Password policies
- Group policies

The following tools can be used for enumeration:

- *GetAcct*: This tool allows a user to enumerate user account information on Windows NT/2000 systems by providing the IP address or NetBIOS name of the target machine, bypassing "RestrictAnonymous=1."
- *Winfingerprint*: This allows a user to enumerate NetBIOS shares, users, services, null IPC$ sessions, local and global groups, etc., by providing an IP address range. The user can also identify the domains that exist on the network.

Step 7: Sniff the Network Using Wireshark

Packet sniffing is listening (with software) to a raw network device for packets that are of interest. When the software sees a packet that fits certain criteria, it logs it to a file. The most common criterion for an interesting packet is one that contains words like *login* or *password*.

The penetration tester should sniff the network and extract the following information:

- Usernames and passwords
- Sensitive information

- Network mapping
- Operating system fingerprinting

The following tools are used to sniff the network:

- *Wireshark*: This tool sniffs the packets that pass through the target machine. This tool is also useful for troubleshooting, network analysis, and protocol development.
- *Tcpdump*: This tool analyzes packet headers, captures packets related to a specific file, and saves the file for later analysis.
- *EtherPeek*: This tool determines the systems that are communicating over the network. EtherPeek also pinpoints network problems and simplifies network analysis.

Step 8: Sniff POP3/FTP/Telnet Passwords

Password sniffing refers to gathering passwords and user information by using sniffing tools. A penetration tester should try to sniff POP3/FTP/telnet passwords by connecting to the network. A penetration tester sniffs passwords to analyze how strong those that protect sensitive information are. Passwords are also sniffed to examine how secure they are against guessing and other password-cracking attacks. Passwords can be sniffed using the following tools:

- *Dsniff*: This tool allows the user to audit the network for common sniffing techniques. This tool handles protocols for FTP, POP3, telnet, HTTP, Symantec pcAnywhere, Microsoft SMB, Oracle SQL*Net, Sybase, Microsoft SQL, and others. The Dsniff software package includes the following tools:
  - arpspoof: Sends out unrequested (and possibly forged) ARP replies
  - dsniff: A password sniffer for several protocols
  - webspy: Sends URLs sniffed from a client to the local browser
  - filesnarf: Saves selected files sniffed from NFS traffic
  - dnsspoof: Forges replies to arbitrary DNS address/pointer queries on the LAN
  - macof: Floods the local network with random MAC addresses
- *Ace Password Sniffer*: This tool listens on the LAN and captures passwords for POP3, FTP, HTTP, telnet, and other protocols.

Step 9: Sniff E-Mail Messages

Penetration testers can test the privacy of Internet communications by sniffing e-mail messages. They can connect systems to the hub and listen to SMTP and POP traffic to sniff e-mail messages that go through the network. Internet communications can be sniffed using the following tools:

- *mailsnarf*: The mailsnarf tool allows a user to save the e-mail messages that are sniffed from SMTP and POP traffic. Messages are stored in the Berkeley mbox format.
- *Dsniff*: Dsniff consists of a collection of tools for sniffing passwords, e-mail, and HTTP traffic. Dsniff's tools include dsniff, arpredirect, macof, tcpkill, tcpnice, filesnarf, mailsnarf, urlsnarf, and webspy. It is an effective sniffer for both switched and shared networks.
- *Linsniff*: Linsniff is a Linux sniffer that captures the first few bytes of each TCP connection to the ports for telnet, FTP, POP, IMAP, and rlogin. Captured information includes date, time, source IP address, destination IP address, destination port, and the first 256 bytes of captured data.
- *Tcpdump*: Tcpdump is a simple, easy-to-use sniffer that enables the user to capture traffic on a network segment. Tcpdump only offers a command-line interface. Using different options, the user can configure Tcpdump to look for specific traffic.
- *BUTTSniffer*: BUTTSniffer is a Windows NT packet sniffer. BUTTSniffer's filters can be used to sniff specific ports or to capture all data on a segment.
- *SessionWall-3*: SessionWall-3 is a commercial sniffing tool and intrusion detection product. Although the product is sold as an intrusion detection system, it also works well as a sniffing tool for testing a network. Using sniffing technology, SessionWall-3 records and displays HTTP, FTP, SMTP, POP, NNTP, and telnet traffic. The tool reassembles the network traffic into legible documents. Telnet and

FTP traffic tends to be the most useful, since usernames and passwords are displayed in clear text and commonly enable the user to gain administrator access to the target system.

Step 10: Attempt Replay Attacks

In this step of internal penetration testing, the penetration tester attempts to exploit the security weaknesses in the LM hash encryption to capture passwords. LM hash password usage is inherently weak, as it stores passwords in two 7-bit sections, which are quite easy to crack. Once a user's credentials are captured, a tester can use them to "replay" the original login and enter the system pretending to be the user. The following tools are used for this attack:

- *L0phtCrack*: This tool allows the user to recover, assess, and decode hashes, and judge passwords through password scanning, dictionary lookup, and brute force attacks.
- *RainbowCrack*: The RainbowCrack hash cracker tool audits password policies. This tool operates by comparing the precalculated password hash value with that of the operating system.
- *Cain & Abel*: Passwords can be sniffed using the Cain & Abel tool. This password recovery tool uses password calculators and decoders to crack common hashes and specific authentication hashes, as well as to calculate common hash algorithms.

Step 11: Attempt ARP Poisoning

ARP resolves IP addresses to MAC (hardware) addresses. When a network device sends an ARP request, it does not verify whether the ARP reply received came from the intended device. In fact, many operating systems implement ARP so trustingly that devices that have not made any ARP requests will still accept ARP replies from other devices.

The attacker can craft a malicious ARP reply that contains arbitrary IP and MAC addresses. Since the victim computer blindly accepts the ARP entry into its ARP table, this reply can force the victim computer to think that any IP is related to the MAC address the attacker wants. The attacker can broadcast this faked ARP reply to the victim's entire network. The following tools can be used to attempt ARP poisoning:

- *arpspoof*: The arpspoof tool comes with the Dsniff collection of tools. Arpspoof redirects packets from a target host (or all hosts) on the LAN to another host on the LAN by forging ARP replies. This is an effective way of sniffing traffic on a switch.
- *Arpoison*: This UNIX-based command-line tool creates ARP replies. It sends spoofed ARP replies to the target by specifying source and destination IP and MAC addresses.
- *Ettercap*: Ettercap allows users to sniff live LAN connections. This tool automates all operations.
- *Parasite*: Parasite allows a user to conduct a man-in-the-middle attack by sniffing network traffic from a switched network. This tool watches ARP requests and automatically sends ARP replies.

Step 12: Attempt MAC Flooding

Penetration testers can try to sniff network traffic by flooding the network switch with false MAC addresses. *MAC flooding* is a computer network enumeration and footprinting technique (attack) that involves the spoofing of a network interface's unique MAC address. The technique focuses on the limited ability of network switches to store MAC addresses to physical port mappings internally. By flooding a switch with packets containing different source MAC addresses, the attack causes the switch to enter a state called failopen mode, in which all incoming packets are broadcast on all ports. This allows the attacking computer to view all legitimate network traffic routed through the affected switch. This visible traffic allows the attacker to gather information about network topology, domain services, and individual machines that would otherwise be hidden by the switch.

The macof tool allows the user to flood the LAN switch with random MAC addresses. macof floods the LAN switch with 150,000 Ethernet packets per minute and tries to alter routing or ARP tables. Changes in these tables facilitate sniffing and entering the network.

Step 13: Conduct Man-In-The-Middle Attacks

A *man-in-the-middle attack* is the most powerful form of gaining control over system resources. The attacker intercepts network traffic flowing between the application and the victim system. Man-in-the-middle attacks can be conducted by spoofing IP, ARP, and MAC addresses. Man-in-the-middle (MITM) attacks can be conducted inside the network by using the following techniques:

- *DNS cache poisoning*: The tester can send false replies to DNS server requests for IP addresses. The tester can then try to direct the victim system to a fake site. The following tools can be used to carry out DNS cache poisoning:
  - DNSA
  - Dnsspoof
  - TinyDNS
  - DNSCache

- *ARP spoofing*: The tester can send spoofed ARP replies to application systems, identifying them as coming from the victim's system. Similarly, he or she can send spoofed ARP replies to the victim's system, identifying them as coming from the application system. The following tools are used for sending spoofed ARP packets:
  - Arpoison
  - Arpspoof
  - Ettercap
  - Parasite

Step 14: Attempt DNS Poisoning

In this step, the penetration tester attempts to poison the DNS server by modifying the file that contains the mappings of IP addresses to host names. In Windows operating systems, the file is at the following location:

`C:\winnt\system32\drivers\etc\hosts`

The tester can poison the IP address DNS entries and replace them with the IP address of a server that is already being controlled, as shown in Figure 9-2. The following tools are used to carry out DNS cache poisoning:

- *Dnsspoof*: This tool can be obtained with the Dsniff package of tools. The tester can forge replies to DNS queries on the LAN by using this tool.
- *DNSA*: This is a Linux-based DNS security tool that is used for injecting forged DNS packets.

```
# Copyright (c) 1993-1999 Microsoft Corp.
#
# This is a sample HOSTS file used by Microsoft TCP/IP for Windows.
#
# This file contains the mappings of IP addresses to host names. Each
# entry should be kept on an individual line. The IP address should
# be placed in the first column followed by the corresponding host
name.
# The IP address and the host name should be separated by at least
one
# space.
#
# Additionally, comments (such as these) may be inserted on
individual
# lines or following the machine name denoted by a '#' symbol.
#
# For example:
#
# 102.54.94.97 rhino.acme.com # source server
# 38.25.63.10 x.acme.com # x client host

127.0.0.1 localhost
XX.XX.XX.XX Citibank.com
```

Figure 9-2   A DNS server can be poisoned by modifying the hosts file.

Step 15: Try Logging In to a Console Machine

In this step, the tester tries to log in to a remote console machine by using default passwords, as shown in Figure 9-3. He or she tries the following easily guessable passwords to log in to a console machine:

- Blank passwords or no passwords
- Name of the user
- Similar or same passwords for all the systems in the network
- The name of the host
- Password related to a detail about the user
- Last name as password
- Temporary passwords (which may be the same for all systems)

Password reminders are also helpful when trying to guess passwords.

Step 16: Boot the PC Using an Alternate OS and Steal the SAM File

The penetration tester can attempt to bypass system authentication by booting the PC using another operating system, such as Knoppix. Knoppix is an open-source Live Linux CD. This Linux software is used to boot and run the PC using only the CD.

The tester then uses the following steps to steal the SAM file using the alternate operating system:

1. *Boot the system using Knoppix*: Insert the Knoppix Live Linux CD and boot the system.
2. *Mount the system drive*: Identify the system drive and mount it.
3. *Copy the SAM file to a floppy*: Figure 9-4 shows the commands for mounting the system drive and copying the SAM file to a floppy.
4. *Shut down the system and remove the Knoppix CD*: Also, remove the floppy on which the SAM file was copied.

Figure 9-3 Passwords can often be guessed by using common default entries.

```
#mount -t vfat -o ro /dev/hda1 /mnt/hda1

#cp /mnt/hda1/windows/system32/config/sam .

#cp sam /dev/fd0
#umount /dev/hda1
#halt
```

Figure 9-4   A Knoppix Live CD can be used to copy the SAM file.

Step 17: Bypass the OS to Obtain Information

A tool like ERD Commander 2005 allows the penetration tester to bypass the operating system and obtain full access to the system resources and configuration settings. This tool gives users read/write access to files and allows them to perform the following functions on the system:

- Remove or replace buggy drivers
- Update out-of-date system files
- Correct misconfigured NTFS or registry security
- Update locked files
- Correct registry problems
- Recover deleted files
- Copy important files from a dead system
- Regain access to a system that the user has been locked out of
- View event logs
- Run CHKDSK on corrupt drives
- Enable and disable services and drivers
- Restore Windows XP restore points
- Compare a working system with a dead system
- Partition and format disks
- Scan a dead system for viruses
- Register COM/DCOM server DLLs

Step 18: Reset Administrator Password

In this step, the penetration tester attempts to reset the administrator password for Windows NT/2000/XP/Server 2003 by using a tool like NTLocksmith. NTLocksmith allows users to access the system under any account and to recover the administrator password. This software requires NTRecover to operate.

The following steps are used to recover administrator passwords:

1. Launch NTLocksmith
2. Select the location of the Windows registry that needs to be changed
3. Select the user account (in this case, administrator) for which the password needs to be changed
4. Enter a new password
5. Close NTLocksmith and reboot the system for which the password was changed
6. Log in with the new password

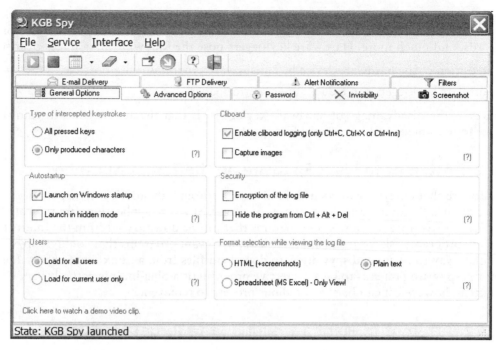

Figure 9-5   KGB Spy is an example of keylogging software.

Step 19: Attempt to Plant a Software Keylogger to Steal Passwords

Keyloggers record all the keystrokes on the target machine. These keystrokes can include passwords as well. Keyloggers store all records in a file and send that file to the attacker via e-mail.

Keyloggers can provide the following information:

- Record of active applications
- Keystrokes
- Screenshots
- Other user actions

The following tools can be used as keyloggers:

- *KGB Spy*: KGB Spy (Figure 9-5) is an example of keylogging software that provides multiple functionalities, such as recording language-specific characters. It also records details such as the time and date of a particular Windows initialization.
- *Realtime-Spy*: Realtime-Spy is a remote spy software solution that requires no physical installation and allows viewing of activity logs from any location at any time.
- *SpyAgent*: Spytech SpyAgent logs everything users do, including all keystrokes, e-mails, applications, windows, Web sites, Internet connections, passwords, chat conversations, and even screenshots. SpyAgent can run in total stealth mode, defeat popular spyware detectors, and provide Web site, chat, and application blocking abilities.
- *Elite Remote Keylogger*: Elite Keylogger works in low-kernel mode as driver-based monitoring software that records every detail of PC and Internet activity.

Step 20: Attempt to Plant a Hardware Keylogger to Steal Passwords

A hardware keylogger is a device that is used to track all keystrokes, even without installing software. This device can be attached between the keyboard and the computer. It keeps track of all activities performed through the keyboard. The moment this device is attached to the system, every keystroke is recorded. These keystrokes may include e-mails, IMs (instant messages), documentation, searches done on the Web, login IDs, passwords, and much more. Hardware keyloggers pose the following advantages over software keyloggers:

- Detection of the hardware device by antispyware programs is not possible.
- Software keyloggers can reduce system performance.

However, the disadvantage of hardware keyloggers is that the attacker has to gain physical access to the machine to both place and retrieve the keylogger.

Step 21: Attempt to Plant Spyware on the Target Machine

Any software that covertly gathers user information through the user's Internet connection without his or her knowledge, usually for advertising purposes, is illegal. Spyware applications are typically bundled as a hidden component of freeware or shareware programs that can be downloaded from the Internet. For example, many shareware programs ask for installation of extra, irrelevant programs that could be spyware.

Another way to download spyware is to download files from an unknown or unsafe source. For example, sometimes spyware pretends to be a corrective program or a plug-in. It is actually very easy to install spyware on a system; however, it can be a very tedious process to remove it.

Step 22: Attempt to Plant a Trojan on the Target Machine

Trojans are malicious programs that hamper security, causing considerable damage to both the hardware and software contents of a system. A Trojan can be a hidden program that runs on the computer without the user's knowledge, or it can be wrapped into a legitimate program. This program may have hidden functionalities that the user is unaware of.

For example, if an attacker sends a Trojan disguised as animated .JPEG files and the recipient opens them on his or her system, the Trojan enters the recipient's system and gradually causes extensive damage to it. A common use of a Trojan horse is to install backdoors to allow a user to come back into a system later, as shown in Figure 9-6. A Trojan can be installed onto a target system in the following ways:

- *Instant messenger applications*: Users can accept files in instant messenger applications, and these files may contain Trojans.
- *IRC (Internet relay chat)*: Files that claim to be free porn utilities or Internet software often contain Trojans.
- *Via attachments*: Trojans can be bundled along with legitimate software and passed to the target.
- *NetBIOS (file sharing)*: If port 139 on the system is open, file sharing is enabled. This is another way for someone to access the system, install a Trojan, and modify a system file so that the Trojan will run the next time the PC is restarted.

The following Trojans have been used in the past to infiltrate systems:

- *Banker.BSK*: Banker.BSK is a Trojan that falls under the category of password stealer. It affects Windows 2003/XP/2000/NT/ME/98/95. The following functions can be performed by Banker.BSK:
  - Opens port 1106 and resides in memory
  - Examines the Web pages accessed by the user that are related to banking in Spanish-speaking countries
  - Records the actions performed by the user after accessing the Web site. These actions can also include logins and entering passwords.
  - Sends the recorded data to the attacker via e-mail
- *Metafile*: Metafile is a Trojan that was written to exploit the vulnerabilities of Windows. It affects Windows 2003/XP/2000/NT/ME/98. Internet Explorer, Outlook, Windows Picture and Fax Viewer, and other programs like these use the library GDI32.DLL. Metafile exploits a vulnerability in this library. Metafile executes random code on the victim's computer. A Windows Metafile (WMF) image is created to exploit the vulnerability and then it is distributed.

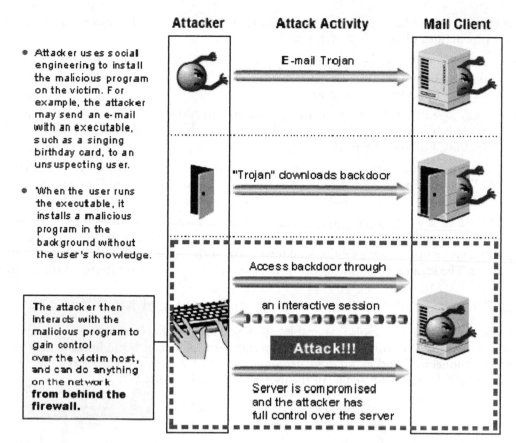

Attacker

Attack Activity

Mail Client

- Attacker uses social engineering to install the malicious program on the victim. For example, the attacker may send an e-mail with an executable, such as a singing birthday card, to an unsuspecting user.

- When the user runs the executable, it installs a malicious program in the background without the user's knowledge.

The attacker then interacts with the malicious program to gain control over the victim host, and can do anything on the network **from behind the firewall.**

E-mail Trojan

"Trojan" downloads backdoor

Access backdoor through
an interactive session

Attack!!!

Server is compromised and the attacker has full control over the server

Figure 9-6   Trojans can be used to install backdoors that can be accessed at a later time.

- *Backdoor.Icmpcmd.10*: Backdoor.IcmpCmd.10 is a remote administration tool. It is a backdoor that allows unauthorized remote access to the target system. Attackers can place server programs in the target system and connect there via client programs. It includes the following features:
  - Hides from the user
  - Resides in the background
  - Permits remote user connections
- *Beast*: Beast is a powerful remote administration tool built with Delphi 7. One of the distinct features of Beast is that it is an all-in-one Trojan (client, server, and server editor are stored in the same application).

Step 23: Attempt to Bypass Antivirus Software Installed on the Target Machine

In this step, penetration testers identify whether antivirus software is configured on the target system. If antivirus software is found, a tester can attempt to bypass the software. Antivirus software uses signatures to detect malware. It is possible to modify or alter the signatures of known Trojans and attempt to bypass antivirus software.

Step 24: Attempt to Send a Virus Using the Target Machine

Penetration testers can inject a virus into the target machine and see how the virus spreads through the network. Any system that accesses the target machine is affected by the virus. These infected machines might, in turn, distribute the virus. The target machine might embed a malicious link in the body of an e-mail message which, when clicked, establishes a connection with the target machine, which is already infected. The following list of viruses give an idea of how they each function:

- *Sober worm*: The Sober worm was discovered on October 23, 2003. It is a mass-mailing worm, which makes use of Simple Mail Transfer Protocol (SMTP) for self-transmission. This worm can compose its e-mails in German or in English.

- *Blaster worm*: The Blaster worm was discovered in 2003. It is a worm that exploits the security of the Remote Procedure Call (RPC). It attacks systems with outdated software. It especially attacks Windows 2000 and Windows XP platforms.

- *Klez worm*: This worm is transferred from system to system through e-mails and attachments. Windows 98, Windows 95, Windows 2000, Windows NT, Windows XP, and Windows ME are the likely victims of this worm.

- *ILOVEYOU virus*: VBS/LoveLetter is a VBScript worm. It spreads over e-mail as a chain letter. The worm uses the Outlook e-mail application to spread. When the script is executed, the virus sends itself to everyone in the user's Outlook address book. It then deletes files of certain types from the user's hard drive. The script also performs other malicious activities, such as altering certain registry settings.

Step 25: Attempt to Plant Rootkits on the Target Machine

A *rootkit* is a collection of tools that enables an attacker to hide the fact that he or she has gained administrative privileges. They are considered the most menacing form of Trojan horse because they can even alter existing system components. Rootkits are installed onto the target system and enable the intruder to enter the system through a backdoor and act as one of the users, as shown in Figure 9-7.

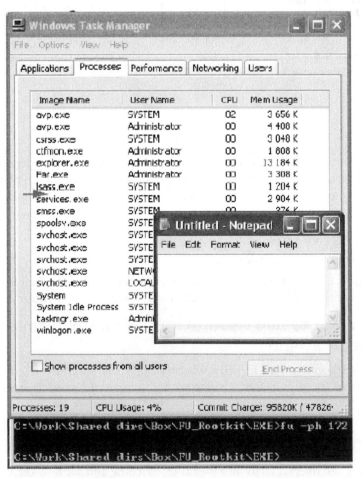

Figure 9-7 Rootkits can be installed on a computer and allow the attacker access to sensitive information.

Intruders gain access to the target system through a known vulnerability. They drop the rootkit files onto the system. Intruders can then include a backdoor and compromise the target system. Most rootkits are installed using administrator-level access. Rootkits enable intruders to perform the following actions:

- Monitor and change the data in files
- Replace system executables to corrupt the system
- Remove traces of their actions after completing their tasks
- Compromise the system so that they can control it at their convenience
- Access the system through the backdoor, even if the system administrator changes the password of the root user

Step 26: Hide Sensitive Data on Target Machines

The following data items should be hidden on target machines:

- *IP addresses*: An IP address is a unique Internet identifier for a local or a remote system connected to the Internet.
- *Source code*: This is the piece of code written by a developer in a high-level language. This code gets converted into machine code after compilation. To prevent this code from getting copied and being misused, it is a good idea to hide the source code.
- *Pictures*: Hide all pictures that carry sensitive information on the system and also hide photographs to prevent morphing, etc.
- *Word documents and spreadsheets*: Word documents and spreadsheets that carry various details, particulars, and other sensitive information should also be hidden.

Figure 9-8 shows the Hide Folder tool, which allows a user to hide files.

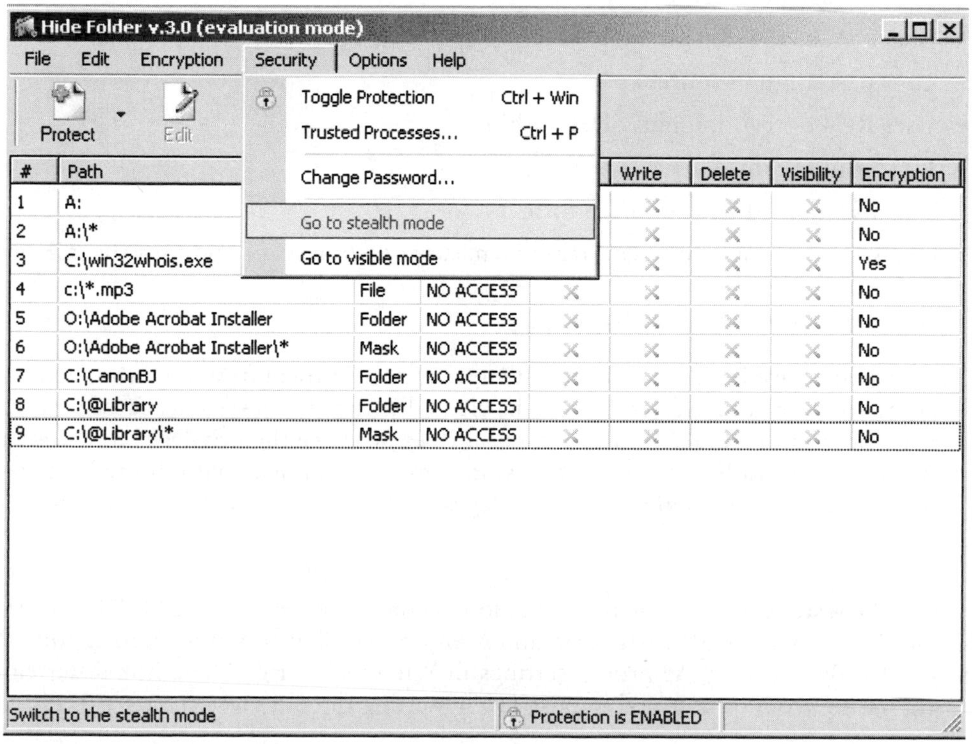

Figure 9-8 Hiding sensitive information is an easy way to prevent a system compromise.

Step 27: Hide Hacking Tools and Other Data on Target Machine

In this step, the penetration tester attempts to hide sensitive documents in hidden directories. Executable files and hacking tools can be easily hidden using Windows NTFS streams. The following tools can be used to hide folders and directories:

- *AB Hide Folder*: AB Hide Folder is file-locking software that can protect personal files and folders. The user can use AB Hide Folder to stop other users from opening personal files, or it can completely hide files until a password is entered.

- *Stealth Folder Hider*: Stealth Folder Hider includes the Folder Hider, Clear Tracks, and File Eradicator utilities. Folders and files cannot be deleted, viewed, modified, or run with Stealth Folder Hider. Stealth Folder Hider is not visible in the taskbar, the Start menu, the system tray, Add/Remove Programs, or the Task Manager.

- *Folder Security Personal*: This security program has the ability to hide and lock folders and files. The user can hide files and folders completely or restrict access by making them read-only, preventing modification or deletion by other users or programs. This powerful program can lock local hard disks as well as floppy drives, CD-ROM drives, and removable disks, and supports FAT, FAT32, and NTFS.

Step 28: Use Various Steganography Techniques to Hide Files on the Target Machine

With steganography, sensitive information can be hidden in images and text. This can prevent the easy recognition of vital files. An intruder cannot see the information hidden inside the images or text.

The following tools allow the user to hide information:

- *ImageHide*: ImageHide hides sensitive data in image files. ImageHide includes the following features:
  - Hides great amounts of text in images
  - Simple encryption and decryption of data
  - Data padding
  - No increase in image size
  - Image looks the same in normal display programs
  - Gets past all mail sniffers
  - Uses RC4 encryption plus SHA hashing
  - Can print the images
  - Can use many different image formats
- *Snow*: Snow exploits the steganographic nature of white space and uses the ICE encryption algorithm.

Step 29: Escalate User Privileges

Operating systems have built-in security systems that protect them from unauthorized access. For this purpose, different types of users and user groups can be created with varying system access powers such as administrator and user, as shown in Figure 9-9. A normal user does not have the privileges to access all the resources of the system. Attackers generally try to get into a system as a normal user with limited privileges and, after entering the attacked system, try to escalate their privileges so that they can further compromise the system.

Step 30: Capture POP3 Traffic

In this step, the tester captures e-mail traffic flowing on the network using POP3 capturing tools. Tools such as Wireshark, PC Network Traffic Monitor, and Analyzer have built-in support to capture POP3 traffic, as shown in Figure 9-10. By selecting the proper settings in Wireshark for example, the tester can tell it to capture any traffic originating from or destined to port 110 by setting the filter to tcp.port == 110.

Step 31: Capture SMTP Traffic

Incoming and outgoing SMTP traffic can be captured using the Tcpdump utility and the output examined with a variety of tools. Radar, shown in Figure 9-11, is a pluggable network-monitoring platform that can capture SMTP traffic along with instant messenger traffic.

Figure 9-9 Obtaining administrative access will allow an intruder to alter a system as he or she sees fit.

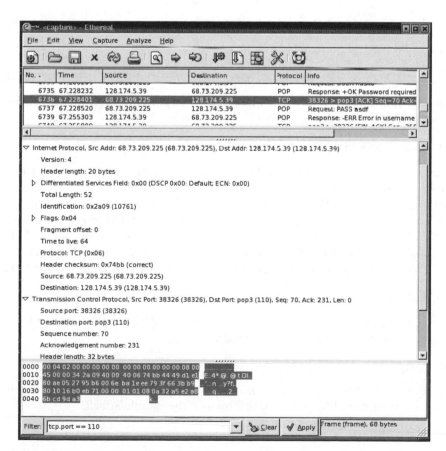

Figure 9-10 POP3 traffic can be intercepted by using tools directed at port 110.

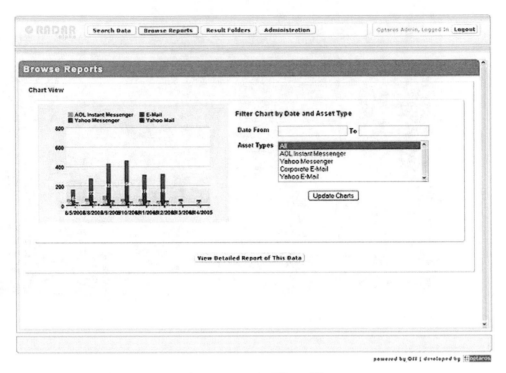

Figure 9-11   Radar can be used to capture SMTP traffic.

Step 32: Capture IMAP E-Mail Traffic

Wireshark can be used to capture IMAP e-mail traffic.

Step 33: Capture Communications Between FTP Client and Server

Penetration testers can use a tool, such as FTP Traffic Capture, to capture the communications between an FTP client and an FTP server.

Step 34: Capture HTTP Traffic

In this step, penetration testers capture HTTP traffic flowing on the target network. Wireshark can be used to capture information such as HTTP headers and content. HTTP traffic can also be captured using Snort in packet-logging mode or the HTTP Analyzer utility. HTTP Analyzer traces and displays details of traffic such as the header, content, cookies, query strings, POST data, request and response streams, and redirection URLs.

EffeTech HTTP Sniffer is another HTTP traffic capture tool. It can capture HTTP traffic and rebuild the HTTP sessions and files sent via HTTP, as shown in Figure 9-12. It has a built in real-time analyzer that enables on-the-fly content viewing as well as capturing, analyzing, parsing, and decoding HTTP traffic.

Step 35: Capture RDP Traffic

Penetration testers can capture Remote Desktop Protocol (RDP) traffic between hosts. VMware Server is a tool that can capture RDP traffic, as shown in Figure 9-13.

Step 36: Capture VoIP Traffic

VoIP traffic can be captured using distributed software agents. Wireshark has the ability to capture VoIP traffic. This traffic can be captured by performing a man-in-the-middle attack.

Step 37: Run Wireshark with Filter -ip.src == ip_address

The following syntax can be used for host filtering:

- host <host>: Host is either the IP address or hostname
- src host <host>: Capture all packets where host is the source

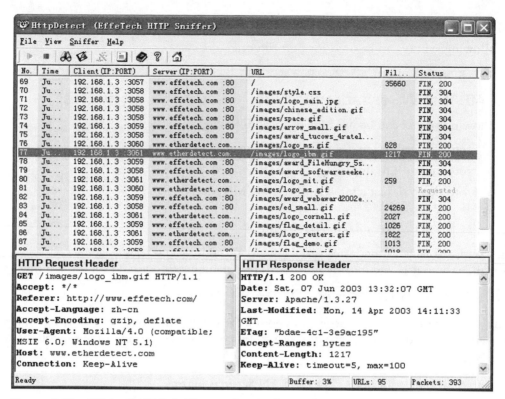

Figure 9-12   Effetech HTTP Sniffer can be used to capture HTTP traffic.

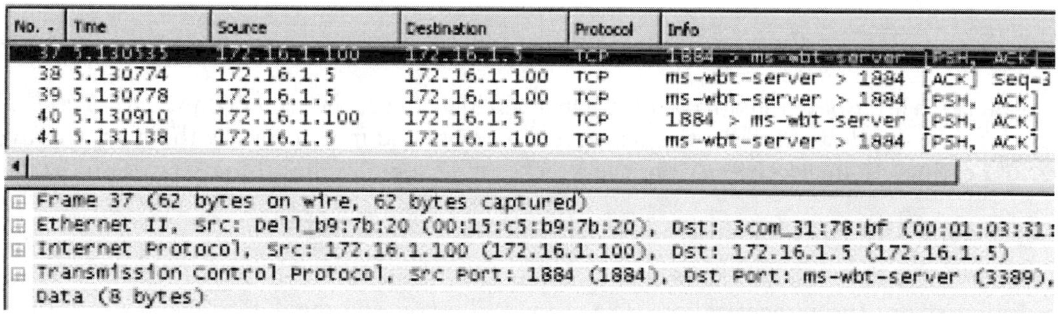

Figure 9-13   VMware Server can capture RDP traffic going to and from the host system.

The following example will capture all packets where 10.10.10.10 is the source:

```
src host 10.10.10.10
```

Step 38: Run Wireshark with Filter -ip.dst == ip_address

The following syntax can be used for host filtering:

- host <host>: Host is either the IP address or hostname
- dst host <host>: Capture all packets where host is the destination

The following example will capture all packets where 10.10.10.10 is the destination:

```
dst host 10.10.10.10
```

Step 39: Run Wireshark with Filter -tcp.dstport == port_no

The following syntax can be used for port filtering:

- port <port>: Capture all packets where port is either the source or destination

Step 40: Run Wireshark with Filter -ip.addr == ip_address

The following syntax can be used for IP-based filtering:

- ip proto \tcp or just tcp: Capture all TCP segments (packets)
- ip proto \udp or just udp: Capture all UDP packets
- ip proto \icmp or just icmp: Capture all ICMP packets

Step 41: Spoof the MAC Address

In this step, the penetration tester spoofs the MAC address and tries to get access to VLANs. SpoofMAC is a powerful, easy to use, and intuitive MAC address changing (spoofing) tool for Windows systems.

Step 42: Poison the Victim's IE Proxy Server

In this step, penetration testers attempt to poison the victim's IE proxy server settings and redirect them to rogue servers. They can add a bogus proxy server to IE's Internet settings by using the following steps:

1. In IE, go to **Tools** and then **Internet Options**.
2. On the Connections tab, click the **LAN Settings** button.
3. In the resulting dialog box, select the following check box in the **Proxy Server** section: **Use a Proxy Server For Your LAN (These Settings Will Not Apply To Dial-up Or VPN Connections)**.
4. Enter **0.0.0.0** in the **Address** text box.
5. Enter **80** in the **Port** text box, and click **OK**.

Step 43: Attempt Session Hijacking on Telnet Traffic

An attacker who is passively hijacking a telnet session can see the telnet commands as the administrator types them into the window. Initially, the session can be observed in real time without attempting to desynchronize the connection. To hijack the session, the attacker must login as the administrator on the telnet server.

Step 44: Attempt Session Hijacking on FTP Traffic

FTP enables users to reliably share files remotely. To transfer a file through FTP, the user is prompted to enter a valid password for authentication. The client and server end the data transfer by closing the data port and control port respectively.

   If an attacker is able to intercept the communication between the FTP client and the server, it is easy to hijack the session. If the attacker forces the client to send a reset to the server and intercepts it before it reaches the server, he or she will have the session ID and can send queries to the server from his or her machine, posing as the client. T-sight is an advanced intrusion detection system that allows users to monitor the network traffic and helps determine possible break-ins or compromises to the system. It also allows users to perform FTP hijacking.

Step 45: Attempt Session Hijacking on HTTP Traffic

HTTP is stateless, which makes it easy to hijack the session ID by masquerading as an alternate user. There are three steps to conduct an HTTP session hijacking attack:

1. Observe (sniff) the HTTP traffic that is transmitted in clear text.
2. Guess the valid session ID by brute-forcing to obtain a valid session ID.
3. The client browser sends the session ID details to a single trusted site for only one time. However, the HTTP REFERER field sends the complete URL in clear text. Cross-site scripting (XSS) can be performed to obtain the session ID by injecting HTML code or HTML script. Often, the session ID is held in the URL or POST fields.

Certain flaws in session ID allocation, such as the sequential allocation of session IDs, too-short session ID values, common hashing techniques, and session obfuscation, can allow attackers to guess the session ID.

Step 46: Document Everything

Penetration testers must document all the findings in this test.

Tools

CORE IMPACT

CORE IMPACT (Figure 9-14) is a penetration testing product for assessing security threats to an organization. It shows how an attacker can get control of valuable information assets. CORE IMPACT actively exploits vulnerabilities within the network, replicating the kinds of access an intruder could achieve. CORE IMPACT makes it possible for network administrators and security engineers to perform a penetration test and identify network assets that can be compromised.

Metasploit

Metasploit (Figure 9-15) is an exploit development tool that is used for writing, testing, and using exploit code in an open-source platform. It provides a concrete platform for penetration testing, shell code development, and vulnerability research. Metasploit is written in Perl and runs on Windows, Linux, BSD, and Mac OS X. It includes the following features:

- Supports various networking options and protocols to develop protocol-dependent code
- Includes tools and libraries to support features such as debugging, encoding, logging, timeouts, and SSL
- Presence of supplementary exploits to help in testing of exploitation techniques and sample exploits produced

There are three work environments for the installed Metasploit Framework (MSF). They are the msfconsole, the msfcli interface, and the msfWeb interface. The primary and most resourceful work area is the msfconsole, which is a command-line interface.

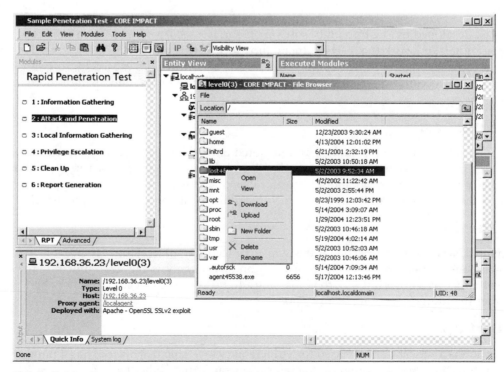

Figure 9-14   Core Impact is an automated penetration testing tool.

Figure 9-15 Metasploit is a tool used to develop exploits.

Canvas

Canvas, developed by the Immunity software team, is a security tool written in Python. Canvas is an inclusive exploitation framework that casts vulnerability information into practical exploits. The main focus of this tool is on creative debugging, i.e., working with unexpected behaviors caused by software bugs and making them reliable. Canvas runs on Windows 2000, Windows XP, and Linux, and operates both in a GUI and at the command line.

Internet Scanner

The Internet Scanner application is an integrated part of Internet Security Systems security management platform and provides comprehensive network vulnerability assessment for measuring online security risks. Internet Scanner performs scheduled and selective probes of communication services, operating systems, applications, and routers to uncover and report system vulnerabilities that might be open to attack.

NetRecon

Symantec NetRecon goes beyond just discovering security vulnerabilities to provide a systematic understanding of their causes. It utilizes a unique root-cause and path-analysis engine to illustrate the exact sequence of steps taken to uncover vulnerabilities, thus enabling administrators to identify exactly where to correct vulnerabilities in order to enforce corporate security policies.

CyberCop

CyberCop is a tool commonly used for vulnerability assessment. This tool has a number of additional features, such as a packet-building program to create a custom vulnerability test.

Nessus

Nessus is a free, open-source security scanner.

Cisco Secure Scanner

Cisco Secure Scanner is an enterprise-class software tool offering network system identification, innovative data management, user-defined vulnerability rules, security reporting capabilities, and Cisco support. Cisco Secure Scanner allows users to measure security, manage risk, and eliminate security vulnerabilities, thus enabling more secure network environments.

Retina

Retina is a network vulnerability scanner and remediation management system that discovers and helps fix all known security vulnerabilities on Internet, intranet, and extranet systems. Retina includes reporting tools to help prioritize and isolate necessary fixes. Retina provides control over auditing open gateways, user security policies, registry settings, as well as a long list of known security vulnerabilities.

Chapter Summary

- Internal network penetration testing is carried out from within a network.
- Port-scanning software, in its most basic form, simply sends out a request to connect to the target computer on each port sequentially and makes a note of which ports respond or seem open to more in depth probing.
- The goal of running a vulnerability scanner is to identify devices on the network that are open to known vulnerabilities.
- Penetration testers test the privacy of Internet communications by sniffing e-mail messages.
- A penetration tester can attempt to bypass system authentication by booting the PC using another operating system, such as Knoppix.
- Keyloggers track all keystrokes on the keyboard of the target machine.
- Penetration testers inject a virus into the target machine and see how the virus spreads through the network.
- Penetration testers capture e-mail traffic flowing on the network using POP3 capturing tools.
- An attacker who is passively hijacking a telnet session can see the telnet commands as the administrator types them into the window.

## Chapter 10

Penetration Testing Deliverables

Objectives

After completing this chapter, you should be able to:

- Understand the components of a penetration testing report
- Prepare a penetration testing report
- Understand how to deliver the report to the client
- Understand how long to retain information related to a penetration test

Key Terms

Common Gateway Interface (CGI) a standard protocol for external application software to interact with a Web server

Computer Emergency Response Team Coordination Center (CERT/CC) an organization that studies Internet security vulnerabilities and often issues advisories

Internet Control Message Protocol (ICMP) one of the principle Internet protocols used to send error messages or test connectivity

Introduction to Penetration Testing Deliverables

This chapter focuses on penetration testing deliverables. It describes the components of a penetration testing report and describes how a tester creates the final report. It also discusses how to deliver the report to the client and how long to retain information about the penetration test after its completion.

Penetration Testing Report

The penetration testing report must contain the following:

- *Summary of test execution*: The summary should provide an overview of the penetration testing process.

- *Scope of the project*: This specifies the scope of the project and provides details about the testing process. This includes a list of the vulnerabilities that were discovered during the course of the testing.

- *Results analysis*: The team should provide the test results along with an analysis of those results, based on the project scope.

- *Recommendations*: The penetration testing team should recommend a set of actions that a client could take to eliminate the vulnerabilities uncovered during the testing process.

- *Added value*: In this section, the team details additional precautions that can be taken to prevent future attacks. Implementations of these recommendations need not be made compulsory. If possible, the penetration tester should suggest mitigating measures for the vulnerabilities that the client is unable to patch.

- *Appendices*: The appendices typically include screenshots, output logs, and the team's contact information.

The goal of the penetration test is to suggest protective controls for the client's network. The penetration testing report should disclose all technical findings as well as an overview of the assessment of the client's network.

The ultimate goals of preparing a penetration testing report include the following:

- Disclosing the vulnerabilities

- Analyzing the available options to mitigate the vulnerabilities

- Suggesting appropriate solutions

- Recommending actions to prevent future attacks

Summary of Test Execution

The test execution summary provides an overview of the penetration testing process. It should contain the following information:

- Client's name

- Name of the organization

- Date on which the test was carried out

- Type of network (public or private)

- Details of ports used

The summary should provide brief information about the following:

- Target systems and their applications

- End users' test results

- Vulnerabilities and exploits discovered

- Estimated cost to fix the vulnerabilities and flaws

Figure 10-1 shows part of a sample of a test execution summary.

Scope of the Project

The scope of the project includes:

- Specifying whether IP addresses and ports were tested

- Specifying whether social engineering techniques were employed

- Specifying whether private and public networks were tested

- Specifying whether Trojans and backdoor applications such as Back Orifice were utilized

This section details the time taken to complete the test process. The report should also include details of the following:

- Vulnerabilities, including the following types:

  - **Common Gateway Interface (CGI)** vulnerabilities; CGI is a standard protocol for external application software to interact with a Web server

  - FTP, Web, and e-mail server vulnerabilities

  - Firewall vulnerabilities

Summary of discovered hosts

Total number of targeted hosts:	3
Total number of compromised hosts: (hosts with known vulnerabilities)	3
Average number of exploited vulnerabilities per compromised host:	1

Summary of targeted users

Total number of targeted users:	1
Total number of users susceptible to social engineering attacks: (This is the number of targeted users who opened the email and thus provided reconnaissance information to the attacker)	1

Summary of Exploited Vulnerabilities

Total number of vulnerabilities successfully exploited	4
Total number of unique vulnerabilities successfully exploited	3
Total number of compromised hosts (hosts with known vulnerabilities)	3
Average number of compromised hosts per vulnerability (Total amount of compromised hosts / Total amount of vulnerabilities successfully exploited)	1
Total number of unique network vulnerabilities successfully exploited	2
Total number of unique client-side vulnerabilities successfully exploited	1

Source: http://www.coresecurity.com. Accessed 2007.

Figure 10-1   The test execution summary provides an overview of the test results.

- Backdoor application vulnerabilities
- Network-based vulnerabilities
- Remote administration vulnerabilities
- Tests performed, including the following:

  - *Internet Control Message Protocol (ICMP)* tests; **ICMP** is one of the principle Internet protocols used to send error messages or test connectivity
  - Bugtraq advisory testing
  - *Computer Emergency Response Team Coordination Center (CERT/CC)* advisory testing; **CERT/CC** is an organization that studies Internet security vulnerabilities and often issues advisories
  - CGI and port scanners
  - Dictionary attacks

Figure 10-2 shows part of a sample showing details of a test. Figure 10-3 shows part of a sample showing details about tested hosts. Figure 10-4 shows details about a vulnerability that was discovered.

Results Analysis

Based on the scope and details of the testing process, the team analyzes the results of the penetration testing. The following list shows how the results are analyzed:

- Domain name and IP address of the host system
- TCP and UDP ports used
- Description of the services provided
- Details of the tests performed
- Vulnerability analysis

Detailed activity report

Module:	**Client-side Attack and Penetration**
Start:	7/25/2007 10:02:38AM
Finish:	7/25/2007 10:39:23AM
Status:	Stopped
Agent:	/localagent
Parameters:	AGENT_PORT: 0
	CONN_METHOD: Connect from target
	EMAIL_BODY_TEMPLATE: C:\Documents and Settings\Don \Application
	EMAIL_BODY_TEMPLATE_TROJAN: C:\Documents and Settings\Don \Application
	EXCEL_FILE_NAME: example.txt
	EXPLOIT_SELECTOR: IE IFRAME Buffer Overflow exploit
	EXPLOIT_TYPE_SEL: WEB_BROWSER
	PACKING_TYPE: notpacked
	SELECTED_EMAIL_FROM: someone@example.com
	SMTP_PORT: 25
	SMTP_SERVER: 192.168.179.99
	SUBJECT: Undelivered Mail Returned to Sender
	SUBJECT_TROJAN: Undelivered Mail Returned to Sender
	TARGET: victimxp@vmcorelab.com

Log:

> Module "Client-side Attack and Penetration" (v46886) started execution on Wed Jul 25 10:02:38 2007
> Note: New email address 'victimxp@vmcorelab.com' added.
> Executing module 'IE IFRAME Buffer Overflow exploit'...
> --
> The module was cancelled after 36 minute(s) and 45 secs.

Source: http://www.coresecurity.com. Accessed 2007.

Figure 10-2   The report includes details about the tests the team performed.

Host IP Address - 192.168.179.99

Entity Name: /192.168.179.132/192.168.179.99

Operating System: Windows 2000 Server SP 3   (i386)

TCP Ports in state listen

25, 42, 53, 80, 110, 135, 139, 389, 443, 445, 636, 3269, 5900

UDP Ports in state listen

53, 135

Services Found

domain (53-tcp)	domain (53-udp)	http (80-tcp)	https (443-tcp)
ldap (389-tcp)	ldapssl (636-tcp)	loc-srv (135-tcp)	loc-srv (135-udp)
microsoft-ds (445-tcp)	msft-gc-ssl (3269-tcp)	nameserver (42-tcp)	netbios-ssn (139-tcp)
pop-3 (110-tcp)	smtp (25-tcp)	vnc (5900-tcp)	

Vulnerabilities

- A NETBIOS/SMB share password is the default, null, or missing. (CVE-1999-0519)

- The Windows Internet Naming Service (WINS) in Windows NT Server 4.0 SP 6a, NT Terminal Server 4.0 SP 6, Windows 2000 Server SP3 and SP4, and Windows Server 2003 does not properly validate the computer name value in a WINS packet, which allows remote attackers to execute arbitrary code or cause a denial of service (server crash), which results in an `unchecked buffer` and possibly triggers a buffer overflow, aka the `Name Validation Vulnerability.` (CVE-2004-0567)

Source: http://www.coresecurity.com. Accessed 2007.

Figure 10-3   The report details the individual hosts that were tested.

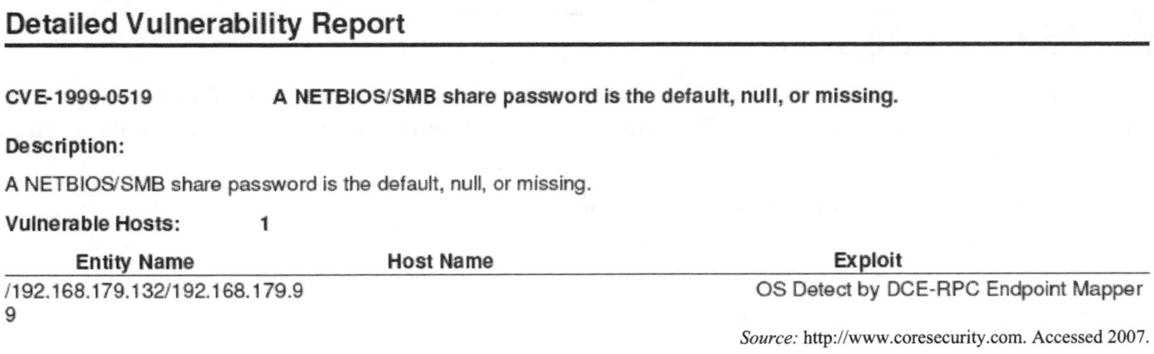

Detailed Vulnerability Report

CVE-1999-0519   **A NETBIOS/SMB share password is the default, null, or missing.**

Description:

A NETBIOS/SMB share password is the default, null, or missing.

Vulnerable Hosts: 1

Entity Name	Host Name	Exploit
/192.168.179.132/192.168.179.9 9		OS Detect by DCE-RPC Endpoint Mapper

Source: http://www.coresecurity.com. Accessed 2007.

Figure 10-4 The report provides details about each vulnerability that was discovered during testing.

The following is part of a sample result analysis:

IP Address: 192.16.22.199
Name: WebSrvr

Port	Service	Description
80	HTTP (Web)	Host appears to be running Microsoft Internet Information Server 5.0. The following penetration attempts were made: 1) MSADC exploit, 2) codebrw.asp exploit, 3) showcode.asp exploit, 4) CGI exploits, 5) webhits.dll/webhits.htw exploits, 6) $data exploit, 7) ASP dot bug exploit, 8) ISM.dll buffer truncation exploit, 9) .idc and .ida exploits, 10) +htr exploits, 11) adsamples exploit, 12) /iisadmnpasswd, 13) dictionary password cracking, 14) brute-force password cracking, and 15) SQL injection.
443	HTTPS (Secure Web)	A 1,024-bit digital certificate is used that will expire December 15, 2009. The certificate is encrypted using RSA SHA-1 encryption and is signed by VeriSign.

Recommendations

The penetration testing team should keep the following in mind when formulating recommendations:

- Penetration testers greatly rely on automated tools and their reports; however, ready-made reports hold no value if not analyzed properly.

- The penetration tester should leave no network component specified in the scope untouched. All relevant network components should be thoroughly examined for exploits.

- The penetration testing report is beneficial only if the suggested recommendations improve the security of the organization. Merely pointing out the network's weaknesses is insufficient.

Appendices

The appendices should include the following:

- Details of contact information
- Screenshots
- Log output
- Tools used
- Security policies implemented

Client-Side Test Reports

The client-side test report contains details about attacks like phishing, spear phishing, spam, and social engineering attacks against end users. The following are the two different types of test reports for client-side penetration testing:

- Client-side penetration report
- User report

Client-Side Penetration Report

Client-side penetration testing reports provide details about the various types of client-side attacks used during the test. The report also includes details about compromised systems. Figure 10-5 shows part of a sample client-side penetration report.

User Report

A user report provides detailed information on the links that were clicked, when the links were clicked, and who clicked them. This report also displays information about users who were identified and targeted by social engineering and client-side attacks during the test process. Figure 10-6 shows part of a sample user report.

All successful client-side attacks

Total number of hosts compromised through email-borne attacks:	0
Total number of hosts compromised through malicious web server attacks:	1
Total number of unique hosts compromised through client-side attacks:	1

Summary of email-borne attacks

Total number of email addresses targeted:	0
Total number of emails sent:	0
Total number of hosts compromised through email-borne attacks:	0
Percentage of successful email-borne attacks:	0.00%

Summary of malicious web server attacks

Total number of malicious web sites deployed:	1
Total number of unique user hits on the malicious web sites:	1
Total number of hosts compromised through malicious web server attacks:	1
Percentage of successful malicious web server attacks:	4.17%

Summary of exploited client-side vulnerabilities

Total number of client-side vulnerabilities successfully exploited:	1
Total number of unique client-side vulnerabilities successfully exploited:	1
Total number of hosts successfully exploited by client-side vulnerabilities:	1

Source: http://www.coresecurity.com. Accessed 2007.

Figure 10-5   The client-side penetration testing includes details about client-side attacks.

Total number of unique email addresses available:	**27**
Total number of email addresses attacked:	**24**
Total number of users who viewed any attack email:	**1**
Percentage of targeted users who viewed any attack email:	**4.17%**
Total number of targeted users whose hosts were successfully compromised:	**1**
Total number of targeted users whose hosts were not compromised:	**23**

Source: http://www.coresecurity.com

Figure 10-6   A user report provides details about end-user results.

Summary of Vulnerabilities found

Total number of vulnerabilities found	31
Total number of compromised web pages	29
Total number of exploited *SQL Injection* vulnerabilities	28
Total number of potential *SQL Injection* vulnerabilities	0
Total number of exploited *PHP Remote File Inclusion vulnerabilities*	3
Average number of compromised web pages per vulnerability	0.94

Source: http://www.coresecurity.com. Accessed 2007.

Figure 10-7   The Web application test report details vulnerabilities found in Web applications.

Test Reports on Web Applications

The Web application test report provides a detailed report about various web application attacks like PHP remote file inclusion attacks and SQL injection. The following are the two different types of Web application reports:

1. *Web application vulnerability report*: This report provides detailed information on each vulnerability uncovered in the Web applications that were tested. The report details the key vulnerable points and any risks related to each Web application vulnerability.

2. *Web application execution report*: This report provides detailed information on vulnerabilities found on every Web page during the process of testing.

Figure 10-7 shows part of a sample Web application test report.

Sign-Off Document

The contract between the client and the penetration testing team is an important document, as it specifies exactly what the team will do as part of the testing process. The costs involved in the penetration test are provided in the contract before testing begins. The client may also ask the penetration tester to verify in writing that the testing has been completed. Doing so can alleviate future controversy.

Creating the Final Report

The final report does not have to be the responsibility of one person. A penetration tester can accept the help of trusted coworkers and other team members when preparing the final report. The penetration tester should keep in mind the abilities of each team member and coworker when seeking help so that skills are appropriately matched to sections of the report. All report writers should possess excellent communication skills and understand all terms related to the penetration testing field. The report should be easy for the client company's management and information security personnel to understand. A report that is too technical is of no use to the upper management; however, it should not be too simplistic or the information security personnel will be unable to properly implement the recommended changes.

The final report should include the following:

- *Final-report delivery date:* The delivery date must be included in the report so the client organization can have that information for its records.
- *Cover letter:* The cover letter should be addressed to the client organization's contact person. It should include the penetration tester's name, the name of the organization the tester works for, and the tester's e-mail address. The cover letter should also include details about the penetration tester and acknowledgments for those who helped in the successful completion of the penetration test.
- *Executive summary:*
  - *Organization synopsis:* A brief description of the organization and its network is given.
  - *Purpose for the evaluation:* The reason for which the testing was performed should be defined.
  - *System description:* The client's organization and its system are described briefly.
  - *Summary of evaluation:* This is a summary of the tests that were carried out.
  - *Major findings and recommendations:* The major findings and any issues that could become the target of future attacks should be included in the final report. The actions that are recommended to mitigate the vulnerabilities must also be included in the report.
  - *Conclusions:* The report should end with the testing team's conclusions. These conclusions include any further suggestions from the penetration testing team.

Report Format

The final report should ideally be provided in PDF format. However, it can be provided in any format the client requests. The PDF format's flexible architecture:

- Makes it easy to transfer files
- Has strong security mechanisms and is resistant to viruses, worms, and other malware
- Allows the testing team to protect the report against modifications
- Can be read by anyone with the freely available Adobe Reader software
- Is compatible with various operating systems

Report Delivery

The final penetration testing report must be delivered personally to prevent the report from falling into the wrong hands. The report should not be sent through e-mail or delivered on a CD-ROM or any other storage media. The report should be delivered only in printed format.

Report Retention

During the course of the penetration test, the tester will have the opportunity to perform the following tasks:

- Access internal resources
- Read restricted files
- Alter restricted files
- Read transaction data
- Execute potentially dangerous programs
- Access user accounts
- Obtain administrative privileges
- Control network management systems
- Demonstrate ability to control resources

Because of this, the penetration testing report must not be exposed to unauthorized personnel. Penetration testing reports include sensitive information about the organization's network infrastructure and layout. Note the following points in relation to report retention:

- The information gathered during the penetration test is very sensitive, as the report includes information related to the following:
  - Existing vulnerabilities
  - Network components
  - Server configurations
  - Personnel
  - Physical security
- The penetration tester should not maintain a report for a prolonged period: at most for 30–45 days. Once the project is no longer active, the penetration tester may lose or misplace the report if it is kept lying around. The penetration tester should also destroy any information related to the client's network within the same time frame.
- The report should be submitted to the client as early as possible, bearing in mind the sensitivity of information the report includes.
- The penetration tester should be available to answer any questions during this period.
- All of the above are usually specified in the contract before the engagement begins.

Chapter Summary

- Penetration testing reports provide details regarding the discovered vulnerabilities, available options, recommendations, and suggestions.
- The penetration testing report must be delivered personally to assure that unauthorized personnel do not see the report.
- The penetration tester should destroy sensitive information within 45 days of delivering the final report.

## Chapter 11

Post-Testing Actions

Objectives

After completing this chapter, you should be able to:

- Prioritize the recommendations of a penetration testing team
- Develop an action plan for improving security
- Create a process for minimizing instances of misconfigurations
- Capture lessons learned and best practices

Key Terms

Misconfiguration   the state of an operating system or application in which it is left vulnerable to attack because of improper or default installation

Patch   a manufacturer-provided fix for a bug or vulnerability found in a previously installed application or code that adds new features to that application

Update   see *Patch*

Introduction to Post-Testing Actions

This chapter focuses on the actions that an organization should take following the completion of a penetration test. These actions will improve the organization's security and are based on the recommendations of the penetration testing team.

Prioritize Recommendations

The organization should prioritize the recommendations that the penetration testing team has made. The following are some post-testing actions an organization should take:

- After the completion of the penetration test, the first focus should be on high-priority security worries.
- Implement technical solutions for security issues that the penetration test has revealed.
- Develop strategies to achieve short-term and long-term security postures.
- Decide on required and available resources to maintain reliable information security.

Develop an Action Plan

The organization should develop an action plan that does the following:

- Addresses the security concerns systematically
- Reduces system misuse and the threat of attacks on the organization
- Decreases the level of vulnerability in the network
- Makes it easier for the organization to handle future vulnerabilities
- Analyzes the network for possible damage

Create a Process for Minimizing Instances of Misconfigurations

A *misconfiguration* is the state of an operating system or application in which it is left vulnerable to attack because of improper or default installation. The organization should create a configuration management process. This is a process that ensures an organization's policy compliance and controls changes made to the network. This process must not delay the timely application of updates and security patches.

The organization should also create their own configuration checklists or use configuration checklists available from product vendors and security organizations. Secure networks can be maintained by implementing the configuration settings provided by these checklists. These checklists can be obtained from federal agencies and other sources.

Apply Updates and Patches

Installing new updates or patches is another action that should be carried out after penetration testing. An *update* is a manufacturer-provided fix for a bug or vulnerability found in an older or legacy application or code that adds new features to that application. A *patch* is a manufacturer-provided fix for a bug or vulnerability found in a previously installed application or code that adds new features to that application. The following are some of the processes that should be developed to improve the patching process:

- Improve the level of control over purchased software by checking for updates and patches from vendors
- Create a policy for applying patches in an appropriate, timely manner
- Ensure continuous updates to counter the latest threats
- Security processes should be updated frequently

Capture Lessons Learned and Best Practices

The organization should create guidelines for best practices to be followed based on the recommendations of the penetration testing report. Regular auditing of an organization reduces exposure to vulnerabilities.

The security policies and guidelines include the following:

- *Organizational standards policy*: Specifies the utilization of technologies, procedures, and parameters
- *Acceptable-use guidelines*: Specifies the acceptable use of organizational resources such as computers and networks
- *Roles and responsibilities*: Specifies roles and responsibilities for administrators, users, and management

Create Security Policies

The organization should create several security policies such as the following:

- Systems security policy
- Information classification policy
- Password policy
- Strong authentication policy
- Virus detection and management policy
- Encryption policy
- Security change management policy
- Remote network access policy
- Firewall security policy

Conduct Training

The organization should organize security education and awareness programs such as the following:

- Conducting general security awareness for new employees and students in the organization
- Creating awareness programs through e-learning and conducting training for analyzing the security posture of a network
- Conducting technical-security training programs for people managing information technology
- Conducting training for application developers to develop secure code and follow best practices to reduce instances of vulnerable code

Conduct a Social Engineering Class

Social engineering is a method by which attackers manipulate employees in order to obtain information about the organization and its security. The organization should conduct social engineering classes for the employees. These classes help employees acquire knowledge about the tactics social engineers use so that the employees can watch for those tactics in the future.

Destroy the Penetration Testing Report

The organization should take precautions so that the penetration testing report is not exposed to anyone until any unauthorized people. A trusted employee in the organization should also destroy the penetration testing report after all the vulnerabilities are repaired.

Chapter Summary

- An organization should prioritize recommendations to focus on high-priority security concerns first.
- Organizations should develop an action plan to address the security concerns systematically.
- The organization should create their own configuration checklists or use configuration checklists available from product vendors and security organizations.
- The organization should follow best practices such as regular auditing to reduce exposure to vulnerabilities.
- Management should conduct training for application developers to develop secure code and follow best practices to reduce instances of vulnerable code.

- The organization should take precautions so that the penetration testing report is not exposed to any unauthorized people.
- Social engineering classes help employees acquire knowledge about the tactics that attackers use to gain knowledge about an organization and its security.

## Chapter 12

Advanced Exploits and Tools

Objectives

After completing this chapter, you should be able to:

- Carry out a buffer overflow
- Carry out a heap overflow
- Exploit format string flaws
- Illustrate the elements of an exploit
- Identify vulnerable code
- Run shellcode
- Utilize null operations (NOPs)
- Use shellcode-generation and payload-generation tools

Key Terms

Buffer   a temporary data storage area used by hardware or software

Buffer overflow   a condition that occurs when the data going into a buffer exceed the capacity of the buffer, and memory adjacent to the buffer is overwritten with the excess data

Delivery code   code designed to deliver shellcode to the target machine

Format string flaw   the result of programmers allowing externally supplied and unsanitized data into the format string argument

Null operations (NOPs)   subroutines that tell the CPU to wait and then go on to the next instruction

Shellcode   small pieces of machine code/assembly language used to start shells

Vulnerable code   code that has a flaw and can be exploited

Introduction to Advanced Exploits and Tools

Advanced penetration testing involves techniques that simulate an attack by experienced hackers. These techniques include initiating buffer overflows, exploiting string format errors, and using null operations. Advanced penetration testing techniques generally involve overwriting a system's memory to find information or gain control of the system. This kind of attack must be carried out to its fullest extent in order to adequately test a system. Advanced penetration testing techniques should only be attempted by experienced penetration testers, because they involve potentially damaging attacks that must be repaired in the postattack phase of testing.

Buffer Overflows

Buffers are temporary data storage areas used by hardware or software. If too much data are put into the buffer, a *buffer overflow* occurs, and memory adjacent to the assigned buffer is overwritten with the excess data, as shown in Figure 12-1. Buffer overflows can be initiated as malicious attacks if the extra data include actual code that is designed to hijack the program.

The following code is an example of a purposeful buffer overflow:

```
void function (char *str)
        {
        char buffer[16];
        strcpy (buffer, str);
        }
        int main ()
        {
        // length of str = 27 bytes
        char *str = "I am greater than 16 bytes";
        function (str);
        }
```

The following code is another example of a purposeful buffer overflow:

```
void main
(int argc, char **argv[])
{
char buffer[256];
strcpy (buffer, argv[1]);
printf("Buffer::%sn", buffer);
}
```

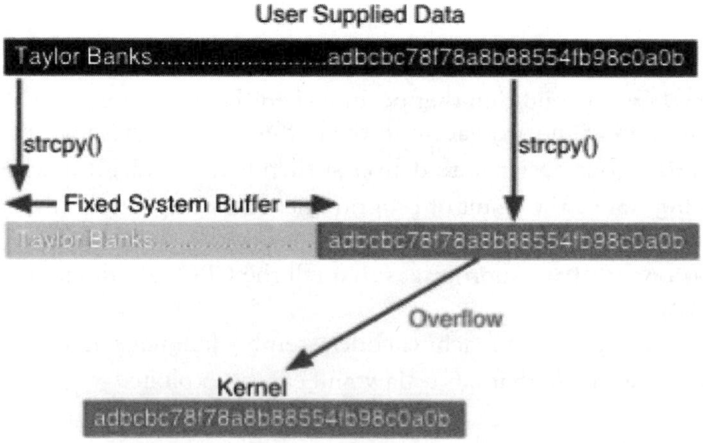

User Supplied Data

Taylor Banks............................adbcbc78f78a8b88554fb98c0a0b

strcpy()   strcpy()

Fixed System Buffer

Taylor Banks adbcbc78f78a8b88554fb98c0a0b

Overflow

Kernel

adbcbc78f78a8b88554fb98c0a0b

Figure 12-1 Data that overflow a buffer will overwrite data stored in the system's memory.

Because there is no bounds checking, anything larger than the buffer runs off into uncontrolled memory space. This gives the potential to overwrite the EIP (enhanced instruction pointer), hijacking the execution flow of the program. With control of the EIP, an attacker can write a new return address in and force the program to execute code under its security context.

For example, code might spawn a remote shell with the privileges of the exploited user context. If this context is root or administrator, the system is completely compromised.

The most common types of buffer overflows are stack-based and heap-based overflows.

Stack Overflows

Call stacks are used to store data on program subroutines. If the stack is overwritten by malicious code through a buffer overflow, the attacker can take over the program.

Heap Overflows

Heaps are another type of buffer used during the runtime of a program. A heap memory segment stores dynamically allocated data and global variables. A heap overflow occurs when more memory than can be handled is allocated and returned by an application using the `malloc()` function at runtime. The `malloc()` function is a routine that returns the address of an unused section of the heap. It slices a chunk off the heap and returns the address of the first byte in the chunk.

The following points should be considered when attempting a heap overflow:

- The pointer must come after the buffer is overflowed, because the heap grows upward.
- Fill the buffer. Overwrite the pointer, and point it to the address of the malicious code.
- Note that the heap must be executable in order for the code to execute.

Stack-Based Versus Heap-Based Overflows

The stack is used for initialization of temporary values, such as variables, arrays, and so on. The heap, however, is used to store things that are expected to persist throughout the execution cycle of the program. Heap overflows are usually more difficult to exploit than traditional stack-based buffer overflows. In a heap, a statically defined buffer and pointer are needed to carry out an overflow, as shown in Figure 12-2. The following code is an example of this:

```
static char buf[BUFSIZE];
static char *ptr_to_something;
```

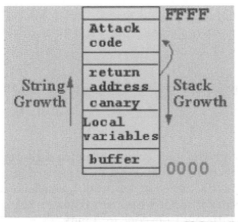

Figure 12-2 A statically defined buffer and pointer are needed to exploit a heap.

Format String Flaws

Format string flaws are the result of programmers allowing externally supplied and unsanitized data into the format string argument. If a buffer is made up of user input, attackers can use formatting tokens (%s, %x) to start exploring the stack space and return memory addresses. This technique can be used to map out memory space, return addresses, shellcode, and so on.

The following code examples use format strings to print the buffer:

```
static char find_me[] = "..Buffer was lost in memory/n";
main()
{
char buf[512]; char tmp[512]; while(1) {
memset(buf, '0', 512);
read(0, buf, 512); sprintf(tmp ,buf); printf("%s", tmp);
}
}
```

Format Strings: Writing into Memory

%n is a very useful formatting token. It takes an integer pointer as an argument and writes the number of bytes already written, to that location. By carefully controlling the number of bytes written, and breaking the writes up into small operations, a user can construct a memory address to be written to an arbitrary location using %n.

The Anatomy of an Exploit

Exploits involve the following elements:

- *Vulnerable code*: Code that has a flaw and can be exploited.
- *Shellcode*: Small pieces of machine code/assembly language used to start shells.
- *Delivery code*: The delivery code is designed to deliver the shellcode to the target machine. Any network communication code can be used, such as code for generating an HTTP request or filling in a login field.
- Debuggers: A debugging tool is essential for discovering and exploiting these vulnerabilities.

Vulnerable Code

The following code is an example of vulnerable code that can be exploited:

```
int main(int argc, char *argv[])
{
char buffer[500];
if(argc>=2) strcpy(buffer, argv[1]);
return 0;
}
```

This code includes a basic program that creates a 500-byte buffer and puts the first command-line argument into it.

Shellcode

Shellcode is small pieces of assembly language used to launch shells, especially as a result of buffer overflows. Shellcode contains a list of instructions that allows it to be injected into an application at runtime. Shellcode is created in the format of raw opcode (operation code), which is executed directly by the CPU. Shellcode is often architecture- and OS-dependent. Code written for Linux on Sparc will not work on an x86 Linux system. Likewise, code for Windows is different from code for Linux.

The following code is an example of shellcode:

```
char shellcode[]=
"x31/xc0" // xorl %eax,%eax "/x50" // pushl %eax
"/x68/x6e/x2f/x73/x68" // pushl $0x68732f6e "/x68/x2f/x2f/x62/x69"
```

```
// pushl $0x69622f2f "/x89/xe3" // movl %esp,%ebx "/x99" // cltd
"/x52" // pushl %edx "/x53" // pushl %ebx "/x89/xe1" // movl
%esp,%ecx "/xb0/x0b" // movb $0xb,%al "/xcd/x80" // int $0x80
```

This code results in a root shell spawned with the execve() call for Linux.

The following tools can be used to write shellcode:

- *env-overflow*: This tool automatically exploits vulnerable code and includes copying the data of an environment variable into a fixed-size buffer with no bounds checking. The env-overflow tool includes the following options:
  - *--target*: Set the name of the target program
  - *--size*: Set the size of the buffer to use
  - *--args*: Set the argument string to use
  - *--env*: Set the environment variable to overflow
  - *--verbose*: Show diagnostics
  - *--payload*: Choose the shellcode to run
  - *--test*: Execute the desired shellcode and exit

- *cmd-overflow*: This tool automatically exploits vulnerable code by copying the contents of a command-line argument into a fixed-size buffer. The following options can be used with this tool:
  - *--target*: Set the name of the target program
  - *--size*: Set the size of the buffer to use
  - *--args*: Set the argument string to use
  - *--verbose*: Show diagnostics
  - *--payload*: Choose the shellcode to run
  - *--test*: Execute the selected shellcode only

- *objdump*: This tool converts binary code to disassembled output. The following shows part of the result of objdump being run on the UNIX ls utility:

```
/bin/ls: file format elf32-i386
Disassembly of section .init:
0804945c <.init>:
804945c: 55 push %ebp
804945d: 89 e5 mov %esp,%ebp
804945f: 83 ec 08 sub $0x8,%esp
8049462: e8 0d 06 00 00 call 0x8049a74
8049467: e8 74 06 00 00 call 0x8049ae0
804946c: e8 2f ce 00 00 call 0x80562a0
8049471: c9 leave
8049472: c3 ret
```

- *dasm*: This is a small Perl script that uses the objdump program to disassemble binaries and gives a cross-referenced dump of unknown binaries with string references.

Null Operations (NOPs)

Null operations (NOPs) are subroutines that tell the CPU to wait and then go on to the next instruction. Because it is difficult to find the exact starting point of shellcode, NOPs can be used to pad the code. With a 500-byte buffer, there would be plenty of room for, for example, 50 bytes of shellcode to be stored until a NOP is hit somewhere in the buffer.

Because it is difficult to tell where the code starts, the attacker can stick in 450 bytes of null operations before the shell code. He or she can then redirect the execution flow to point somewhere toward where the beginning of the buffer is. The CPU will hit the NOPs and "slide" through them until it hits the shellcode payload, thus giving rise to the term "NOP slide." In this way, the attacker does not need to know precisely where the shell-code starts in the buffer. He or she can pad the buffer with NOPs so that the exploited return address just has to point to one of the NOPs.

Delivery Code

Delivery code is designed to deliver the shellcode to the target machine. This can be any network communication code, such as code generating an HTTP request or filling in a login field. Delivery code loads the code into memory and fills up the vulnerable buffers.

The following snippet of code is an example of delivery code that sets up the connection for an RPC overflow:

```
FD_ZERO(&fdreadme); FD _ SET(sockfd, &fdreadme); FD _ SET(0, &fdreadme);
while(1) {
FD_SET(sockfd, &fdreadme); FD_SET(0, &fdreadme);
if(select(FD_SETSIZE, &fdreadme, NULL, NULL, NULL) < 0 )
break;
if(FD_ISSET(sockfd, &fdreadme)) {
if((i = recv(sockfd, rb, sizeof(rb), 0)) < 0{
printf("[-] Connection lost../n");
exit(1);}
if(write(1, rb, i) < 0) break;}
if(FD_ISSET(0, &fdreadme)) {
if((i = read(0, rb, sizeof(rb))) < 0){ printf("[-] Connection lost../n");
exit(1);}
if (send(sockfd, rb, i, 0) < 0) break;}
usleep(10000);}
printf("[-] Connection closed by foreign host../n");
exit(0);
}
```

Linux Exploits Versus Windows Exploits

Windows has a much more complex, monolithic code base than most Linux systems. Linux is a kernel, and Windows is an entire integrated OS. This presents a larger attack surface. Windows is the most widely used operating system in the world. This makes it a higher profile target. Writing exploits for Windows, however, is somewhat more difficult than for Linux. Writing shellcode is more complex for Windows because of the following reasons:

- Windows shellcode does not generally get much smaller than about 800 bytes. This places a lower limit on the size of the buffer that can be exploited. Denial-of-service attacks are still possible with smaller buffers, however.

- Windows does not use syscalls; the Windows API must be directly manipulated.

- There are no clean methods for spawning a shell. All of this combines to greatly increase the size of the shellcode necessary for a successful exploit.

- Offsets and return addresses can change from service pack to service pack as well, further complicating issues.

Debuggers

A debugging tool is essential for discovering the following:

- The location of exploitable buffers

- The location of shellcode

- The return point, once control of the execution flow has been established

- What exactly is happening in memory

OllyDbg and GDB are some of the more commonly used debuggers for the nefarious purposes of exploitation. Standard practice is to set up a machine as close to the target as possible, run the vulnerable application through a debugger, and analyze the results.

Tools

GDB

GDB is a GNU Project debugger that allows the user to see what is going on inside another program while it executes. GDB performs the following functions:

- Starts the program, specifying anything that might affect its behavior
- Makes the program stop on specified conditions
- Examines what has happened when the program stops
- Changes things in the program, so the user can experiment with correcting the effects of one bug and go on to learn about another

GDB can be launched in the following ways:

- To launch GDB with an executable, run **gdb <binary>**.
- To load a core file, type **gdb <core-file>**.
- To attach to a running process, first launch GDB. Then type **attach <pid>**.
- The following are some example commands for searching through memory at the GDB command prompt:
  - **x/d <address>**: Show decimal at address
  - **x/100d <address>**: Show next 100 decimals at address
  - **x/d 0x0804846c**: Show decimal at 0x0804846c
  - **x/s <address>**: Show strings at address
  - **x/105s 0x0804846c**: Show 105 strings at 0x0804846c
  - **x/x <address>**: Show hexadecimal address
  - **x/10x 0x0804846c**: Show 10 addresses at 0x0804846c
  - **x/b 0x0804846c**: Show byte at 0x0804846c
  - **x/10b 0x0804846c-10**: Show 10 bytes at 0x0804846c – 10
  - **x/10b 0x0804846c+20**: Show 10 bytes at 0x0804846c + 20
  - **x/20i 0x0804846c**: Show 20 assembler instructions at 0x0804846c

GDB can also be used to set breakpoints. Breakpoints are useful for freezing the execution flow of a binary and analyzing the memory state. For example, if there was a known vulnerability in the function foo(), a breakpoint could be set on the execution of foo(). The debugger would freeze the program and allow the user to dissect and analyze foo() and determine the precise addresses necessary for the exploit. Breakpoints can be utilized in the following ways:

- To set a breakpoint:
  - Type **break <name of function or memory address>**.
  - Type **run** to run the loaded executable.
  - Execution will continue until the breakpoint reaches the matched function.
- To delete breakpoints, type **delete breakpoints** at the GDB command prompt.

The following commands are also useful:

- To show the value of a register, type **print $<register>**.
- To show all registers at a given point, type **info registers**.

- To list the sections of an executable, type **maintenance info sections**.
- To attempt to disassemble a function, type **disassemble <function>**.

Metasploit

The Metasploit Framework (Figure 12-3) is an open-source platform for doing vulnerability research and development, IDS signature development, and exploit research and penetration testing. Metasploit handles building shellcode and delivery code. The user selects the payload and then selects the exploit to use. The user can then exploit the targeted remote service.

One of the features of the Metasploit client API is the ability to read and write the memory of any accessible process on the exploited system, all from inside a Ruby shell. When combined with a Meterpreter script (started with the run command from inside Meterpreter), this feature can be used to backdoor running applications or steal in-memory credentials.

Some of the exploits that Metasploit includes are the following:

- AppleFileServer LoginExt PathName Buffer Overflow
- Apache Win32 Chunked Encoding
- ISS PAM.dll ICQ Parser Buffer Overflow
- DistCC Daemon Command Execution
- Exchange 2000 MS03-46 Heap Overflow
- Frontpage fp30reg.dll Chunked Encoding
- IA WebMail 3.x Buffer Overflow
- IIS 5.0 nsiislog.dll POST Overflow
- IIS 5.0 Printer Buffer Overflow

Source: http://www.metasploit.com. Accessed 2007.

Figure 12-3   Metasploit can create payloads and carry out exploits.

- IIS 5.0 WebDAV ntdll.dll Overflow
- IMail LDAP Service Buffer Overflow
- Microsoft LSASS MSO4-011 Overflow
- Mercantec SoftCart CGI Overflow
- Microsoft RPC DCOM MSO3-026
- MSSQL 2000 Resolution Overflow
- Poptop Negative Read Overflow
- RealServer Describe Buffer Overflow
- Samba Fragment Reassembly Overflow
- Samba trans2open Overflow
- Sambar 6 Search Results Buffer Overflow
- Serv-U FTPD MDTM Overflow
- SMB Password Capture Service
- Solaris sadmind Command Execution
- Squid NTLM Authenticate Overflow
- Subversion Date Svnserve
- Unreal Tournament 2004 "secure" Overflow (Linux)
- Unreal Tournament 2004 "secure" Overflow (Win32)
- War-FTPD 1.65 PASS Overflow
- Windows SSL PCT Overflow

Metasploit uses the following user-interface modes:

- *Msfconsole*
  - Msfconsole is the Metasploit interactive shell user interface.
  - The console interface supports tab completion of known commands.
  - The Msfconsole interface requires that Ruby was built with the Readline library.
- *Msfcli*
  - Msfcli is the command-line interface.
  - It is not as user-friendly but provides for easy scripting and is good for batch jobs.
  - This interface takes a module name as the first parameter, followed by the options in a VAR=VAL format, and finally an action code to specify what should be done.
  - The module name is used to determine which exploit or auxiliary module should be launched.
- *Msfweb*
  - Msfweb (Figure 12-4) is the Web interface.
  - This interface is a standalone Web server that allows the user to harness the power of the framework through a browser.
  - Exploited machine connections are proxied to a random port on the Web server, and the user is given a telnet link to the listener.

Metasploit Environment

The environment system is a core component of the Metasploit Framework; the interfaces use it to configure settings, the payloads use it patch opcodes, the exploits use it to define parameters, and it is used internally to pass options between modules. The environment system is divided into global and temporary environments.

- Global environment
  - To interact with the Global environment, use the commands setg and unsetg.

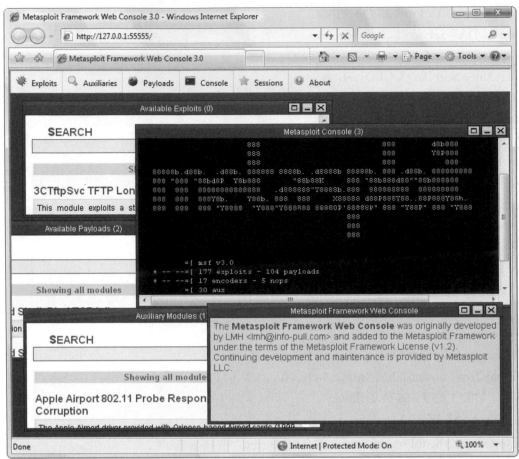

Figure 12-4   Msfweb is the Web interface for Metasploit.

- The setg command, by itself, displays the current global environment. To set a variable, use **setg <foo> <bar>**, where foo is the variable and bar is its value.
- The unsetg command clears the entire global environment.

  The following example shows the global environment state after a fresh installation:

  ```
  AlternateExit: 2
  DebugLevel: 0
  Encoder: Msf::Encoder::PexFnstenvMov
  Logging: 0
  Nop: Msf::Nop::Pex
  RandomNops: 1
  ```

- Temporary environment
  - The temporary environment is accessed through the set and unset commands.
  - Variables that are set are specific to the exploit that is loaded.
  - This environment only applies to the currently loaded exploit module; switching to another exploit via the use command will result in the temporary environment for the current module being swapped out with the temporary environment of the new module.
  - If no exploit is currently active, the set and unset commands will not be available.
  - Switching back to the original exploit module will result in the original environment being restored.
  - Inactive environments are simply stored in memory until the exploit they are associated with is loaded.

The following example shows how the use command selects an active exploit and how the back command reverts to the main mode:

```
msf > use wins_ms04_045
msf wins_ms04_045 > set
msf wins_ms04_045 > set FOO BAR FOO -> BAR
msf wins_ms04_045 > set
FOO: BAR
msf wins_ms04_045 > back
msf > use openview_omniback
msf openview_omniback > set RED BLUE RED -> BLUE
msf openview_omniback > set
RED: BLUE
msf openview_omniback > back
msf > use wins_ms04_045
msf wins_ms04_045 > set
FOO: BAR
msf wins_ms04_045 >
```

Metasploit includes the following options:

- Logging:
  - This variable is used to enable or disable session logging.
  - Session logs are stored in /.msf/logs by default; the directory can be changed by using the LogDir environment variable.
  - The msflogdump utility can be used to view the generated session logs.
  - These logs contain the complete environment for the exploit as well as per-packet time stamps.
- LogDir:
  - This option specifies what directory the log files should be stored in.
  - It defaults to /.msf/logs. There are two types of log files, the msfconsole log and the session logs.
  - The msfconsole log records each significant action performed by the console interface.
  - A new session log will be created for each successful exploit attempt.
- Encoder:
  - This variable can be set to a comma-separated list of preferred encoders.
  - The framework will try this list of encoders first (in order) and then fall through to any remaining encoders.
  - The encoders can be listed with show encoders.
- NOP:
  - This has similar behavior to the Encoder entry except it is used to specify the list of preferred NOP generator modules.
  - The NOP generators can be listed with show nops.
- RandomNops:
  - This option allows randomized NOP sleds to be used instead of the standard NOP opcode.
  - Not all architectures and NOP generator modules support randomization.
- Proxies:
  - This environment variable forces all TCP sockets to go through the specified proxy chain.
  - The format of the chain is type:host:port for each proxy, separated by commas.
- NinjaHost:
  - This environment variable can be used to redirect all payload connections to a socketNinja server.
  - This value should be the IP address of the system running the socketNinja console.

- NinjaDontKill:
  - This option can be used to exploit multiple systems at once and is particularly useful when firing a UDP-based exploit at a network broadcast address.
- EnablePython:
  - This is required to use the InlineEgg Python payloads.

Metasploit includes the following informational commands:

- Help
- Show:
  - show exploits: Shows loaded exploits
  - show payloads: Shows payloads available
  - show encoders: Shows the available encoding engines
  - show nops: Shows the available NOP engines
  - show options: Shows the configurable options for an exploit
  - show advanced: Shows advanced options for an exploit
- Info: Gives detailed information on a payload or an exploit

Exploits can be set up using the following steps:

1. Use **show exploits** to list the loaded exploits.
2. Once you find an exploit, load it by typing **use <name of exploit>**.
3. Configure the exploit.
4. Type **show options** to see what variables can be set for the exploit.
5. Use RHOST or RPORT to specify the target and port number.
6. Once the options are set, test them with the check command.
   - The check command verifies all the options and attempts to verify that the target is actually vulnerable, if possible.
   - Not all exploits have check functionality built in.
   - The check command should never result in harm to the remote machine.

7. Set the payload, as shown in Figure 12-5.
   - Select a payload from the list, and link it to the exploit with **set payload <name of payload>**.
   - The **show options** command can be used to show any options.

8. Now select a target.
   - If an exploit supports multiple platforms, then the target variable will need to be set.
   - The default is brute-forcing the remote system's type, which often is not desirable.

Some of the advanced features of Metasploit include the following:

- InLineEgg Python payloads
  - InLineEgg is a Python class designed for generating small ASM programs.
  - This is commonly used for generating custom payloads.
  - The exploit payloads are dynamically generated based off of Python scripts in the payloads/external directory.
  - The EnablePython environment variable must be set to use this.
  - The Metasploit Framework supports InlineEgg payloads through the External Payload module interface; this allows transparent support if the Python scripting language is installed.

Source: http://www.metasploit.com. Accessed 2007.

Figure 12-5 Metasploit allows the user to choose from a variety of payloads.

- Impurity ELF injection
  - Metasploit supports loading and running an ELF executable in memory.
  - This allows for very complex payload code to be written and compiled using standard C.
  - The framework includes a Linux loader for impurity executables; the payload is named Linux ia32 reverse impurity and requires the PEXEC option to be set to the path of the executable.
- Proxy chaining
  - The proxy variable allows chaining of multiple proxies to mask the user's presence.
  - The framework includes transparent support for TCP proxies.
  - To use a proxy with a given exploit, the Proxies environment variable needs to be set.
  - Each server must be in the format type:host:port, where type is either HTTP or SOCKS4.
  - The chaining functionality has tested stable with over 500 proxies configured in a random chain.
- Win32 DLL injection payloads
  - Metasploit is able to execute staged payloads that can inject custom DLLs into memory, using any Win32 exploit.
  - The DLLs are not written to disk and reside only in memory, forked off the owned process.
  - To create a DLL that can be used with this payload, use the development environment of choice and build a standard Win32 DLL.
  - This DLL exports a function called init() and has it take a single argument, an integer, which is the socket descriptor of the connection.

- The init() function is launched in a new thread when the process is exploited.
- When processing is complete, it should return and allow the loader stub to exit the process according to the EXITFUNC environment variable.

- VNC DLL injection
  - To demonstrate the capabilities of DLL injection, Metasploit ships with the ability to load a VNC server on the target, as shown in Figure 12-6.
  - This payload starts up a VNC server on exploitation. It will first attempt to grab control of the user's desktop. If it fails, then it will fall back to "read-only" mode, where the user can view the desktop, but not interact with it.
  - If access is gained, then VNC will spawn a command shell, with the privileges of the user the exploited process was running as.

CANVAS

CANVAS (Figure 12-7) is a commercial shellcode and payload generator that allows the user to test compliance. With packaged vulnerability modules for scripting and a powerful framework for developing original security checks, Immunity CANVAS provides a way for any organization to have a concrete picture of its security posture.

CANVAS includes the following features:

- More than 50 exploits, written and tested by Immunity's team
- Completely open design allows a team to adapt CANVAS to its environment and needs
- Does not restrict the use of CANVAS to any particular IP range
- Delivery of CANVAS is purely over the Internet

Source: http://www.metasploit.com. Accessed 2007.

Figure 12-6   Metasploit includes VNC injection capabilities as one of its advanced features.

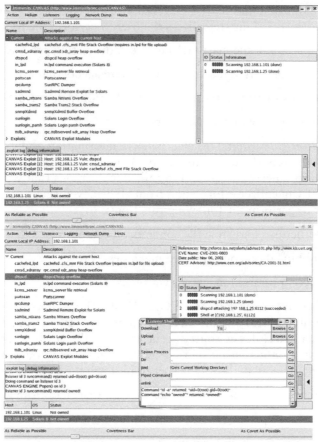

Source: http://www.metasploit.com. Accessed 2007.

Figure 12-7   CANVAS creates shellcodes and payloads to test compliance.

CORE IMPACT

CORE IMPACT (Figure 12-8) is a commercial shellcode and payload generator. CORE IMPACT allows the user to ensure compliance with industry and government regulations. CORE IMPACT can be run completely autonomously. This process includes the following steps:

1. *Information gathering*: The information-gathering step collects data about the targeted network, typically using Network Discovery, Port Scanner, and OS and Service Identification modules. This step can also be completed by importing information from a network mapping tool or vulnerability scanner. Access to a vulnerability scanner is not required. This step allows the user to perform the following functions:

   • Identify the operating system and services running on targeted machines

   • Control the IP ranges that need to be scanned

   • Select from a variety of network discovery and port-scanning methods, including TCP connect, fast SYN, and ICMP

2. *Attack and penetration*: During an attack and penetration, CORE IMPACT automatically selects and launches remote attacks leveraging IP, OS, architecture, port, and service information obtained in the information-gathering step. The user can choose to launch every potential attack against each target host, or have the system stop once it successfully deploys a single agent, which carries the attack payload. The user maintains full control over which hosts are attacked and the order in which exploits are launched.

In addition, exploits that may leave a target service unavailable or take a long time to run can be excluded to speed up the process. This step allows the user to perform the following functions:

- Launch multiple simultaneous attacks to speed the testing process

- Interact with compromised machines via discrete agents that are installed only in system memory

- Run local exploits to attack machines internally, rather than from across the network

- Maintain control over which exploits are applied

3. *Local information gathering*: This step collects information about hosts that have agents deployed on them. During this step, the deployed agents interact with the compromised hosts to gather information about OS, agent privileges, users, and installed applications that were not previously visible to the user. CORE IMPACT can collect information from all deployed agents or only from those specified. This step allows the user to perform the following functions:

- Browse file structures and view file contents on compromised machines

- View rights obtained on compromised machines

- Interact with compromised machines via shells

4. *Privilege escalation*: During this step, CORE IMPACT attempts to penetrate deeper into a compromised computer by running local exploits in an attempt to obtain administrative privileges. After privilege escalation, the user can shift the source agent to one of the newly compromised systems and cycle back to the initial information-gathering step, thereby establishing an outpost from which to run attacks deeper into the network. This step allows the user to perform the following functions:

- Run local exploits to attack systems internally, rather than from across the network

- Gain administrative privileges on compromised systems

- View the networks to which a compromised computer is connected

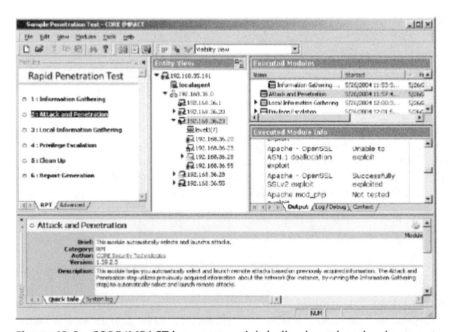

Figure 12-8 CORE IMPACT is a commercial shellcode and payload generator.

- Launch attacks from any compromised system to other computers on the same network, gaining access to systems with increasing levels of security

5. *Clean up*: This step automatically uninstalls every connected agent. Agents are uninstalled in post order to support complex agent chains. In addition, all agents are automatically uninstalled when closing the active workspace, regardless of whether the clean-up step is executed. This step allows the user to perform the following functions:

- Run tests without installing modules or tools on compromised systems (or altering them in any way)

- Quickly and easily remove all agents from compromised machines, leaving the network in its original state

6. *Report generation*: CORE IMPACT generates clear, informative reports that provide data about the targeted network and hosts, audits of all exploits performed, and details about proven vulnerabilities. The user can view and print reports using Crystal Reports or export them in popular formats such as HTML, PDF, Microsoft Word, and Microsoft Excel. CORE IMPACT provides the following reports:

- *Executive report*: A high-level snapshot of all activities and test results

- *Activity report*: A report of all executed exploits (available in three levels of detail)

- *Host report*: Detailed host information, including the number of compromised hosts, the average number of vulnerabilities exploited on each host, and the CVE (Common Vulnerabilities and Exposures) names of vulnerabilities found on each host

- *Vulnerability report*: A detailed report of successfully exploited, versus potential, vulnerabilities on each host

CORE IMPACT can be used for the following purposes:

- Advanced penetration testing scenarios (Figure 12-9):
  - External attacker with no previous knowledge
  - Internal attacker with access to internal network

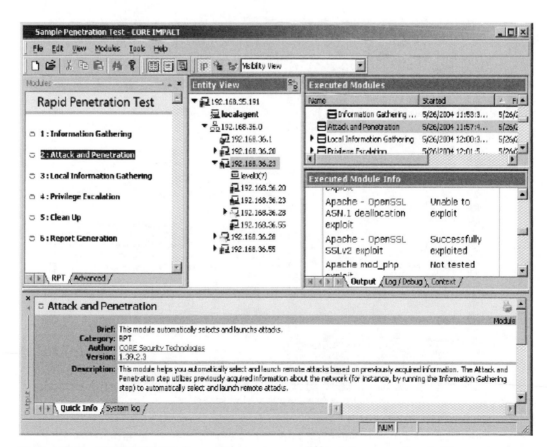

Figure 12-9 CORE IMPACT allows the user to run different penetration testing scenarios.

- Verification of IDS and other security controls:
  - Verify external and internal taps
  - Tune rule sets to an appropriate threshold: This reduces false positives and increases responsiveness
- Intrusion-response-team testing:
  - Generates actual events that create a realistic intrusion
- Researching new areas and technologies

Microsoft Baseline Security Analyzer (MBSA)

Microsoft Baseline Security Analyzer (MBSA) is a security analyzer used to help small- and medium-sized businesses determine their security state in accordance with Microsoft security recommendations. MBSA (Figure 12-10) detects common security misconfigurations and missing security updates on computer systems.

MBSA can be used from a graphical user interface (GUI) executable file, MBsa.exe, and from the command-line executable file, Mbsacli.exe. To verify the updates that are needed, MBSA makes use of Microsoft Update and Windows Server Update Services (WSUS) technologies. In order to perform a vulnerability assessment scan, it uses ports 138 and 139. It consists of a secured connection using DCOM through the Windows Firewall to execute the security update scans. MBSA needs administrator rights for the computers that have MBSA installed on them and the target computer that is to be scanned.

The secured configuration scan is performed in the following stages:

1. *Performing the scan*: Run MBSA and clear the **Check for security update** check box while the scanning is performed.

2. *Analyzing the scan*: A resulting report page details the issues found, the solutions for the issues, and the steps to correct the issues.

3. *Correcting the issues that were found*: Clicking the **How to correct this** link for any issue in the scan report provides the solution and instructions for correcting the issue.

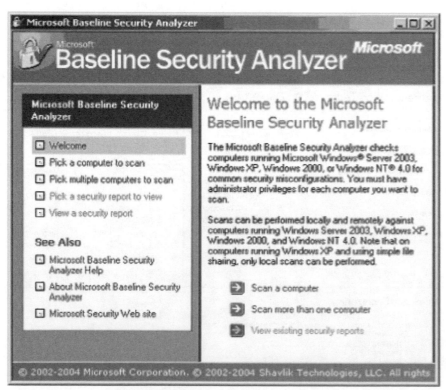

Source: http://www.microsoft.com/technet/security/tools/mbsahome.mspx. Accessed 2007.

Figure 12-10 Microsoft Baseline Security Analyzer (MBSA) is a security analyzer used to help small- and medium-sized businesses determine their security state in accordance with Microsoft security recommendations.

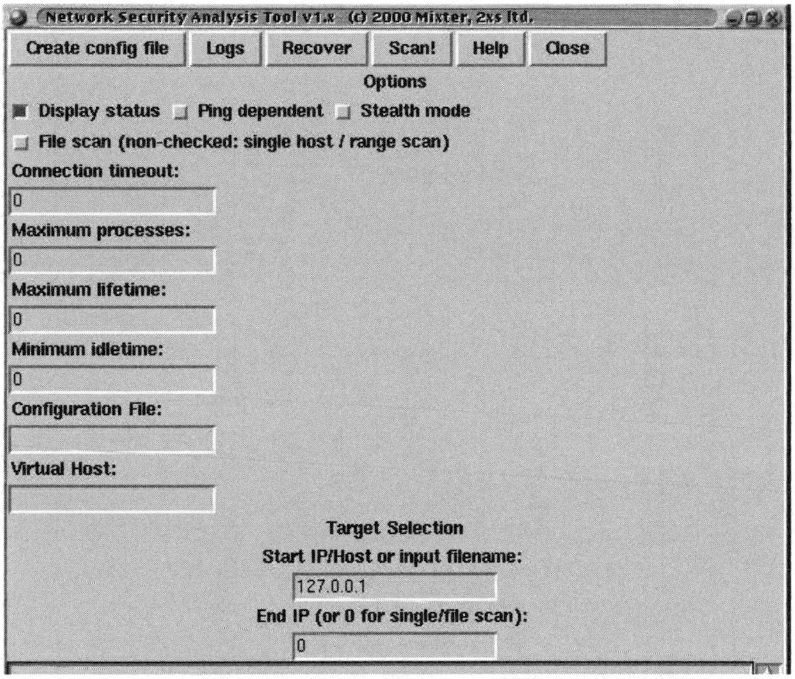

Source: http://nsat.sourceforge.net. Accessed 2007.

Figure 12-11 NSAT is a bulk security scanner that is designed to audit remote network services.

Network Security Analysis Tool (NSAT)

The Network Security Analysis Tool (NSAT) is a bulk security scanner that is designed to audit remote network services, check for versions and security problems, and get information on the servers and machines. NSAT (Figure 12-11) can perform the following functions:

- Different types of wide-ranging scans
- Scanning on multiuser boxes (local stealth and nonpriority scanning options)
- Professional-grade penetration testing and comprehensive auditing
- Full-scale archiving of vulnerability and version information for further purposes
- Virtual host support, host/network exclusion support
- Flexibility and configurable scanning

Sunbelt Network Security Inspector (SNSI)

Sunbelt Network Security Inspector (Figure 12-12) is a vulnerability scanner and commercial-grade database. The vulnerabilities that are scanned are database-based, providing high-level scan results that give short descriptions of each scan for quick reference.

SNSI uses a complete vulnerability database and also the latest CERT, CIAC, and FedCIRC advisories. It holds the latest SANS/FBI top 20 vulnerability list. It detects 4,000+ vulnerabilities and provides consolidated management reports. It provides the ability to easily export reports to multiple formats such as PDF, XLS, DOC, HTML, XML, and DB. It works with TCP/IP, which works over the Internet. It recognizes machine names and NT domain names, as well as IP addresses. It checks for vulnerabilities associated with Microsoft Server Applications and applications like Microsoft Word, Microsoft Excel, Internet Information Server (IIS), ColdFusion, Microsoft SQL Server, and Web browsers.

SNSI will run on a system even if it does not have Internet connectivity. When the user clicks on **updates**, it will show a URL that the user can go to, download the update from another machine, and then get it to the system via a CD, e-mail, etc.

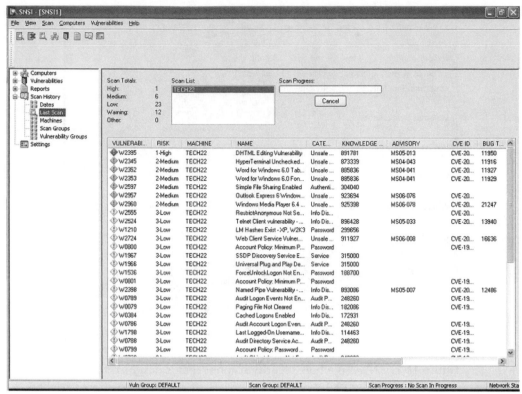

Source: http://www.sunbelt-software.com/documents/unbelt_network_security_inspector_user_guide.pdf. Accessed 2007.

Figure 12-12 Sunbelt Network Security Inspector is a vulnerability scanner and commercial-grade database.

Network Security Inspector includes the following features:

- A large number of vulnerabilities in its database
- Flexible, scalable, and easy to use
- Scans and analyzes the entire domain or selected systems in the domain
- Selects specific vulnerabilities with the help of configuration files
- Performs frequent vulnerability database updates
- Searches specific vulnerabilities, groups them, and then scans them
- Provides a detailed report after scanning
- Performs field-based searching for vulnerabilities
- Eliminates the vulnerabilities by providing recommended solutions
- Ensures the elimination of the vulnerability by rescanning for it
- Provides review and print reports for previously performed scans
- Scans IP address ranges
- Creates a new group of computers for future scanning

Chapter Summary

- Buffer overflows occur when excess data overload the buffer and the data are written into adjacent memory.

- Buffer overflows can be accidental, but they are often used maliciously.

- The most common types of buffer overflows are stack-based and heap-based overflows.

- Heap-based overflows are usually more difficult to exploit than traditional stack-based buffer overflows.

- Format strings can be used to print the contents of buffers.

- Shellcode is often architecture- and OS-dependent.

- Windows presents a larger target for shellcode exploits, but it is easier to write shellcode for Linux.

- Because it is difficult to find the exact starting point of shellcode, NOPs can be used to pad the code.

Hands-On Projects

1. Compile and execute a simple buffer overflow program.

   - Boot the computer using the BackTrack CD-ROM bootable Linux disc.

   - When the console screen appears, type **startx** to launch the GUI interface.

   - Open a command shell, as shown in Figure 12-13.

Figure 12-13   Open a command shell.

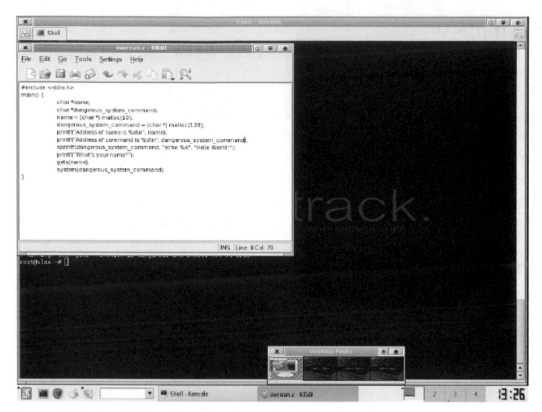

Figure 12-14 Type **kedit** to launch the Knoppix editor.

- To launch the Knoppix editor, type **kedit,** as shown in Figure 12-14.
- Type the following in kedit (note: the code is case sensitive):

```
#include <stdio.h>
main() {
char *name;
char *dangerous_system_command;
name = (char *) malloc(10);
dangerous_system_command = (char *) malloc(128);
printf("Address of name is %dn", name);
printf("Address of command is %dn", dangerous_system_command);
sprintf(dangerous_system_command, "echo %s", "Hello world!");
printf("What's your name?");
gets(name);
system(dangerous_system_command);
}
```

- Save the program by choosing **File → Save in/root/overrun.c.**
- Compile the code, as shown in Figure 12–15, by running:

```
gcc overrun.c -o overrun
```

- If there are any errors during compilation, load the program in kedit to fix them.
- Execute the program by typing **./overrun,** as shown in Figure 12-16.

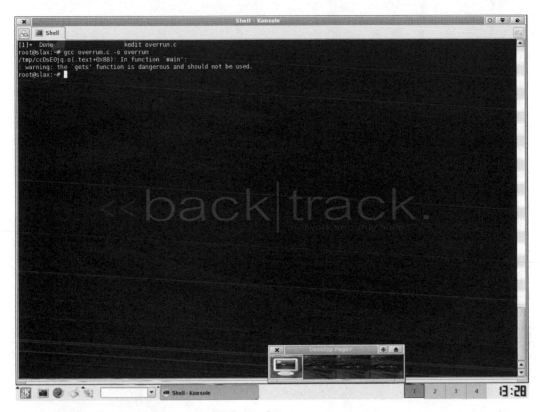

Figure 12-15 Save and then compile the code.

Figure 12-16 Execute the program.

Figure 12-17 In the **What's Your Name?** field, type **james bond**.

- In the **What's Your Name?** field, type **james bond**, as shown in Figure 12-17.
- "Hello World" should display.
- Now, overflow the buffer and execute system commands.
- Run the program again by typing **./overrun**.
- Type the following in the **What's Your Name?** field:

    `0123456789123456cat /etc/passwd`

- The password file should display, as shown in Figure 12-18.
- Now, obtain a command shell.
- Run the program again and type the following in the What's Your Name? field, as shown in Figure 12-19:

    `0123456789123456/bin/sh`

- You should see a shell launch. Press Ctrl+C to exit the shell.

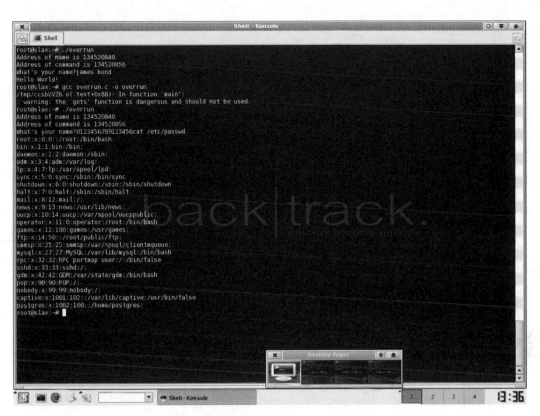

Figure 12-18   The password file should display.

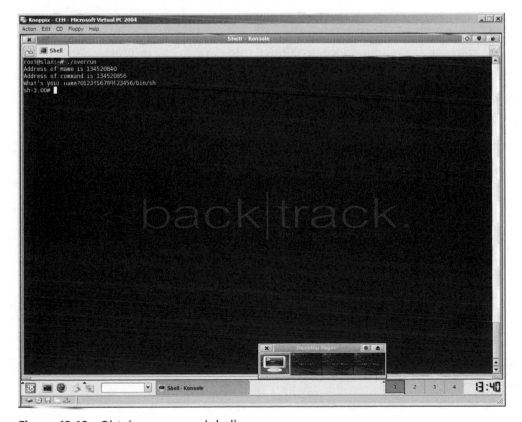

Figure 12-19   Obtain a command shell.

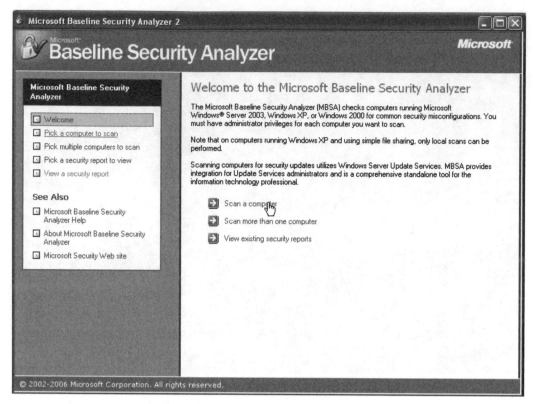

Figure 12-20 Install and launch MBSA.

2. Use MBSA to check for common security configuration drawbacks in Windows:
   - Navigate to Chapter 12 of the Student Resource Center.
   - Install and launch the MBSA program, as shown in Figure 12-20.
   - Pick a computer to scan and provide the IP address, as shown in Figure 12-21.
   - Scan the computer to find the security configuration drawbacks, as shown in Figure 12-22.
   - Check the security report, as shown in Figure 12-23.

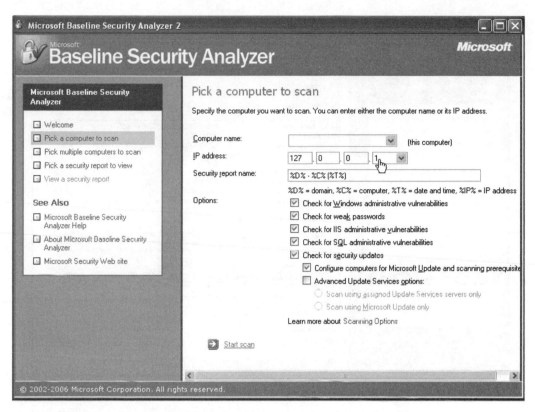

Figure 12-21 Provide the IP address for the computer to be scanned.

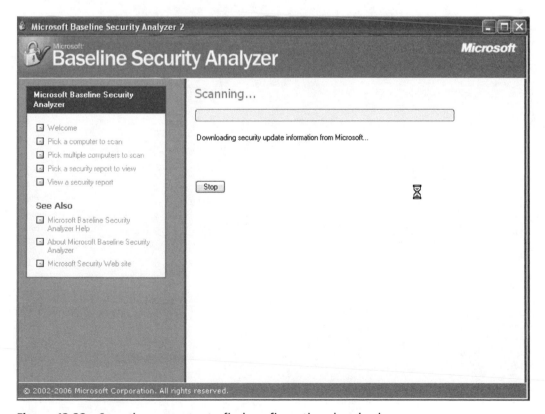

Figure 12-22 Scan the computer to find configuration drawbacks.

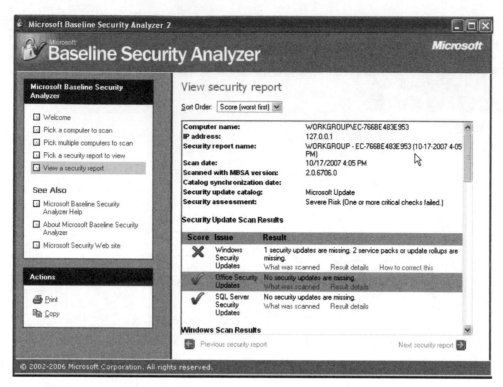

Figure 12-23   Check the security report.

Index